At the end of each chapter you will find a Knowledge diagnostic, which is a summary of the main learning points from the chapter to allow you to check you have understood the key concepts. You will also find a Further study guidance which contains suggestions for ways in which you can continue your learning and enhance your understanding. This can include: recommendations for question practice from the Further question practice and solutions, to test your understanding of the topics in the Chapter; suggestions for further reading which can be done, such as technical articles; and ideas for your own research.

Introduction to the Essential reading

The electronic version of the Workbook contains additional content, selected to enhance your studies. Consisting of revision materials and further explanations of complex areas (including illustrations and activities), it is designed to aid your understanding of key topics which are covered in the main printed chapters of the Workbook.

A summary of the content of the Essential reading is given below.

Chapter		Summary of Essential reading content
1	International regulatory environments for audit and assurance services	• Legal and professional framework in place (uses the UK as an illustrative example) • Corporate governance and audit committees (again, using UK examples as illustrations)
2	Code of ethics and conduct	• An overview of the various ethical threats and how the firm should respond to them using the ACCA and IESBA Codes • Specific guidance on confidentiality and conflicts of interest
3	Fraud and professional liability	• A summary of the relevant legal cases used to determine auditor liability • Advantages and disadvantages of different structures for firms
5	Obtaining and accepting professional appointments	• Ethical requirements from AA and acceptance/continuance factors from ISQC 1 plus money laundering and PEPs and their impact on acceptance decisions • Contents of an engagement letter
6	Planning and risk assessment	• Business risks related to emerging trends in IT and e-commerce • Planning issues: risks of material misstatement, documentation, materiality, initial audits and audit risk • Professional scepticism and additional information required • Analytical procedures as substantive procedures
7	Evidence	• Various additional elements of evidence: external confirmations; opening balances; documentation • Further detail on the auditor's responses to risks presented by related parties, the use of experts and the use of internal audit by the external auditor
8	Evaluation and review – matters relating to specific accounting issues	• A revision of the accounting and financial reporting issues associated with relevant IAS/IFRS from SBR plus suggested auditing issues relevant to each area covered
9	Group audits and transnational audits	• A recap on group accounting including associates and joint ventures, plus an overview of consolidation problems and procedures • Communication with the component auditor
10	Completion	• Further reading on ISA 220 and quality control for audits • Additional details on how to apply ISA 560 *Subsequent Events*

ACCA

Strategic Professional

Advanced Audit and Assurance – International (AAA – INT)

Workbook

For exams in September 2021, December 2021, March 2022 and June 2022

Third edition 2021

ISBN 9781 5097 3705 5

ISBN (for internal use only): 9781 5097 3703 1

e-ISBN 9781 5097 3953 0

British Library Cataloguing-in-Publication Data

A catalogue record for this book is available from the British Library.

Published by

BPP Learning Media Ltd

BPP House, Aldine Place

142–144 Uxbridge Road

London W12 8AA

learningmedia.bpp.com

Printed in the United Kingdom

Your learning materials, published by BPP Learning Media Ltd, are printed on paper sourced from sustainable, managed forests.

The contents of this book are intended as a guide and not professional advice. Although every effort has been made to ensure that the contents of this book are correct at the time of going to press, BPP Learning Media makes no warranty that the information in this book is accurate or complete and accept no liability for any loss or damage suffered by any person acting or refraining from acting as a result of the material in this book.

Contains public sector information licensed under the Open Government Licence v3.0.

We are grateful to the Association of Chartered Certified Accountants for permission to reproduce past examination questions and extracts from the syllabus. The suggested solutions in the practice answer bank have been prepared by BPP Learning Media Ltd, except where otherwise stated.

BPP Learning Media is grateful to the IASB for permission to reproduce extracts from the International Financial Reporting Standards including all International Accounting Standards, SIC and IFRIC Interpretations (the Standards). The Standards together with their accompanying documents are issued by:

The International Accounting Standards Board (IASB) 30 Cannon Street, London, EC4M 6XH, United Kingdom. Email: info@ifrs.org Web: www.ifrs.org

Disclaimer: The IASB, the International Financial Reporting Standards (IFRS) Foundation, the authors and the publishers do not accept responsibility for any loss caused by acting or refraining from acting in reliance on the material in this publication, whether such loss is caused by negligence or otherwise to the maximum extent permitted by law.

Contents

Helping you to pass

BPP Learning Media – ACCA Approved Content Provider

As an ACCA Approved Content Provider, BPP Learning Media gives you the opportunity to use study materials reviewed by the ACCA examining team. By incorporating the examining team's comments and suggestions regarding the depth and breadth of syllabus coverage, the BPP Learning Media Workbook provides excellent, ACCA-approved support for your studies.

These materials are reviewed by the ACCA examining team. The objective of the review is to ensure that the material properly covers the syllabus and study guide outcomes, used by the examining team in setting the exams, in the appropriate breadth and depth. The review does not ensure that every eventuality, combination or application of examinable topics is addressed by the ACCA Approved Content. Nor does the review comprise a detailed technical check of the content as the Approved Content Provider has its own quality assurance processes in place in this respect.

BPP Learning Media do everything possible to ensure the material is accurate and up to date when sending to print. In the event that any errors are found after the print date, they are uploaded to the following website: www.bpp.com/learningmedia/Errata.

The PER alert

Before you can qualify as an ACCA member, you not only have to pass all your exams but also fulfil a three-year practical experience requirement (PER). To help you to recognise areas of the syllabus that you might be able to apply in the workplace to achieve different performance objectives, we have introduced the 'PER alert' feature (see the next section). You will find this feature throughout the Workbook to remind you that what you are learning to pass your ACCA exams is equally useful to the fulfilment of the PER requirement. Your achievement of the PER should be recorded in your online My Experience record.

Chapter features

Studying can be a daunting prospect, particularly when you have lots of other commitments. This Workbook is full of useful features, explained in the key below, designed to help you get the most out of your studies and maximise your chances of exam success.

Key term
Central concepts are highlighted and clearly defined in the Key terms feature.
Key terms are also listed in bold in the Index, for quick and easy reference.

PER alert
This feature identifies when something you are reading will also be useful for your PER requirement (see 'The PER alert' section above for more details).

Illustration
Illustrations walk through how to apply key knowledge and techniques step by step.

Activity
Activities give you essential practice of techniques covered in the chapter.

Essential reading
Links to the Essential reading are given throughout the chapter. The Essential reading is included in the free eBook, accessed via the Exam Success Site (see inside cover for details on how to access this).

Chapter		Summary of Essential reading content
11	Reporting	• Discussion documents from the IAASB on the auditor's report, including the use of KAMs • Illustrations of unmodified and modified auditor's reports • Further considerations when reporting to those charged with governance and management
12	Audit-related services and other assurance services	• Examples of various assurance and audit-related reports for information • Further detail on how to apply the various assurance and audit-related services standards
14	Forensic audits	• Further detail on how to plan and conduct a forensic audit engagement
15	Social, environmental and public sector auditing	• An overview of the difficulties encountered by firms when measuring social and environmental performance • A reminder of the capitals used in the Integrated Reporting framework as well as some practical issues from their use
16	Current issues	• Topical issues relevant to the audit profession, including reforms to the regulation of auditing, big data and data analytics, professional scepticism and audit quality

Introduction to Advanced Audit and Assurance – International (AAA – INT)

Overall aim of the syllabus

To analyse, evaluate and conclude on the assurance engagement and other audit and assurance issues in the context of best practice and current developments.

Brought forward knowledge

The AAA syllabus uses a lot of content that you will have already seen in Audit and Assurance (AA) and Strategic Business Reporting (SBR) but the crucial difference here is that it is all tested in the context of more detailed scenarios and requires higher level skills to pass. There are also some new areas of content that you will need to learn, so you should treat AAA as an exercise in itself, rather than an extension of AA.

The syllabus

The broad syllabus headings are:

A	Regulatory environment
B	Professional and ethical considerations
C	Quality control and practice management
D	Planning and conducting an audit of historical financial information
E	Completion, review and reporting
F	Other assignments
G	Current issues and developments
H	Employability and technology skills

Main capabilities

On successful completion of this exam, you should be able to:

A	Recognise the legal and regulatory environment and its impact on audit and assurance practice
B	Demonstrate the ability to work effectively on an assurance or other service engagement within a professional and ethical framework
C	Assess and recommend appropriate quality control policies and procedures in practice management and recognise the auditor's position in relation to the acceptance and retention of professional appointments
D	Identify and formulate the work required to meet the objectives of audit assignments and apply the International Standards on Auditing
E	Evaluate findings and the results of work performed and draft suitable reports on assignments
F	Identify and formulate the work required to meet the objectives of non-audit assignments
G	Understand the current issues and developments relating to the provision of audit-related and assurance services
H	Demonstrate employability and technology skills

Links with other exams

The diagram shows where direct (solid line arrows) and indirect (dashed line arrows) links exist between this exam and other exams preceding or following it.

The Advanced Audit and Assurance syllabus assumes knowledge acquired in Audit and Assurance and develops and applies this further in greater depth. AAA also assumes accounting knowledge from SBR.

Achieving ACCA's Study Guide Learning Outcomes

This BPP Workbook covers all the Advanced Audit and Assurance – International (AAA – INT) syllabus learning outcomes. The tables below show in which chapter(s) each area of the syllabus is covered.

A	Regulatory environment	
A1	International regulatory frameworks for audit and assurance services	Chapter 1
A2	Money laundering	Chapter 1
A3	Laws and regulations	Chapter 1

B	Professional and ethical considerations	
B1	Code of Ethics for Professional Accountants	Chapter 2
B2	Fraud and error	Chapter 3
B3	Professional liability	Chapter 3

C	Quality control and practice management	
C1	Quality control (firm-wide)	Chapter 4
C2	Advertising, tendering and obtaining professional work and fees	Chapter 5
C3	Professional appointments	Chapter 5

D	Planning and conducting an audit of historical financial information	
D1	Planning, materiality and assessing the risk of material misstatement	Chapter 6
D2	Evidence and testing considerations	Chapter 7
D3	Audit procedures and obtaining evidence	Chapter 8

D4	Using the work of others	Chapter 7
D5	Group audits	Chapter 9

E	**Completion, review and reporting**	
E1	Subsequent events and going concern	Chapter 10
E2	Completion and final review	Chapter 10
E3	Auditor's reports	Chapter 11
E4	Reports to those charged with governance and management	Chapter 11

F	**Other assignments**	
F1	Audit-related and assurance services	Chapter 12
F2	Specific assignments: • Due diligence • Review of interim financial information • Prospective financial information • Forensic audits	Chapter 12 Chapter 12 Chapter 13 Chapter 14
F3	The audit of social, environmental and integrated reporting	Chapter 15
F4	The audit of performance information (pre-determined objectives) in the public sector	Chapter 15
F5	Reporting on other assignments	Chapters 12 and 13

G	**Current issues and developments**	
G1	Professional and ethical developments	Chapters 1 and 2
G2	Other current issues	Chapter 16

H	**Employability and technology skills**	
H1	Use computer technology to efficiently access and manipulate relevant information	You will find more guidance on how to achieve these learning outcomes within 'Exam success skills'.
H2	Work on relevant response options, using available functions and technology, as required by the workspace	
H3	Navigate windows and computer screens to create and amend responses to exam requirements, using the appropriate tools	
H4	Present data and information effectively, using the appropriate tools	

The exam

Computer-based exams

With effect from the March 2020 sitting, ACCA have commenced the launch of computer-based exams (CBEs) for this exam with the aim of rolling out into all markets internationally over a short period. Paper-based examinations (PBE) will be run in parallel while the CBEs are phased in. BPP materials have been designed to support you, whichever exam option you choose. For more information on these changes, when they will be implemented and to access Specimen Exams in the Strategic Professional CBE software, please visit the ACCA website. Please note that the Strategic Professional CBE software has more functionality than you will have seen in the Applied Skills exams.

www.accaglobal.com/gb/en/student/exam-support-resources/strategic-professional-specimen-exams-cbe.html

Approach to examining the syllabus

The exam lasts 3 hours and 15 minutes and consists of two sections. Questions will have a global focus and will require no more than basic calculations at most (for example, to assess materiality and calculate relevant ratios where appropriate) so candidates should always aim to have a calculator handy when attempting any study for AAA.

35% Knowledge > 65% Application

Format of the exam	Marks
Question 1 will comprise a Case Study, worth 50 marks, set at the planning stage of the audit, for a single company, a group of companies or potentially several audit clients. Candidates will be provided with detailed information, which will vary between examinations, but is likely to include extracts of financial information, strategic, operational and other relevant financial information for a client business, as well as extracts from audit working papers, including results of analytical procedures. Candidates will be required to address a range of requirements, predominantly from syllabus Sections A, B, C and D, thereby tackling a real-world situation where candidates may have to address a range of issues simultaneously in relation to planning, risk assessment, evidence gathering and ethical and professional considerations. Other syllabus areas, excluding Section E, may also be drawn on as part of the Case Study. Four professional marks will be available in Question 1 and will be awarded based on the level of professionalism with which a candidate's answer is presented, including the structure and clarity of the answer provided.	50
The remainder of the exam will contain two compulsory 25-mark questions, with each being predominately based around a short scenario which may relate to more than one client. One question will always predominantly come from syllabus Section E, and consequently candidates should be prepared to answer a question relating to completion, review and reporting. There are a number of formats this question could adopt, including, but not limited to, requiring candidates to assess going concern, the impact of subsequent events, evaluating identified misstatements and the corresponding effect on the auditor's report. Candidates may also be asked to critique an auditor's report or evaluate the matters to be	50

Format of the exam		Marks
	included in a report which is to be provided to management or those charged with governance. The other 25-mark question can be drawn from the remaining areas of the syllabus, including Sections A, B, C, D and F.	
Quality control and ethics	The auditor's assessment of effective quality control procedures and consideration of ethical issues are fundamental to all stages of the audit and therefore these concepts could be examined in any section of the exam.	
Current issues	Content from Section G on current issues is unlikely to form the basis of any question on its own but instead will be incorporated into any of the three questions, dependent on that question's content and the topical issues affecting the profession at the time of writing.	
		100

Analysis of past exams

The table below provides details of when each element of the syllabus has been examined in the ten most recent sittings and the question number and section in which each element was examined.

Note that in exams before September 2018 there were two compulsory and three optional questions (of which two had to be answered) so five questions in total are referenced for those exams.

Workbook Chapter		Sep/Dec 2020 (AAA)	Mar 2020 (AAA)	Sep/Dec 2019 (AAA)	Mar/Jun 2019 (AAA)	Dec 2018 (AAA)	Sept 2018 (AAA)	Mar/Jun 2018 (P7)	Sep/Dec 2017 (P7)	Mar/Jun 2017 (P7)	Sep/Dec 2016 (P7)
	REGULATORY ENVIRONMENT										
1	International regulatory frameworks for audit and assurance services										5(a)
1	Money laundering					3(a)	2(a)				
1	Laws and regulations										
	PROFESSIONAL AND ETHICAL CONSIDERATIONS										

Workbook Chapter		Sep/Dec 2020 (AAA)	Mar 2020 (AAA)	Sep/Dec 2019 (AAA)	Mar/Jun 2019 (AAA)	Dec 2018 (AAA)	Sept 2018 (AAA)	Mar/Jun 2018 (P7)	Sep/Dec 2017 (P7)	Mar/Jun 2017 (P7)	Sep/Dec 2016 (P7)
2	Codes of ethics for professional accountants		3(b)	1(d)	1(d)	3(b)	1(d), 2(b), 3(b)	2(a)		3(a)	4, 5(a)
3	Fraud and error		2(a)	3(c)		1					
3	Professional liability										
	QUALITY CONTROL AND PRACTICE MANAGEMENT										
4	Quality control	2(a)					3(b)	3	4	2	
5	Advertising, tendering, obtaining professional work and fees	1(c)									
5	Professional appointments	2(b)	3(a)			1					
	ASSIGNMENTS										
6, 7, 8	The audit of historical financial information including: (a) (i) Planning, materiality and assessing the risk of misstatement (b) (ii) Evidence	1	1, 2	1, 2	1, 3	1	1	1, 4	1, 2	1, 4	1, 2, 3
9	Group audits		1					1(b), 4	1(c)		
	COMPLETION,										

Workbook Chapter		Sep/Dec 2020 (AAA)	Mar 2020 (AAA)	Sep/Dec 2019 (AAA)	Mar/Jun 2019 (AAA)	Dec 2018 (AAA)	Sept 2018 (AAA)	Mar/Jun 2018 (P7)	Sep/Dec 2017 (P7)	Mar/Jun 2017 (P7)	Sep/Dec 2016 (P7)
	REVIEW AND REPORTING										
10	Completion	3				2(a), 2(b)	2(a)		5(a)	2	3
11	Auditor's reports	3	2(b)	2(b)	2(a)	2(c)	2(a)	5	5(b)	5(a)	5(b)
11	Communications to management				2(b)			3			
11	Other reports										
	OTHER ASSIGNMENTS										
12	Audit-related services					1(e)			3(a)		
12	Assurance services										
13	Prospective financial information		3(a)				3(a)	2(b)		5(b)	
14	Forensic audits			3(a), 3(b)							
15	Social and environmental auditing	1(c)									
15	Public sector audit of performance information									3(b) –(c)	
	CURRENT ISSUES AND DEVELOPMENTS										
1, 2, 3	Professional, ethical and corporate governance		1(c)		3(a)						

Workbook Chapter		Sep/Dec 2020 (AAA)	Mar 2020 (AAA)	Sep/Dec 2019 (AAA)	Mar/Jun 2019 (AAA)	Dec 2018 (AAA)	Sept 2018 (AAA)	Mar/Jun 2018 (P7)	Sep/Dec 2017 (P7)	Mar/Jun 2017 (P7)	Sep/Dec 2016 (P7)
16	Other current issues	1(d)			3(a)						

IMPORTANT! The table above gives a broad idea of how frequently major topics in the syllabus are examined. It should **not** be used to question spot and predict, for example, that Topic X will not be examined because it came up two sittings ago. The examining team's reports indicate that they are well aware that some students try to question spot. They avoid predictable patterns and may, for example, examine the same topic two sittings in a row, particularly if there has been a recent change in legislation.

Understanding the question verbs

Verbs that are likely to be frequently used in this exam are listed below, together with their intellectual levels and guidance on their meaning. Bold text denotes verbs used most frequently in AAA.

Intellectual level		
3	**Evaluate/critically evaluate**	Determine the value of, in the light of the arguments for and against (critically evaluate means weighting the answer towards criticisms/arguments against)
3	**Design**	To devise in order to execute a plan
3	Assess	Determine the strengths/weaknesses/importance/significance/ability to contribute
3	Examine	Critically review in detail
3	**Discuss**	Examine by using arguments for and against
3	Explore	Examine or discuss in a wide-ranging manner
3	**Criticize**	Present the weaknesses of/problems with the actions taken or viewpoint expressed, supported by evidence
3	Construct the case	Present the arguments in favour or against, supported by evidence
3	**Recommend**	Advise the appropriate actions to pursue in terms the recipient will understand
2	Distinguish	Define two different terms, viewpoints or concepts on the basis of the differences between them
2	Compare and contrast	Explain the similarities and differences between two different terms, viewpoints or concepts
2	Contrast	Explain the differences between two different terms, viewpoints or concepts

Intellectual level		
2	**Analyse**	Give reasons for the current situation or what has happened
1	Define	Give the meaning of
1	Explain	Make clear
1	Identify	Recognise or select
1	Describe	Give the key features

A lower level verb such as define will require a more **descriptive answer**. A higher-level verb such as evaluate will require a more **applied, critical answer**. The examining team has stressed that **higher-level requirements and verbs** will be most significant in this exam, such as critically evaluating a statement and arguing for or against a given idea or position. The examining team is looking to set questions that provide evidence of student understanding.

Certain verbs have given students particular problems.

(a) **Identify and explain**

Although these verbs are both Level 1, the examining team sees them as requiring different things. You have to go into more depth if you are asked to **explain** than if you are asked to **identify**. An explanation means giving more detail about the problem or factor identified, normally meaning that you have to indicate **why** it's significant. If you were asked to:

- **Identify the main problem with the same person acting as chief executive and chair** – you would briefly say excessive power is exercised by one person.

- **Explain the main problem with the same person acting as chief executive and chair** – you would say excessive power is exercised by one person and then go on to say it would mean that the same person was running the board and the company. As the board is meant to monitor the chief executive, it can't do this effectively if the chief executive is running the board. Also, you may be asked to explain or describe something complex, abstract or philosophical in nature.

(b) **Evaluate**

Evaluate is a verb that the examining team uses frequently. Its meaning may be different from the way that you have seen it used in other exams. The examining team expects to see arguments for **and** against, or pros **and** cons for what you are asked to evaluate.

Thus, for example, if a question asked you to:

'Evaluate the contribution made by non-executive directors to good corporate governance in companies'

You would not only have to write about the factors that help non-executive directors make a worthwhile contribution (independent viewpoint, experience of other industries), you would also have to discuss the factors that limit or undermine the contribution non-executive directors make (lack of time, putting pressure on board unity).

If the examining team asks you to critically evaluate, you will have to consider both viewpoints. However, you will concentrate on the view that you are asked to critically evaluate, as the mark scheme will be weighted towards that view.

The examining team has stated that 'Evaluate' is likely to be used for risk-based questions, ie Question 1.

Examinable documents

Knowledge of new examinable regulations issued by 31 August will be examinable in examination sessions being held in the following exam year. Documents may be examinable even if the effective date is in the future. This means that all regulations issued by 31 August 2020 will be examinable in the September 2021 to June 2022 examinations.

The Workbook offers more detailed guidance on the depth and level at which the examinable documents should be examined. The Workbook should therefore be read in conjunction with the examinable documents list.

Accounting Standards

All questions set will be based on IFRS Standards.

The accounting knowledge that is assumed for Advanced Audit and Assurance is the same as that examined in Strategic Business Reporting (SBR). Therefore, candidates studying for AAA should refer to the IFRS Standards listed under SBR.

Note. AAA will only expect knowledge of accounting standards and financial reporting standards from SBR. Knowledge of exposure drafts and discussion papers will not be expected.

Auditing standards

	Title
	International Standards on Auditing (ISAs)
	Glossary of Terms
	International Framework for Assurance Engagements
	Preface to the International Quality Control, Auditing, Review, Other Assurance and Related Services Pronouncements
ISA 200	Overall Objectives of the Independent Auditor and the Conduct of an Audit in Accordance with ISAs
ISA 210	Agreeing the Terms of Audit Engagements
ISA 220	Quality Control for an Audit of Financial Statements
ISA 230	Audit Documentation
ISA 240	The Auditor's Responsibilities Relating to Fraud in an Audit of Financial Statements
ISA 250 (Revised)	Consideration of Laws and Regulations in an Audit of Financial Statements
ISA 260 (Revised)	Communication with Those Charged with Governance
ISA 265	Communicating Deficiencies in Internal Control to Those Charged with Governance and Management
ISA 300	Planning an Audit of Financial Statements
ISA 315 (Revised 2019)	Identifying and Assessing the Risks of Material Misstatement
Amendments	Conforming amendments to other ISAs
ISA 320	Materiality in Planning and Performing an Audit
ISA 330	The Auditor's Responses to Assessed Risks
ISA 402	Audit Considerations Relating to an Entity Using a Service Organisation
ISA 450	Evaluation of Misstatements Identified during the Audit
ISA 500	Audit Evidence
ISA 501	Audit Evidence – Specific Considerations for Selected Items

	Title
ISA 505	External Confirmations
ISA 510	Initial Audit Engagements – Opening Balances
ISA 520	Analytical Procedures
ISA 530	Audit Sampling
ISA 540 (Revised)	Auditing Accounting Estimates and Related Disclosures
ISA 550	Related Parties
ISA 560	Subsequent Events
ISA 570 (Revised)	Going Concern
ISA 580	Written Representations
ISA 600	Special Considerations - Audits of Group Financial Statements (Including the Work of Component Auditors)
ISA 610 (Revised)	Using the Work of Internal Auditors
ISA 620	Using the Work of an Auditor's Expert
ISA 700 (Revised)	Forming an Opinion and Reporting on Financial Statements
ISA 701	Communicating Key Audit Matters in the Independent Auditor's Report
ISA 705 (Revised)	Modifications to the Opinion in the Independent Auditor's Report
ISA 706 (Revised)	Emphasis of Matter Paragraphs and Other Matter Paragraphs in the Independent Auditor's Report
ISA 710	Comparative Information – Corresponding Figures and Comparative Financial Statements
ISA 720 (Revised)	The Auditor's Responsibilities Relating to Other Information
	International Standards on Assurance Engagements (ISAEs)
ISAE 3000 (Revised)	Assurance Engagements other than Audits or Reviews of Historical Financial Information
ISAE 3400	The Examination of Prospective Financial Information
ISAE 3402	Assurance Reports on Controls at a Service Organisation
	International Auditing Practice Notes
IAPN 1000	Special Considerations in Auditing Financial Instruments
	International Standards on Quality Control (ISQCs)
ISQC 1	Quality Control for Firms that Perform Audits and Reviews of Financial Statements, and Other Assurance and Related Services Engagements
	International Standards on Related Services (ISRSs)

	Title
ISRS 4400 (Revised)	Agreed-Upon Procedures Engagements
ISRS 4410 (Revised)	Compilation Engagements
	International Standards on Review Engagements (ISREs)
ISRE 2400 (Revised)	Engagements to Review Historical Financial Statements
ISRE 2410	Review of Interim Financial Information Performed by the Independent Auditor of the Entity
	Exposure Drafts (EDs)
	IAASB – Proposed International Standard on Auditing 220 (Revised) Quality Management for an Audit of Financial Statements
	IAASB – Proposed International Standard on Quality Management 1, Quality Management for Firms that perform Audits or Reviews of Financial Statements, or Other Assurance or Related Services Engagements
	IAASB – International Standard on Quality Management 2, Engagement Quality Reviews
	IAASB – Proposed International Standard on Auditing (ISA) 600 (Revised), Special Considerations – Audits of Group Financial Statements (Including the Work of Component Auditors)
	IESBA – Proposed Revisions to the Code to Promote the Role and Mindset Expected of Professional Accountants
	IESBA – Proposed Revisions to the Fee-Related Provisions of the Code
	IESBA – Proposed Revisions to the Non-Assurance Services Provisions of the Code
	Ethical Guidelines
	ACCA's Code of Ethics and Conduct (January 2020)
	IESBA's International Code of Ethics for Professional Accountants (Revised August 2018)
	Other documents – Corporate Governance
	The UK Corporate Governance Code as an example of a code of best practice (Revised July 2018)
	FRC Guidance on Audit Committees (Revised April 2016) as an example of guidance on best practice in relation to audit committees
	Other documents – IAASB
	Towards Enhanced Professional Skepticism (August 2017)
	The New Auditor's Report – Questions and Answers (November 2016)
	Feedback Statement – Exploring the Growing Use of Technology in the Audit with a Focus on Data Analytics (January 2018)

Title
Support Material Related to Technology: Audit Documentation when using Automated Tools and Techniques
Determining and Communicating Key Audit Matters (July 2016)
More Informative Auditor's Reports – What Audit Committees and Finance Executives Need to Know (March 2016)
IAASB A Framework for Audit Quality: Key Elements that Create an Environment for Audit Quality (February 2014)
IAASB Auditor Considerations Regarding Significant Unusual or Highly Complex Transactions (September 2010)
IAASB Questions and Answers Professional Scepticism in an Audit of Financial Statements (February 2012)
IAASB Integrated Reporting Working Group: Supporting Credibility and Trust in Emerging Forms of External Reporting: Ten Key Challenges for Assurance Engagements (January 2018)
Other documents – IESBA and ACCA
ACCA's Anti-money Laundering Guidance for the Accountancy Profession

Note. Topics of exposure drafts are examinable to the extent that relevant articles about them are published in *Student Accountant*.

Essential skills areas to be successful in Advanced Audit and Assurance

We think there are three areas you should develop in order to achieve exam success in AAA – INT:

(a) Knowledge application

(b) Specific AAA skills

(c) Exam success skills

These are shown in the diagram below.

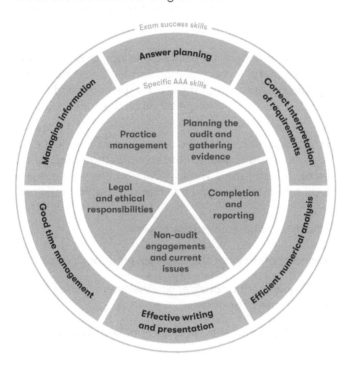

Specific AAA skills

These are the skills specific to AAA that we think you need to develop in order to pass the exam.

In this Workbook, there are five **Skills Checkpoints** which define each skill and show how it is applied in answering a question. A brief summary of each skill is given below.

Note. You will see the term 'write' used when discussing the preparation of an answer – obviously this can include both handwriting and typing, depending on whether you are attempting a practice question by hand or typing your answers in the CBE!

Skill 1: Legal and ethical responsibilities

The AAA exam will always test the application of your knowledge of this area. Candidates tend to remember enough to be able to identify when something's not right in a scenario – however, explaining why something is not right and how the firm should respond appears to be more challenging. You therefore need to be able to develop an approach that will assist you, both in advance of the exam and on the day itself.

While the context and complexity of scenarios testing legal and ethical responsibilities may be different to those you would have seen in the Audit and Assurance exam, the knowledge that you require for AAA should not be new to you – it is therefore important that you refresh your memory using the technical knowledge presented in this Workbook before you attempt more exam standard questions.

A step-by-step technique for applying these techniques is outlined below.

Step 1	Think about the requirement and consider all the tasks that you are being asked to undertake.

Step 2	Read the scenario and identify all the areas of legal and/or ethical concern that you can.
Step 3	For each of the areas that you have identified, list the reasons why you think they may be of concern to you.
Step 4	Add suitable responses to each of the matters listed and their reasons.
Step 5	Write your answer.

Skills Checkpoint 1 covers this technique in detail through application to a preparation question.

Skill 2: Practice management

This area of the syllabus could either be tested in a discrete, stand-alone way or as part of a larger question testing professional issues in general – practice management includes both quality control as well as tendering, fees and acceptance so these could be combined too. There is sometimes even a cross-over with ethical issues as well, so questions on this topic could vary and you need to be prepared.

Answering questions related to practice management do require some learned knowledge to inform your approach – this will also help you identify areas of the scenario that may not look quite right and which will need some further investigation. The AAA skills and exam success skills in this checkpoint will help you to develop an approach that you can apply throughout the rest of your studies.

A step-by-step technique for applying these techniques is outlined below.

Step 1	Isolate the verbs and confirm what the requirement is looking for.
Step 2	For theory-based requirements, consider whether there is a list that can be used to help you create your answer.
Step 3	For application-based requirements, what information do you need to focus on?
Step 4	Create an approach that takes steps 1, 2 and 3 into account.
Step 5	Write your answer.

Skills Checkpoint 2 covers this technique in detail through application to an exam-standard question.

Skill 3: Planning the audit and gathering evidence

Question 1 in the exam will be a 50-mark scenario question with a number of requirements that should test some, if not all, of the following:

- Risks (audit risks, risks of material misstatement or business risks)
- Other planning issues
- Audit procedures and evidence required to verify specific parts of the scenario
- Ethical and professional points related to the scenario

In this skills checkpoint, we will go through an audit risk question, showing you how to use the scenario to draw up a detailed answer. We will also show you all of the exam success skills as they relate to Question 1 so you can start to practise them as part of your home study.

A step-by-step technique for applying these techniques is outlined below.

Step 1	Confirm the requirement (such as evaluating audit risk) by reference to the verb, the marks and the timing.
Step 2	Annotate the scenario with ideas of audit risks.
Step 3	Perform analytical procedures on the data supplied (including

	conclusions).
Step 4	Create an answer plan that takes steps 1, 2 and 3 into account.
Step 5	Write your answer.

Skills Checkpoint 3 covers this technique in detail through application to an exam-standard question.

Skill 4: Completion and reporting

The ACCA has confirmed that one of the 25-mark questions will always come from syllabus section E, and consequently candidates should be prepared to answer a question relating to completion, review and reporting. As a result, this skills checkpoint will cover some of the topics most likely to be seen in these types of questions and the skills required to produce great answers.

Questions on completion and reporting tend to go well together – when you consider issues such as going concern, subsequent events and the evaluation of the auditor's findings, inevitably they will need to considered in the context of the auditor's report and any other communication that might be necessary.

A step-by-step technique for applying these techniques is outlined below.

Step 1	Determine which parts of the syllabus the requirement is testing.
Step 2	Actively read the scenario to identify the key issues.
Step 3	Consider the implications of the issues identified in Step 2 for the auditor's opinion (both cause and extent).
Step 4	Consider whether there are any additional impacts on the auditor's report from the issues identified in Step 2.
Step 5	Write your answer.

Skills Checkpoint 4 covers this technique in detail through application to an exam-standard question.

Skill 5: Non-audit engagements and current issues

Remember that although this is an audit exam, the words '...and Assurance' are also in the title. The syllabus contains a number of non-audit elements that you could be tested on, so this checkpoint will consider how you can prepare for these if required. Part F of the syllabus covers these subjects.

The AAA examining team also periodically publishes technical articles on subjects deemed to be of interest to candidates: in some cases, they may recommend exam techniques for syllabus topics that have been poorly answered in previous exam sittings; in others, they may relate to current issues which the examining team want candidates to be aware of.

Traditionally, whenever a technical article is published, the content is often examined within the next couple of sittings, so keeping up to date with these technical articles is essential. You will find references to relevant technical articles with the 'Further reading' sections of this workbook.

A step-by-step technique for applying these techniques is outlined below.

Step 1	Think about the question and list all the things that you will need to do.
Step 2	Read the scenario and identify all the areas that are relevant to producing an answer.
Step 3	Is there any other technical knowledge that will help you to produce and answer?
Step 4	Draw up an answer plan based on your outputs from Steps 1, 2 and 3.

BPP LEARNING MEDIA

Step 5	Write your answer.

Skills Checkpoint 5 covers this technique in detail through application to an exam-standard question.

Exam success skills

Passing the AAA exam requires more than applying syllabus knowledge and demonstrating the specific AAA skills; it also requires the development of excellent exam technique through question practice.

We consider the following six skills to be vital for exam success. The Skills Checkpoints show how each of these skills can be applied specifically to the AAA exam. You will also find details on how to apply these skills in the context of the CBE and Syllabus Area H 'Employability and technology skills'.

1 Exam success skill 1

Managing information

Questions in the exam will present you with a lot of information. The skill is how you handle this information to make the best use of your time. The key is determining how you will approach the exam and then actively reading the questions.

Advice on developing this skill

Approach

The exam is 3 hours 15 minutes long. There is no designated 'reading' time at the start of the exam, however, one approach that can work well is to start the exam by spending 10–15 minutes carefully reading through all of the questions to familiarise yourself with the exam paper.

Once you feel familiar with the exam paper consider the order in which you will attempt the questions; always attempt them in your order of preference. For example, you may want to leave to last the question you consider to be the most difficult.

If you do take this approach, remember to adjust the time available for each question appropriately – see Exam success skill 6: Good time management.

If you find that this approach doesn't work for you, don't worry – you can develop your own technique.

Active reading

You must take an active approach to reading each question. Focus on the requirement first, highlighting key verbs such as 'prepare', 'comment', 'explain', 'discuss', to ensure you answer the question properly. Then read the rest of the question, identifying important and relevant information as you go, making notes of any relevant technical information you think you will need.

The CBE

At first glance, the CBE is quite daunting as the screenshot of the workspace below illustrates:

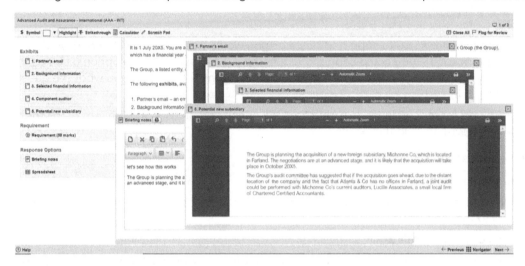

Managing this information is quite a challenge – however, on the left-hand side of the screen is all the information you need:

- The exhibits (for Question 1 of the AAA exam, the partner's email will usually outline the requirements so is a good place to start)
- The requirement (for other questions, you will find the requirements here)
- The response options (in most cases you will just need the word processing document but if presented with more complex financial statements extracts, the spreadsheet option may be of use)

You will also note that the various windows can be re-sized and moved around the screen to help you navigate each of the exhibits as you make sense of the question.

2   Exam success skill 2

Correct interpretation of the requirements

The active verb used often dictates the approach that written answers should take (eg 'explain', 'discuss', 'evaluate'). It is important you identify and use the verb to define your approach. The **correct interpretation of the requirements** skill means correctly producing only what is being asked for by a requirement. Anything not required will not earn marks.

Advice on developing this skill

This skill can be developed by analysing question requirements and applying this process:

Step 1	**Read the requirement** Firstly, read the requirement a couple of times slowly and carefully and highlight the active verbs. Use the active verbs to define what you plan to do. Make sure you identify any sub-requirements.
Step 2	**Read the rest of the question** By reading the requirement first, you will have an idea of what you are looking out for as you read through the scenario and exhibits. This is a great time saver and means you don't end up having to read the whole question in full twice. You should do this in an active way – see Exam success skill 1: Managing Information.
Step 3	**Read the requirement again** Read the requirement again to remind yourself of the exact wording before starting your written answer. This will capture any misinterpretation of the requirements or any missed requirements entirely. This should become a habit in your approach and, with

repeated practice, you will find the focus, relevance and depth of your answer plan will improve.

The CBE

The workspace allows you to copy and paste as you would normally do within any word processing package – you could copy the requirement into your response option (such as the briefing note shown in the screenshot) and it will then be there to remind you what the question is asking for.

There is a 'flag for review' function within the CBE which can be used to highlight areas that you may wish to revisit later in the exam.

3 Exam success skill 3

Answer planning: Priorities, structure and logic

This skill requires the planning of the key aspects of an answer which accurately and completely responds to the requirement.

Advice on developing this skill

Everyone will have a preferred style for an answer plan. For example, it may be a mind map, bullet-pointed lists or simply annotating the question. Choose the approach that you feel most comfortable with, or, if you are not sure, try out different approaches for different questions until you have found your preferred style.

For a discussion question, annotating the question is likely to be insufficient. It would be better to draw up a separate answer plan in the format of your choosing (eg a mind map or bullet-pointed lists). For a risk question, you should annotate the scenario, noting which areas present the type of risk being examined and explain why.

The CBE

In the screenshot below, you can see that some of the text has been highlighted:

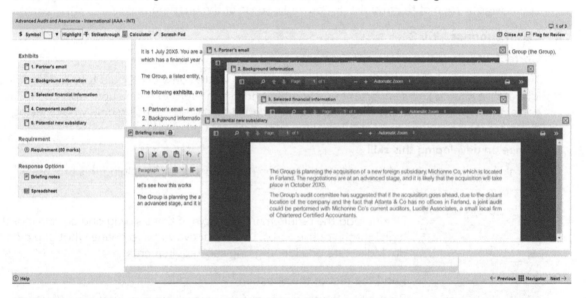

You can use a variety of colours to highlight different parts of the exhibits to address separate aspects of the requirements.

There is a 'scratch pad' that you can also use to organise your thoughts and make rough workings. You can copy and paste content from the scratch pad into your response option, but the scratch pad itself is not submitted for marking at the end of the exam. The answer space can also be used for rough workings.

4 Exam success skill 4

Efficient numerical analysis

This skill aims to maximise the marks awarded by making clear to the marker the process of arriving at your answer. This is achieved by laying out an answer such that, even if you make a few errors, you can still get some credit for your calculations. It is vital that you do not lose marks purely because the marker cannot follow what you have done.

Advice on developing this skill

This skill can be developed by applying the following process:

Step 1	**Explain your workings where relevant**
	Materiality calculations or other forms of analytical procedure should have a brief explanation of their purpose so the examining team can understand what your calculations are trying to tell them. Remember, for AAA, calculations are just a way of quantifying a part of your answer (such as a form of risk assessment or when considering going concern indicators).
Step 2	**Show your workings**
	Keep your workings as clear and simple as possible and ensure they are cross-referenced to the main part of your answer. Where it helps, provide brief narrative explanations to help the marker understand the steps in the calculation. This means that if a mistake is made you do not lose any subsequent marks for follow-on calculations.
Step 3	**Keep moving!**
	It is important to remember that, in an exam situation, it is difficult to get every number 100% correct. The key is therefore ensuring you do not spend too long on any single calculation. If you are struggling with a solution then make a sensible assumption, state it and move on. It's also important to remember that for AAA, you will not be expected to generate a large number of calculations: usually, only key ratios, trends or materiality calculations will be required.

The CBE

Although the spreadsheet function exists to help you perform calculations more quickly and efficiently than using the onscreen calculator, there may not always be enough of them to merit using the spreadsheet function. It is probably best to practise using the CBE software as part of your revision so you can settle on a style that you feel comfortable with.

5 Exam success skill 5

Effective writing and presentation

Written answers should be presented so that the marker can clearly see the points you are making, presented in the format specified in the question. The skill is to provide efficient written answers with sufficient breadth of points that answer the question, in the right depth, in the time available.

Advice on developing this skill

Step 1	**Use headings**
	Using the headings and sub-headings from your answer plan will give your answer structure, order and logic. This will ensure your answer links back to the requirement and is clearly signposted, making it easier for the marker to understand the different points you are making. Underlining your headings will also help the marker.
Step 2	**Write your answer in short, but full, sentences**
	Use short, punchy sentences with the aim that every sentence should say something different and generate marks. Write in full sentences, ensuring your style is professional.

Step 3	**Do your calculations first and explanation second**
	Questions sometimes require an explanation with suitable calculations, such as materiality. The best approach is to prepare the calculation first but present it on the bottom half of the page of your answer, or on the next page. Then add the explanation before the calculation. Performing the calculation first should enable you to explain what you have done.

The CBE

Within the workspace, the response option does allow you to format your answer as you would in any word processing package: eg **bold**, <u>underline</u> or *italics*. These will help you provide emphasis on different parts of your answer (and in the case of Question 1, will help you earn the professional marks by use of sub-headings etc).

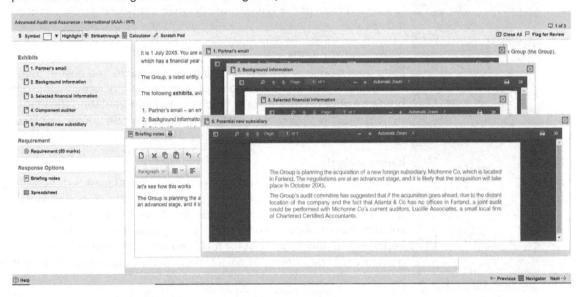

Tables and bullets can also be introduced into your response (although you should only be using these if you feel it still helps you to address the requirement fully).

6 Exam success skill 6

Good time management

This skill means planning your time across all the requirements so that all tasks have been attempted at the end of the 3 hours 15 minutes available and actively checking on time during your exam. This is so that you can flex your approach and prioritise requirements which, in your judgement, will generate the maximum marks in the available time remaining.

Advice on developing this skill

The exam is 3 hours 15 minutes long, which translates to 1.95 minutes per mark. Therefore a 10-mark requirement should be allocated a maximum of 20 minutes to complete your answer before you move on to the next task. At the beginning of a question, work out the amount of time you should be spending on each requirement and write the finishing time next to each requirement on your exam paper. If you take the approach of spending 10–15 minutes reading and planning at the start of the exam, adjust the time allocated to each question accordingly; eg if you allocate 15 minutes to reading, then you will have 3 hours remaining, which is 1.8 minutes per mark.

Keep an eye on the clock

Aim to attempt all requirements, but be ready to be ruthless and move on if your answer is not going as planned. The challenge for many is sticking to planned timings. Be aware this is difficult to achieve in the early stages of your studies and be ready to let this skill develop over time.

If you find yourself running short on time and know that a full answer is not possible in the time you have, consider recreating your plan in overview form and then add key terms and details as time allows. Remember, some marks may be available, for example, simply stating a conclusion which you don't have time to justify in full.

Question practice

Question practice is a core part of learning new topic areas. When you practice questions, you should focus on improving the Exam success skills – personal to your needs – by obtaining feedback or through a process of self-assessment.

The CBE

Sitting this exam as a computer-based exam and practising as many exam-style questions as possible in the ACCA CBE practice platform will be the key to passing this exam. You should attempt questions under timed conditions and ensure you produce full answers to the discussion parts as well as doing the calculations. Also ensure that you attempt all mock exams under exam conditions.

ACCA have launched a free on-demand resource designed to mirror the live exam experience helping you to become more familiar with the exam format. You can access the platform via the Study Support Resources section of the ACCA website navigating to the CBE question practice section and logging in with your myACCA credentials.

International regulatory environments for audit and assurance services

Learning objectives

On completion of this chapter, you should be able to:

	Syllabus reference no.
Explain the need for laws, regulations, standards and other guidance relating to audit, assurance and related services.	A1(a)
Outline and explain the need for the legal and professional framework including: (a) Public oversight of audit and assurance practice (b) The impact of corporate governance principles on audit and assurance practice.	A1(b)
Discuss the role of the audit committee and its impact on audit and assurance practice in relation to: (a) The relationship with the external auditor, including the appointment, removal and monitoring of effectiveness; and (b) The oversight and approval of the provision of non-audit services.	A1(c)
Define 'money laundering' and discuss international methods for combatting money laundering.	A2(a)
Explain the scope of criminal offences of money laundering and how professional accountants may be protected from criminal and civil liability.	A2(b)
Explain the need for ethical guidance in this area.	A2(c)
Describe how accountants meet their obligations to help prevent and detect money laundering including record keeping and reporting of suspicion to the appropriate regulatory body.	A2(d)
Explain the importance of customer due diligence (CDD) also referred to as know your customer (KYC) and recommend the information that should be gathered as part of CDD/KYC.	A2(e)
Recognise potentially suspicious transactions and assess their impact on reporting duties.	A2(f)
Describe, with reasons, the basic elements of an anti-money laundering program.	A2(g)
Compare and contrast the respective responsibilities of management and	A3(a)

	Syllabus reference no.
auditors concerning compliance with laws and regulations in an audit of financial statements.	
Describe the auditors' considerations of compliance with laws and regulations and plan audit procedures when possible non-compliance is discovered.	A3(b)
Discuss how and to whom non-compliance should be reported.	A3(c)
Recognise and recommend when withdrawal from an engagement is necessary.	A3(d)

Business and exam context

This chapter covers a wide range of regulations that affect the work of audit and assurance professionals. You need to be aware of the international nature of the audit and assurance market and the main issues driving the development of regulatory frameworks.

The detailed requirements relating to money laundering are then discussed. You should be prepared to explain the responsibilities of professional accountants in this area and to outline the procedures that audit firms should implement.

The final section looks at the auditor's responsibilities in respect of laws and regulations that apply to an audit client. This is a topic that could be built into a practical case study question. The technical content of this part of the syllabus is mainly drawn from your earlier studies. Questions in this exam are unlikely to ask for simple repetition of this knowledge, but are more likely to require explanation or discussion of the reasons behind the regulations.

Chapter overview

International regulatory environments for audit and assurance services

International regulatory environment

Money laundering

Money laundering offences

ACCA guidance

Risk-based approach

ISA 250 (revised) *Consideration of Laws and Regulations in an Audit of Financial Statements*

1 International regulatory environment

Activity 1: Regulating the audit profession

What factors have led to the growth in regulation of the audit profession?

Solution

PER alert

One of the competencies you require to fulfil **Performance Objective 18** of the PER is the ability to use up to date auditing standards and legal and ethical frameworks. You can apply the knowledge you obtain from this section of the Workbook to help you demonstrate this competency.

Essential reading

See Chapter 1 of the Essential reading for more detail on the legal and professional framework (including the role of regulators, standard-setters and those responsible for oversight, as well as a recap of corporate governance and the audit committee).

The Essential reading is available as an Appendix of the digital edition of the Workbook.

2 Money laundering

Money laundering: The **process** by which criminals attempt to **conceal the true origin** and ownership of **the proceeds of their criminal activity,** allowing them to maintain control over the proceeds and, ultimately, providing a cover for their sources of income.

Money laundering usually consists of **three stages:**

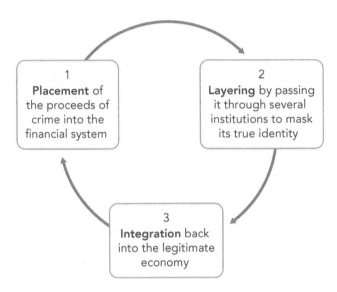

2.1 Money laundering offences

The Financial Action Task Force (FATF) has clarified a number of criminal offences relating to money laundering. Many of these have a **significant impact** on the auditor and it is therefore **imperative** that firms are aware of them and consider the risk that they may be committing an offence. The key offences are as follows:

(a) **Acquiring, using, possessing** or **concealingcriminal property** (this includes arranging, or becoming involved in an arrangement which might facilitate the acquisition of criminal property).

(b) **Failing to report** knowledge or suspicion of money laundering to the appropriate authority. For example, in the UK, the National Crime Agency (NCA) receives over 300,000 suspicious activity reports each year.

(c) **Tipping off** a client of suspicions relating to money laundering or disclosing any information that may prejudice an investigation.

2.1.1 International efforts to combat money laundering

Since 1989, FATF has acted as an intergovernmental body to set standards and develop policies to combat money laundering and terrorist financing.

FATF has made **40 recommendations** designed to combat money laundering and these have been adopted across the world.

2.2 ACCA guidance

In order to assist members, the ACCA has included **guidance on anti-money laundering** within the ACCA Rulebook (2020) alongside the *Code of Ethics and Conduct*.

2.2.1 The key elements of the guidance:

Internal controls and policies	Members should ensure their staff receive **regular training** to ensure that **client identification procedures** are carried out correctly and that knowledge and suspicions of money laundering or terrorist financing are reported. Firms should identify to their staff a clear procedure for reporting suspected money laundering and appoint an individual through whom reports of suspicions can be channelled to the relevant authority (**Money Laundering Reporting Officer** or **MLRO**; in the UK this role can also be fulfilled by a separate officer known as a **Money Laundering Compliance Principal** or **MLCP**, although one person can fulfil both roles if sufficiently senior within the firm).

Client identification	Before any work is undertaken, members should verify the identity of the potential client – this is known as either **'know your client' (KYC)** or **'customer due diligence' (CDD)** and requires awareness of the client's **identity**, their **ownership** structure and their operating **cash-flows**. This is discussed in more detail below.
Record keeping	Members should **retain all client identification records** for at least **five years** after the end of the client relationship. Records of all transactions and other work carried out, in a full audit trail form, should be retained for at least five years after the conclusion of the transaction.
Recognition of suspicion	Suspicion can be described as being **more than speculation** but **falling short of proof based on firm evidence**. The key to recognising a suspicious transaction or situation is for members to have sufficient understanding of clients and their activities. Special attention should be paid to any transactions **without** any visible **lawful** or **economic purpose**.
Reporting suspicious transactions	Where members know or suspect that funds are the proceeds of crime or relate to terrorist financing, they should request that their MLRO **promptly report their suspicions** to the relevant authority (such as the NCA in the UK).
Tipping off	Members **should not 'tip off' a client** that a report has been made. If a suspicion has arisen during the course of client identification procedures, members should take extra care that carrying out those procedures will not tip off the client. However, attempts to **discourage** a client from breaking the law will **not** be seen as tipping off.

Activity 2: Ethics and money laundering

Why is there a need for ethical guidance for accountants in respect of money laundering?

Solution

2.2.2 Client identification

The guidance on members' responsibilities mentions the requirement to gather CDD/KYC information. This includes:

Who the client is (company or individual?)	Who controls it	The purpose and intended nature of the business relationship
The nature of the client	The client's source of funds	The client's business and economic purpose

KYC enables the audit firm to understand its client's business well enough to spot any **unusual** business activity. This assists the firm in identifying **suspicions** of money laundering.

In the UK, the Money Laundering Regulations extended the circumstances under which customer due diligence (CDD) must be carried out from new to existing clients.

CDD is the term used in the Money Laundering Regulations for the steps that businesses must take to:

(a) **Identify the customer** and verify their identity using documents, data or information obtained from a reliable and independent source: for individuals, this could be a passport and proof of address; for a company, obtaining proof of incorporation or similar.

(b) **Identify any beneficial owner who is not the customer**. This is the individual (or individuals) behind the customer who ultimately owns or controls the customer or on whose behalf a transaction or activity is being conducted.

(c) Where a business relationship is established, you will need to understand the **purpose and intended nature of the relationship**, such as details of the customer's business or the source of the funds.

Businesses must also conduct ongoing monitoring to identify large, unusual or suspicious transactions as part of CDD. The requirement to confirm the identity of customers and other individuals clearly links to the concept of KYC described above.

If a potential client's identity cannot be established, no work should be done by the professional accountant.

2.3 Risk-based approach

On any assignment, the auditor should assess the risk of money laundering activities. Clearly, every circumstance is different, but the following diagram illustrates some key risk factors:

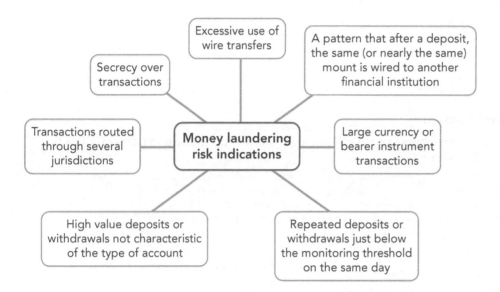

3 ISA 250 (revised) *Consideration of Laws and Regulations in an Audit of Financial Statements*

Companies are increasingly subject to laws and regulations with which they must comply. Here are some examples:

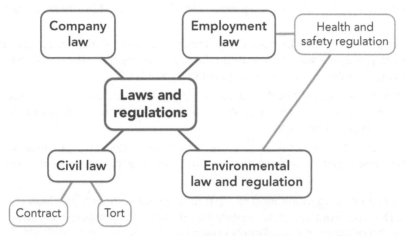

When designing and performing audit procedures and in evaluating and reporting the results thereof, the auditor should recognise that **non-compliance** by the entity with law or regulations may **materially affect the financial statements**.

> **Non-compliance:** Refers to acts of omission or commission, intentional or unintentional, committed by the entity, or by those charged with governance, by management or by other individuals working for or under the direction of the entity, which are contrary to the prevailing laws or regulations. Non-compliance does not include personal misconduct unrelated to the business activities of the entity.
>
> (ISA 250 (revised): para. 11)
>
> Non-compliance with laws and regulations is sometimes referred to as **NOCLAR**.

3.1 Responsibilities of management

It is management's responsibility to ensure that the **entity's operations** are conducted in accordance with laws and regulations. The responsibility for the **prevention** and **detection** of non-compliance also rests with management.

The following policies and procedures, among others, may assist management in discharging its responsibilities for the prevention and detection of non-compliance:

Monitoring legal requirements and any changes therein and ensuring that operating procedures are designed to meet these requirements

Instituting and operating appropriate systems of **internal control**

Developing, publicising and following a **Code of Conduct**, and ensuring employees are properly trained and understand the Code of Conduct

Monitoring **compliance** with the Code of Conduct and acting appropriately to discipline employees who fail to comply with it

Engaging **legal advisers** to assist in monitoring legal requirements

Maintaining a **register of significant laws and regulations** with which the entity has to comply within its particular industry and a record of complaints

In **larger entities**, these policies and procedures may be supplemented by assigning appropriate responsibilities to:

- An internal audit function
- An audit committee
- A compliance function

3.2 The auditor's consideration of compliance with laws and regulations

The auditor is not, and cannot be, held responsible for preventing NOCLAR. The fact that an audit is carried out may, however, act as a deterrent. The auditor needs to consider the **impact** of any non-compliance on the financial statements, and assess the risk of material misstatement by considering the various laws and regulations which clients must comply with and how the auditor should **respond**.

- Those that have a **direct effect** on determining material amounts in the financial statements (such as tax laws) require the auditor to obtain evidence of **compliance**.
- Those that are fundamental to the operating aspects of the client which have a **material (but not direct) effect** on the financial statements (such as compliance with an operating licence) require the auditor to undertake procedures to identify any **non-compliance**.

The auditor has no formal responsibility for NOCLAR that has neither a direct nor material effect on the financial statements, but should respond appropriately should such cases be detected. Maintaining an **awareness** of such laws and regulations for clients is obviously a challenge for auditors, especially if clients attempt to deliberately **conceal** NOCLAR.

Examples of laws and regulations that may have either a direct or material effect on the financial statements include those that relate to:

In order to determine whether or not NOCLAR has occurred, the auditor needs to obtain a **general understanding** of the **legal** and **regulatory framework** and whether the client is **complying** with this framework. This takes the form of **enquiries** of management and **reviews** of correspondence with the appropriate regulatory and/or licensing authorities (although ISA 250 (revised) points out that **other testing** during the audit might provide valuable evidence of non-compliance, so the team needs to be alert throughout the audit).

3.3 Audit procedures when possible NOCLAR is discovered

When the auditor becomes aware of information concerning a possible instance of non-compliance, the auditor should obtain an **understanding** of the **nature** of the act and the **circumstances** in which it has occurred, and seek **further information** to **evaluate** the possible effect on the financial statements. This may require **amendments** to both **amounts** and **disclosures** (as well as casting doubt on the entity's **going concern status** if sufficiently serious). All such information and evaluations should be fully **documented**.

ISA 250 (revised) sets out examples of the type of information that might come to the auditor's attention that may indicate non-compliance.

Investigation by a **regulatory organisation** or **government department** or payment of fines or penalties
Payments for **unspecified services** or loans to consultants, related parties, employees or government employees
Sales commissions or agents' fees that appear excessive in relation to those normally paid by the entity or in its industry or to the services actually received
Purchasing at **prices significantly above** or **below market price**
Unusual payments in **cash**, purchases in the form of cashiers' cheques payable to bearer or transfers to numbered bank accounts
Unusual transactions with companies registered in **tax havens**
Payments for goods or services made other than to the country from which the goods or services **originated**
Payments without proper exchange control documentation
Existence of an **information system** that **fails**, whether by design or by accident, to **provide an adequate audit trail** or sufficient evidence
Unauthorised transactions or improperly recorded transactions
Adverse media comment

(ISA 250: para. A13)

When evaluating the possible effect on the financial statements, the auditor should consider:

The **potential financial consequences**, such as fines, penalties, damages, threat of expropriation of assets, enforced discontinuation of operations and litigation
Whether the **potential financial consequences** require **disclosure**
Whether the potential financial consequences are so serious as to call into question the **fair presentation** given by the financial statements, or otherwise make the financial statements misleading

(ISA 250: para. A14)

The auditor should also **report** any cases of NOCLAR to the appropriate level of **management** and, where appropriate, to **those charged with governance**. However, ISA 250 (revised) does also state that if there are laws and regulations that **prohibit** this (for example, where reporting to either management or those charged with governance would constitute 'tipping off') or if the auditor suspects that **management or those charged with governance are involved in NOCLAR**, then the auditor should communicate the matter to the next higher level of authority (such as an audit committee or regulator), usually after seeking suitable legal or professional advice to confirm who this is.

In extreme cases, the auditor may feel compelled to make disclosures about NOCLAR in the **public interest** (for example, if a client is wilfully polluting public land) but is still bound by the fundamental ethical duty of **confidentiality**. Both ISA 250 (revised) and the IESBA Code of Ethics specifically encourage auditors to seek legal advice before deciding on how to proceed in such cases.

3.4 Withdrawal from the engagement

The auditor may conclude that withdrawal from the engagement is necessary when the **entity does not take the remedial action that the auditor considers necessary** in the circumstances, even when NOCLAR is not material to the financial statements. However, ISA 250 (revised) and the IESBA Code also emphasise that **withdrawal should not be used by firms as a substitute for responding appropriately to any NOCLAR at a client** (in other words, the auditor cannot just keep quiet about any NOCLAR they discover, regardless of how difficult it may be for them to do so).

The process for dealing with laws and regulations can be summarised for auditors like this:

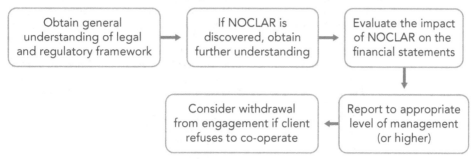

3.5 The auditor's report

3.5.1 Material misstatement

Where the auditor concludes that the non-compliance (**such as failing to disclose certain items within the financial statements**) has a material effect on the financial statements which have not been amended, they should express a **qualified** or **adverse opinion**.

3.5.2 Insufficient or inappropriate audit evidence

Where adequate information about compliance or suspected non-compliance cannot be obtained (either due to **obstruction by the client** or **any other circumstance**), the auditor may need to express a **qualified opinion** or **disclaimer of opinion** due to inability to obtain sufficient, appropriate audit evidence.

Chapter summary

International regulatory environments for audit and assurance services

International regulatory environment

- International Federation of Accountants (IFAC)
- International Auditing and Assurance Standards Board
  - ISAs
  - ISREs
  - ISAEs
  - ISRSs

Money laundering

Money laundering offences

- Acquiring, using, possessing, dealing with or concealing criminal property
- Failure to report knowledge or suspicion
- Tipping off
- Concealing the true origin and ownership of the proceeds of crime
- Consists of three stages:
  - Placement
  - Layering
  - Integration
- Financial Action Task Force role

ACCA guidance

- Internal controls and policies, including Money Laundering Reporting Officer (MLRO) role (Money Laundering Compliance Principal or MLCP in the UK) and training
- Client identification (identity, ownership and cash flows) via CDD or KYC
- Record keeping – at least five years
- Recognition of suspicion – more than speculation but falling short of firm proof
- Reporting suspicious transactions
- Tipping off should not be done, even by accident

Risk-based approach

- Secrecy over transactions
- Transfers via several jurisdictions
- High value transactions not in line with business model
- Excessive use of wire transfers
- Patterns between deposits and transfers
- Transactions of great value
- Repeated transactions below monitoring threshold on same day

ISA 250 (revised) *Consideration of Laws and Regulations in an Audit of Financial Statements*

- Non-compliance with laws and regulations (omission, commission, deliberate, accidental) is sometimes referred to as **NOCLAR**
- Management is responsible for **operational compliance** and also for prevention and **detection of non-compliance**
- Auditors are responsible for the **impact** of any non-compliance on the financial statements, and for assessing the **risk of material misstatement** due to the following:
  - Those that have a **direct effect** on the financial statements (eg compliance with enacted laws) require evidence of compliance
  - Those that have a **material (but not direct) effect** on the financial statements (eg compliance with an operating licence) require evidence of any non-compliance
  - Those that have **neither a direct nor material effect** on the financial statements require an awareness of any NOCLAR and an appropriate response
- Auditors need a **general understanding** of the legal and regulatory framework in place (see ISA 315) including environmental/public health and safety, fraud, corruption, bribery, data protection or other financial crime (such as money laundering)

- If NOCLAR is discovered, the following steps should take place:
  - The auditor must **understand** the matter fully and document their findings
  - They must **report** cases of NOCLAR to the appropriate level of management or those charged with governance (TCWG) unless prohibited by law
  - If management and/or TCWG are suspected of involvement in NOCLAR, the auditor **may report to next most higher level of authority** (eg audit committee or regulator)
  - They may need to **disclose** to others in the **public interest**
  - In all cases, especially when reporting or disclosing NOCLAR, **legal advice** should be sought due to the need for confidentiality
- If NOCLAR has not been addressed by a client, the auditor may **withdraw** from the engagement, but this should not be seen by auditors as a suitable way of responding to NOCLAR without any further action being taken
- Material NOCLAR can lead to a **modified audit opinion**:
  - Failure to comply with a requirement could lead to a **misstatement**
  - An obstruction by the client or poor record keeping could lead to **insufficient or inappropriate audit evidence**

Knowledge diagnostic

1. International regulatory environment

The various **laws, standards, governance structures** and **regulations** in place within the financial community are essential to protect and enhance the **reputation** of the profession within the society it serves.

2. Money laundering

A key area where guidance and regulations exist is **money laundering**. Auditors are at risk of committing various **criminal offences** regarding money laundering, for example **not reporting** suspicious transactions and/or **tipping off** the client that suspicion has arisen – as such they must know the requirements before acting in any engagement.

3. Customer due diligence

There are **three key areas** that need to be covered when performing customer due diligence (CDD) or know your client (KYC) procedures: the **identity** of the customer; the **ownership** of the customer's business; and the likely **cash flows** of the business.

4. Laws and regulations

Auditors should ensure they are familiar with the **laws and regulations** that the client has to comply with, and have considered the risk of non-compliance (NOCLAR) at all stages of the audit.

5. NOCLAR

Auditors must also know how to **respond** to such cases of **NOCLAR**, including the need to **disclose** to an appropriate level of authority.

Further study guidance

Question practice

Now try the following from the Further question practice bank (available in the digital edition of the Workbook):

- Question 1 'Mr Roy and Mr Fox' is an opportunity to practise some of the theory discussed in this chapter in an applied situation.

Further reading

There are technical articles on the ACCA website written by members of the AAA examining team which are relevant to some of the topics covered in this chapter that you should read:

- *Responding to non-compliance with laws and regulations (NOCLAR)*
- *Laws and regulations*
- *Corporate governance and its impact on audit practice*

Own research

Consider your own organisation or one that you are familiar with – what can you learn from the following to help you with topics from this chapter?

- Which laws and regulations matter most? Why do you think this is?
- How does an audit committee actually work? Are you aware of its impact?
- Have you received training on anti-money laundering procedures? If so, what did it include and are you aware of any instances of reports that needed to be made to the appropriate authority?

Activity answers

Activity 1: Regulating the audit profession

> **Approach**
>
> This question is designed to get you thinking about why there is so much regulation within the audit profession. Your answer needs to have considered the reasons why people rely on auditors; however, you also need to consider why people may find their trust in auditors has been damaged in recent years and how the profession has responded.
>
> This type of requirement is possible within a larger question, especially if it relates to the content of an ACCA examining team technical article. The AAA specimen exam (available on the ACCA website) contains an illustration of how a subject like this could be examined.

Suggested solution

- The reputation of the audit profession has, in recent years, suffered due to high profile audit failures (eg Carillion, BHS, Patisserie Valerie, Autonomy, the financial crisis of 2008 – and of course the classic examples of Enron, Parmalat and WorldCom) and somehow the public's trust needs to be re-established.

- The existence of auditing standards and other regulations should protect/enhance the reputation of the profession amongst all stakeholders by ensuring a consistently high level of work across all firms.

- Businesses have become more complex and global, and firms have expanded their range of services beyond traditional assurance and tax advice. This has led to a great deal of re-examination of regulatory and standard-setting structures both nationally and internationally in recent years.

- The competitiveness in the public audit sector (or lack thereof, especially in UK FTSE 350 audits for example) has led to downward pressure on fees and a consequent impact on quality, which has led some to consider the regulatory role of ethical codes as key (eg stopping firms from offering non-audit services to their audit clients).

Activity 2: Ethics and money laundering

> **Approach**
>
> As with the activity on regulation, there is a balance to be struck here between the duty of care owed by auditors to their clients (and to themselves, as they are not charities!) and the duty to society overall, to demonstrate that they can be trusted to act in the public interest.
>
> Requirements of this type are seen in the AAA exam but usually in the context of something topical.

Suggested solution

- In many countries, the legal requirements are onerous and the penalties for non-compliance are severe (For example, in the UK auditors risk long prison sentences if they commit an offence).

- Money laundering is widely defined and it is not always obvious that an offence has been committed.

- Without the guidance in issue, accountants may be used unwittingly to launder criminal funds.

- In many countries, the law creates a conflict between the ethical duty of confidentiality to the client and the legal duty to report money laundering offences. The guidance helps to clarify the members' professional duty to report offences.

- The reputation of accountants is poor, leading many in society to question whether they are acting in their own (or their clients') best interests, rather than those of society as a whole. For example, if accountants are to be paid for tax advice that reduces the liability of the client, is this in the best interests of society? Ethical guidance is vital for accountants to maintain their reputation.

2

Code of ethics and conduct

Learning objectives

On completion of this chapter, you should be able to:

	Syllabus reference no.
Explain the fundamental principles and the conceptual framework approach.	B1(a)
Identify, evaluate and respond to threats to compliance with the fundamental principles.	B1(b)
Discuss and evaluate the effectiveness of available safeguards.	B1(c)
Recognise and advise on conflicts in the application of fundamental principles.	B1(d)
Discuss the importance of professional scepticism in planning and performing an audit.	B1(e)
Consider the ethical implications of the external auditor providing non-audit services to a client including an internal audit service.	B1(f)
Assess whether an engagement has been planned and performed with an attitude of professional scepticism, and evaluate the implications.	B1(g)
Discuss emerging ethical issues and evaluate the potential impact on the profession, firms and auditors.	G1(a)
Discuss the content and impact of exposure drafts, consultations and other pronouncements issued by IFAC and its supporting bodies (including IAASB, IESBA and TAC).	G1(b)

Business and exam context

You have already learnt about ethical principles for auditors in your earlier studies. We will examine the issues in more detail and consider some of the complex ethical issues that auditors may face.

We also refer to the ethical guidance of the International Federation of Accountants. This is similar to the ACCA's guidance. Both approach issues of ethics in a conceptual manner.

Some of this chapter is likely to be revision, but that does not mean you should ignore it. Ethics is a key syllabus area. Complex ethical issues are introduced in this chapter. You particularly need to work through the questions given so that you practise applying ethical guidelines in given scenarios, as this is how this topic will be tested in the exam.

Professional ethics are of vital importance to the auditing and assurance profession and a major area of the syllabus, so this is likely to be a regular feature of the exam. Ethics can be tested in either Section A or Section B.

Questions are likely to be practical, giving scenarios where you are required to assess whether the situations presented are acceptable. Some of these can be answered by reference to specific guidance in the IESBA International Code of Ethics but others may require you to apply your understanding of the fundamental principles underlying the Code. Ethics may be examined alongside other areas within scenarios; commonly, practice management.

Chapter overview

1 Sources of regulation

The IESBA's International Code of Ethics for Professional Accountants gives the key reason why accountancy bodies produce ethical guidance: the **public interest**.

'A distinguishing mark of the accountancy profession is its acceptance of the responsibility to act in the public interest. A professional accountant's responsibility is not exclusively to satisfy the needs of an individual client or employing organisation.' (IESBA Code: para. 100.1 A1)

> **Public interest:** Considered to be the **collective wellbeing** of the community of people and institutions the professional accountant serves, including clients, lenders, governments, employers, employees, investors, the business and financial community, and others who rely on the work of professional accountants.

The key reason **why** accountants need to have an ethical code is that people **rely** on them and their expertise. Accountants deal with a range of issues **on behalf of clients**. They often have access to confidential and sensitive information. Auditors also claim to give an **independent** opinion. It is therefore critical that accountants and particularly auditors are, and are seen to be, independent.

As the auditor is required to be, and seen to be, ethical in their dealings with clients, the **ACCA** publishes guidance for its members in its **Code of Ethics and Conduct**. This guidance is given in the form of fundamental principles, guidance and explanatory notes. (This guidance is contained within the ACCA Rulebook, which can be found on the ACCA website and which is of crucial importance for ACCA members.)

The **IESBA** (International Ethics Standards Board for Accountants), a body of IFAC, also lays down fundamental principles in its **International Code of Ethics for Professional Accountants**. The fundamental principles of the two associations are extremely similar (much of the ACCA Code is drawn directly from the IESBA Code). The IAASB also issues quality control standards and auditing standards (ISAs), which work together to promote auditor independence and audit quality.

> **PER alert**
>
> One of the competencies you require to fulfil **Performance Objective 1** of the PER is the ability to act diligently and honestly, following codes of conduct, taking legislation into account and keeping up to date with legislation. You can apply the knowledge you have obtained from this chapter of the Workbook to help demonstrate this competency.

2 The fundamental principles

> **Integrity:** Members should be **straightforward** and **honest** in all professional and business relationships (so **truth** is fundamental).
>
> **Objectivity:** Members should not allow **bias, conflicts of interest or undue influence of others** to override professional or business judgement (therefore **fairness** is also fundamental).
>
> **Professional competence and due care:** Members have a continuing duty to **attain and maintain** professional **knowledge and skill** at the level required to ensure that a client or employing organisation receives **competent** professional service, based on **current technical and professional standards** and **relevant legislation**. Members should also act **diligently** and in accordance with applicable **technical** and **professional standards**.
>
> **Confidentiality:** Members should respect the confidentiality of **information acquired** as a result of professional and business relationships and **should not disclose** any such information to third parties without proper and specific authority, unless there is a legal or professional right or duty to disclose. Confidential information acquired as a result of professional and business relationships should not be used for the **personal advantage** of members or third parties.

Professional behaviour: Members should comply with relevant laws and regulations and should avoid any action that **discredits** the profession.

(ACCA Code: para 110.1 A1)

3 The conceptual framework

Activity 1: Ethical threats

The ACCA Code identifies five circumstances which have the potential to threaten a member or professional accountant's compliance with the fundamental principles. These are:

- The self-interest threat
- The self-review threat
- The advocacy threat
- The familiarity threat
- The intimidation threat

Required

What real-world situations could lead to the above threats to compliance with the fundamental principles?

Solution

3.1 Responding to threats

Having identified threats to compliance with the fundamental principles, the IESBA Code goes on to give guidance as to appropriate conditions, policies and procedures that may be relevant in **evaluating** the level of threats – examples of these include the following:

- Corporate governance requirements
- Education, training and experience requirements for the profession
- Effective complaint systems which enable the professional accountant and the general public to draw attention to unethical behaviour
- An explicitly stated duty to report breaches of ethics requirements
- Professional or regulatory monitoring and disciplinary procedures

(IESBA Code: para. 120.8 A2)

Addressing these threats requires the professional accountant to either eliminate them or reduce them to an acceptable level – this is achieved by one of the following actions:

| Eliminating the circumstances, including interests or relationships, that are creating the threats | Applying safeguards, where available and capable of being applied, to reduce the threats to an acceptable level | Declining or ending the specific professional activity |

(IESBA Code: para. R120.10–11)

Factors that are relevant in responding appropriately include **reviews** of significant **judgements** made or **conclusions** reached and the use of '**the reasonable and informed third party test**' (asking if the conclusion reached by the professional accountant would also have been reached by an independent and informed third party if faced with the same set of circumstances).

The use of **professional scepticism** (see Section 4.2) is also reinforced as being 'inter-related' with the fundamental ethical principles (IESBA Code: para. 120.13 A1).

Activity 2: Ethical responses

Discuss the ethical issues raised by the following scenarios and recommend suitable responses that the auditor should take in each case:

1   An audit partner has recently been asked by the finance director of the firm's longest-standing client to be her son's godfather.

2   A partner of the firm, who is a qualified actuary, wishes to provide valuation services to the firm's audit clients.

Solution

 Essential reading

See Chapter 2 of the Essential reading for more detail on the various ethical threats and responses given by the IESBA Code. You should learn these.

The Essential reading is available as an Appendix of the digital edition of the Workbook.

3.2 Public interest entities

The previous activity required you to consider whether any of the firm's clients were public interest entities. The IESBA Code distinguishes between 'public interest entities' and other entities because the ethical requirements applicable to public interest entities are frequently stricter than for other entities. At this level of your studies, you must be able to **recognise** a public interest entity in a question, and **adapt** your answer accordingly.

The term 'public interest entity' is defined as follows.

Public interest entities:

(a) A listed entity; or

(b) An entity:

    (i)   Defined by regulation or legislation as a public interest entity; or

    (ii) For which the audit is required by regulation or legislation to be conducted in compliance with the same independence requirements that apply to the audit of listed entities. Such regulation may be promulgated by any relevant regulator, including an audit regulator.

(IESBA Code: Glossary)

4 Current issues

4.1 Ethical implications of one firm providing both internal and external audit services

It stands to reason that a **good working relationship** should exist in order to facilitate the external auditor being able to place reliance on the work of internal auditors. Following this through to its logical conclusion, surely the **best** form of relationship would be one in which **two separate teams** from the **same firm** (with the same methodology, systems, knowledge sharing etc) carry out both internal and external audit work simultaneously.

Obviously, this has one major **drawback** – working for the same firm dramatically increases the risk of a **self-review threat** to the external auditor's objectivity. Despite this, however, many companies choose this arrangement and sell it to their shareholders as a way of **improving quality** and **reducing agency costs** – in some cases, savings of around 30% of all audit costs have been reported. It raises the question of what serves a company's stakeholders better – **greater audit objectivity** or **smaller audit fees**?

4.2 Professional scepticism

The IESBA Code explains that in order to follow best practice, all professional accountants (including auditors) are required to exercise professional scepticism when planning and performing audits, reviews and other assurance engagements in order to scrutinise and challenge what is placed before them. The Code cites three categories where this can be applied:

Integrity	'Integrity requires the professional accountant to be straightforward and honest. For example, the accountant complies with the principle of integrity by:
	(a) Being straightforward and honest when raising concerns about a position taken by a client; and
	(b) Pursuing inquiries about inconsistent information and seeking further audit evidence to address concerns about statements that might be materially false or misleading in order to make informed

	decisions about the appropriate course of action in the circumstances. In doing so, the accountant demonstrates the critical assessment of audit evidence that contributes to the exercise of professional scepticism.'
Objectivity	'Objectivity requires the professional accountant not to compromise professional or business judgement because of bias, conflict of interest or the undue influence of others. For example, the accountant complies with the principle of objectivity by: (a) Recognising circumstances or relationships such as familiarity with the client, that might compromise the accountant's professional or business judgement; and (b) Considering the impact of such circumstances and relationships on the accountant's judgement when evaluating the sufficiency and appropriateness of audit evidence related to a matter material to the client's financial statements. In doing so, the accountant behaves in a manner that contributes to the exercise of professional scepticism.'
Professional competence and due care	'Professional competence and due care requires the professional accountant to have professional knowledge and skill at the level required to ensure the provision of competent professional service, and to act diligently in accordance with applicable standards, laws and regulations. For example, the accountant complies with the principle of professional competence and due care by: (a) Applying knowledge that is relevant to a particular client's industry and business activities in order to properly identify risks of material misstatement; (b) Designing and performing appropriate audit procedures; and (c) Applying relevant knowledge when critically assessing whether audit evidence is sufficient and appropriate in the circumstances. In doing so, the accountant behaves in a manner that contributes to the exercise of professional scepticism.'

(IESBA Code: para 120.13 A2)

4.3 Management responsibilities

In general, firms cannot accept any management responsibilities for an audit client (IESBA Code: para. 600.7) and must always actively consider risk factors such as the nature of the engagement, the nature of the client and the perception of a reasonable and informed third party in determining the extent of any ethical threats. The Code also prohibits a firm from assuming any management responsibility for an audit client as it creates self-interest, self-review, advocacy and familiarity threats (ISEBA Code: para. 600.7.A2).

Activity 3: Aventura International

Aventura International, a listed company, manufactures and wholesales a wide variety of products including fashion clothes and audio-video equipment. The company is audited by Voest, a firm of Chartered Certified Accountants, and the Audit Manager is Darius Harken. The following matters have arisen during the audit of the group's financial statements for the year to 31 December 20X7 which is nearing completion:

(1) During the annual inventory count of fashion clothes at the company's principal warehouse, the audit staff attending the count were invited to purchase any items of clothing or equipment at 30% of their recommended retail prices.

(2) The Chief Executive of Aventura International, Armando Thyolo, owns a private jet. Armando invoices the company, on a monthly basis, for that proportion of the operating costs which reflects business use. One of these invoices shows that Darius Harken was flown to Florida in March 20X7 and flown back two weeks later. Neither Aventura nor Voest have any offices or associates in Florida.

(3) Last week Armando announced his engagement to be married to his personal assistant, Kirsten Fennimore. Before joining Aventura in September 20X7, Kirsten had been Voest's senior in charge of the audit of Aventura.

Required

Discuss the ethical, professional and quality control issues raised and the actions which might be taken by the auditor in relation to these matters.

Note. Assume it is 6 March 20X8.

Solution

Chapter summary

Code of ethics and conduct

Sources of regulation

- IESBA and ACCA guidance substantially harmonised
- Supports the public interest

The fundamental principles

- Integrity (straightforward, honest or **TRUE**)
- Objectivity (no bias or conflicts of interest – **FAIR**)
- Professional competence and due care (knowledge, skills, CPD etc)
- Confidentiality (no personal advantage)
- Professional behaviour (no discredit to the profession)

The conceptual framework

- Threats to compliance with the fundamental principles:
  - Self interest
  - Self-review
  - Advocacy
  - Familiarity
  - Intimidation

Responding to threats

- Eliminate the circumstances
- Apply safeguards
- Decline the engagement

Public interest entities

- More stringent than other entities
- Either listed or regulated as though listed

Current issues

Ethical implications of one firm providing both internal and external audit services

- Advantages:
  - Good working relationship
  - Efficiencies in approach
  - Reduced combined fees
- Disadvantages:
  - Significant self-review threat

Professional scepticism

Challenge and scrutinise sufficiently to obtain the right evidence

Management responsibility

Firms cannot accept any management responsibilities

Knowledge diagnostic

1. Codes of Ethics in force

The **ACCA Code of Ethics and Conduct** and **IESBA International Code of Ethics for Professional Accountants** explain how accountants should act in the public interest.

2. Fundamental principles

Both the ACCA and IESBA Codes are based on **five fundamental principles** which govern the general behaviour and characteristics of members: integrity; objectivity; professional competence and due care; confidentiality; and professional behaviour.

3. Conceptual framework

The fundamental principles are themselves underpinned by a **conceptual framework** which identifies **threats** in compliance with the fundamental principles (self-interest, self-review, advocacy, familiarity and intimidation).

4. Responses

Responses to ethical threats require them to be **evaluated** and suitable **responses** adopted: removing the circumstances leading to the threat; applying safeguards to reduce the threats to an acceptable level; and declining the activity that leads to the ethical threat.

5. Professional scepticism

Professional scepticism is used to challenge and scrutinise the subject matter placed before the auditor to ensure engagements are undertaken using best practice.

6. One firm providing both types of audit?

Provision of combined 'internal and external' audit by the same firm can deliver **savings** and provide a more '**joined-up**' service, but does present **threats to audit objectivity**.

Further study guidance

Question practice

Now try the following from the Further question practice bank (available in the digital edition of the Workbook):

- Question 2 'Fundamental principles' is an opportunity to practise some of the theory discussed in this chapter in an applied situation.
- Question 3 'Business assurance' is a discussion question that tests how well you have understood the theory regarding certain non-audit services.

Further reading

There are technical articles on the ACCA website written by members of the AAA examining team which are relevant to some of the topics covered in this chapter that you should read:

- *Exam technique for Advanced Audit and Assurance: Part 1 – ethics*
- *Professional scepticism*

Own research

Consider your own organisation or one that you are familiar with – what can you learn from the following to help you with topics from this chapter?

- Do you have a Code of Ethics that you are expected to follow? If so, obtain a copy and see how closely it matches the content presented here.
- Start to keep a diary of events where you believe you needed to consider the ethical implications of your actions – in each case, do you think you behaved as you should have done? If not, why do you think this was?

Note. You may find the **ACCA Rulebook** helpful to refer to. The Rulebook is updated periodically to reflect changes in policy, regulation, standards and legislation. The most recent update took effect from **1 January 2020** and related to regulatory issues that are not expected to have any impact on your studies, hence the details have not been included in your Workbook. Should you wish to access the ACCA Rulebook at any time, it is available on the **ACCA website**: www.accaglobal.com/lk/en/about-us/regulation/rulebook.html

Activity answers

Activity 1: Ethical threats

> **Approach**
>
> This activity serves as something of a refresher for you, as you should have seen the ethical threats in your earlier studies. Use this as a way of reminding yourself what each threat means and how it could be present from the situations you suggest.
>
> Note that in the real exam, you are likely to consider this from the opposite direction: a scenario will present a set of circumstances that you will need to analyse in order to find the appropriate ethical threat.

Suggested solution

Self-interest threat

This would arise in situations where the audit firm or a member of the engagement team has some financial or other interest in the audit client. For example:

- Providing a loan to a client
- Earning fees on a contingent basis, ie profit related
- Owning shares in a client
- Undue dependence on fees from a client

Self-review threat

The self-review threat occurs when a previous judgement needs to be re-evaluated by members responsible for that judgement. The situation tends to arise when the auditor has provided other services to a client. Key examples would be:

- The auditor providing a specialist valuation (eg pension liabilities)
- The audit firm providing internal audit services and subsequently relying on the work for the external audit
- Reporting on the operation of financial systems after being involved in their design or implementation

Advocacy threat

The advocacy threat occurs when members promote a position or opinion to the point that subsequent objectivity may be compromised. Specific examples would be:

- Acting as an advocate on behalf of an assurance client in litigation or disputes with third parties
- Promoting shares in a listed entity when that entity is a financial statement audit client

Familiarity threat

The familiarity threat occurs when, because of a close relationship, members become too sympathetic to the interest of others. Circumstances which would create a familiarity threat would include:

- Long association with a client
- Acceptance of gifts or preferential treatment unless the value is clearly insignificant
- Overfamiliarity with the management of the organisation such that judgement could be compromised

Intimidation threat

The intimidation threat occurs when members are deterred from acting objectively by threats, actual or perceived. Such a threat will occur in the following circumstances:

- The threat of dismissal or replacement of the member, or a close or immediate family member, over a disagreement about the application of an accounting principle or the way in which financial and performance information is to be reported
- A dominant personality attempting to influence the decision-making process or controlling relations with auditors
- Being threatened with litigation
- Being pressured to reduce inappropriately the extent of work performed in order to reduce fees

Activity 2: Ethical responses

> **Approach**
>
> This is similar to the way that such content would be examined in the AAA exam, albeit with slightly less detail than an exam standard scenario would present. The approach you should follow needs to cover two things: firstly, the **threat(s)** presented by the scenario with **reasons** why this represents the threat(s) identified; and secondly, the **response(s)** that should be taken, along with **justifications**.

1 **Suggested solution**

Godfather

Threats: There is a risk that the partner's personal relationship with the client will result in **self-interest**, **familiarity** and **intimidation** threats. This is because the partner has been involved with the client for many years and evidently has a **personal relationship** with a senior member of client staff, despite the fact that this should be an independent audit assignment. We are not told whether or not the partner involved is the engagement partner for this client, so our responses will need to consider both possibilities, but any partner would be able to exert significant influence on the conduct of the audit.

Responses: The risk arising here is **significant**, because both the engagement partner of the firm and the finance director of the client are in senior positions, meaning that any lack of objectivity could affect the financial statements. The firm should therefore implement **safeguards** to mitigate against these threats. If it is the engagement partner who has been asked to be godfather, that partner should be **rotated** away from this engagement immediately. If it is not the engagement partner who has been asked to be godfather, an independent partner should provide an **engagement quality control review** (sometimes called a 'hot review' or pre-issuance review) of the audit to ensure there has been no undue influence on conduct of the audit.

(IESBA Code: section 521)

2 **Suggested solution**

Actuarial services

Threats: Actuarial services are covered by **valuation services** in the IESBA Code, which state that the provision of such services may give rise to a **self-review** or **advocacy** threat. For clients that are not public interest entities, if the service involves evaluating matters that are **material** to the financial statements and the valuation involves a **significant degree of subjectivity**, then the threat to objectivity and independence **cannot be reduced to an acceptable level by appropriate safeguards** and the service should not, therefore, be provided.

For public interest entities, valuation services for material items shall not be provided by a firm, regardless of the level of subjectivity.

Responses: Undertaking this service for an audit client that is not a public interest entity, for amounts that are neither separately, nor in aggregate, material to the financial statements, or that do not involve a significant degree of subjectivity, could still create a **self-review** or **advocacy** threat. However, safeguards could be applied, such as the involvement of an **additional accountant** who is not a member of the assurance team to review the work done, and ensuring that **members** doing the valuation work **do not also undertake the audit work for that client**.

(IESBA Code: section 603)

Activity 3: Aventura International

> ### Approach
>
> As this is an exam-standard question, you should consider the basics of exam technique here:
>
> - **Timing**: 15 marks = 29 minutes, split roughly into 8 minutes of thinking and planning, and 21 minutes of writing.
> - **Planning**: The question requires you to find issues to discuss and recommend suitable responses – assuming an average of 5 marks for each scenario, you should consider 2–3 issues and 2–3 responses in each case.
> - **Content**: Use the knowledge from the chapter and the Essential reading (available in the digital edition of the Workbook) to inform your answer with the content of the various Codes of Ethics.
> - **Tone**: You should get used to writing for a critical audience and consider the higher-level judgement skills of communication, scepticism and logic.

Suggested solution

Ethical situations arising in connection with the audit of Aventura International

(1) Offer of goods

At the inventory count, the auditors attending were invited to purchase inventory at 30% of RRP, that is, at a 70% discount.

ACCA's guidance on accepting goods states that such benefits should only be accepted on 'normal commercial terms' or if the value is 'trivial and inconsequential' (*ACCA Code*: section 250.11 A2; IESBA Code: para R906.3). What constitutes trivial and inconsequential will be a matter of judgement for the auditor.

Benefit

It is possible that this offer does approximate to offers made to staff at Aventura, as clothes commonly retail at prices with a substantial mark-up on cost. It would not be unreasonable for a clothes retailer to give staff a 'cost' benefit. The auditor should determine whether such a benefit is made available to staff. If it is not made to staff it should not be accepted by the auditor. The ethical threat most likely to be relevant here is **self-interest**, although enjoying a discount that client staff may also have access to could introduce a **familiarity** threat too.

The term 'trivial and inconsequential' should be considered in terms of materiality to both the auditor and the company. The offer is not material to Aventura, for whom clothes retail is only one division. However, the offer of unlimited fashion at a 70% discount is extremely likely to be material to junior audit staff (who are the grade most likely to be allocated to the inventory count). In this context, the benefit is clearly not inconsequential.

Timing

It would be inappropriate to take up the offer at the inventory count, not least because this would constitute movement of inventory during the count, which would be wrong.

Also, the junior staff members should not accept such goods without having first discussed the matter with the audit partner (it is assumed in this answer that this is the first time such an offer has been made).

Lastly, if mistakes were to be made on the inventory count, the audit might be open to charges of negligence if it appeared its staff members indulged in a shopping trip when they should have been auditing.

BPP
LEARNING
MEDIA

Action to be taken

The audit staff members should not take up the offer at the inventory count.

The audit partner should discuss the matter with management, ascertain whether a similar benefit is offered to Aventura staff and decide whether he feels it is appropriate for his staff to take up the offer. It may be inappropriate as Aventura might become perceived to be a 'reward' job by audit staff. Alternatively, it might be appropriate if the audit firm imposed a financial limit to the benefits their staff could accept.

(2) Hospitality

An invoice to the company for business use of the Chief Executive's jet shows that the Audit Manager was flown to Florida and back for a stay of two weeks.

Issues arising

(1) If the invoice was ostensibly for 'business use', what was the business? (Neither the client nor the auditor have offices in Florida.)

(2) If the invoice was not for business, the Chief Executive is wrong to invoice it to the company. Is this common practice?

(3) If it was for business, the cost of the auditor's flight should not have been charged directly to the company, but to the audit firm instead, which could then have recharged it. Was Darius Harken working for the weeks in question, or is it recorded as holiday in the audit firm's records?

(4) Does the invoice actually represent a significant example of hospitality being accepted by the Audit Manager?

(5) Did the Audit Manager travel alone, with family, or even with the Chief Executive? Does this indicate that the audit manager has a close personal relationship with the Chief Executive?

Hospitality/close personal relationship

It is possible that points (4) and (5) above may be indicated by the invoice.

In terms of accepting hospitality, ACCA's guidance is the same as was discussed above in relation to accepting goods. It is unlikely that paying for an auditor's flight would be considered to be on normal commercial terms, because it would be traditional for the audit firm simply to recharge the cost of a business trip. Taking steps such as these would help to reduce the suggestion that something inappropriate has occurred, if the trip was genuinely business related.

If the trip was for pleasure (a) it should not have been charged to the company, which raises several auditing issues in its own right, and (b) it does not come within the definition of 'trivial and inconsequential'. Ethical threats of **self-interest** and **familiarity** are evidently possible here.

In terms of close business or personal relationships, ACCA's guidance states that these might adversely affect, or appear to affect, the objectivity of the auditor. It seems likely that in this instance, if the Chief Executive and the Audit Manager have been on holiday together, or at least a business 'jolly', then as a minimum, objectivity will **appear** to be threatened.

Action to be taken

(1) The audit firm should review its personnel records and confirm whether Darius Harken was working or holidaying at the relevant time.

(2) If the trip was business related, the audit partner should establish why the cost has been invoiced to the company by the Chief Executive and not by the audit firm.

(3) If the trip was personal, then the Audit Manager appears to have threatened the objectivity of the audit and, indeed, given that the trip appears to have been taken around the time the prior year audit was taking place, that audit is also adversely affected.

(4) The prior year audit files should be subjected to a 'post-issuance' or 'cold' review and the Audit Manager should be replaced on this year's audit, which should also be subject to a quality control review.

(5) All invoices rendered to the company in respect of the jet should be scrutinised by the audit team, for further evidence of personal expenses being charged to the company.

(3) The impending marriage of the Chief Executive

The Chief Executive's assistant is the former accountant in charge of the audit of Aventura, who is likely to have been involved with the audit of the previous year end. She has just announced her engagement to the Chief Executive.

Issues arising

(1) Current year audit – there is a risk of loss of independence as the Chief Executive's assistant is aware of the firm's auditing methods.

(2) Prior year audit – there is a suggestion that the accountant in charge of the audit may have been in a personal relationship with the Chief Executive which may have adversely affected her objectivity.

Movement of audit staff

Ethical guidance states that where a member of the audit team gains employment with an audit client, then **familiarity** and **intimidation** threats may arise. Where a 'significant connection' remains, then no safeguards could reduce the risk to an acceptable level.

If there is no significant connection, then the IESBA Code suggests a number of safeguards in this situation, such as:

- Considering the appropriateness of modifying the plan for the engagement
- Assigning the audit team to someone of sufficient experience in relation to the person who has left
- Involving an additional accountant not previously associated with the audit to review

In the UK, for example, the FRC's Ethical Standard Section 2 states that in this situation, the following factors should be considered:

(1) The position the individual had in the engagement team or firm

(2) The position the individual has taken at the audit client

(3) The amount of involvement the individual will have with the engagement team (especially where it includes former colleagues)

(4) The length of time since the individual was a member of the engagement team or employed by the audit firm

Following the assessment of such threats, appropriate safeguards should be applied where necessary.

Action to be taken

Although the accountant in charge was not the most senior staff member on the audit, it would have been prudent to modify the audit plan before this year's audit. However, this does not appear to have been done, and the audit is nearing completion.

Therefore, it is important that Voest conducts a quality control review of this audit.

In relation to the suspicion that Ms Fennimore's objectivity may have been affected last year, it might also be a good idea to conduct a similar review of last year's audit work, evidence obtained and conclusions drawn. However, as the work should have been reviewed by an audit manager and partner after Ms Fennimore's involvement, the risk of a problem on last year's audit appears to be slight.

3

Fraud and professional liability

Learning objectives

On completion of this chapter, you should be able to:

	Syllabus reference no.
Identify and develop an appropriate response to circumstances which indicate a high risk of error, irregularity, fraud or misstatement in the financial statements or a given situation.	B2(a)
Compare and contrast the respective responsibilities of management and auditors for fraud and error.	B2(b)
Describe the matters to be considered and recommend procedures to be carried out to investigate actual and/or potential misstatements in a given situation.	B2(c)
Explain how, why, when and to whom fraud and error should be reported and the circumstances in which an auditor should withdraw from an engagement.	B2(d)
Consider the current and possible future role of auditors in preventing, detecting and reporting error and fraud.	B2(e)
Recognise circumstances in which professional accountants may have legal liability and the criteria that need to be satisfied for legal liability to be recognised.	B3(a)
Describe the factors to determine whether or not an auditor is negligent and discuss the auditor's potential liability in given situations.	B3(b)
Compare and contrast liability owed to a client with liability owed to third parties (ie contract vs establishing a duty of care).	B3(c)
Evaluate the practicability and effectiveness of ways in which liability may be restricted including the use of liability limitation agreements.	B3(d)
Discuss and appraise the principal causes of audit failure and other factors that contribute to the 'expectation gap' (eg responsibilities for fraud and error) and recommend ways in which that gap might be bridged.	B3(e)

Business and exam context

Auditors have responsibilities to several parties. This chapter explores the various **responsibilities** and the **liability that can arise** in respect of each of them. It also looks at ways of restricting liability, including professional indemnity insurance.

The auditors' responsibility to members and other readers of the financial statements in tort and contract can give rise to some form of **liability**, particularly in the event of **negligence**. Case law on this matter is complex and not wholly satisfactory. It results in auditors being liable to some parties and not others. However, **auditors' liability** is a dynamic issue in that it **evolves as cases are brought to court**.

There are some interesting issues for auditors with regard to liability, for example **limited liability partnerships**. The reasons for **audit failure** and other factors contributing to the 'expectation gap' are also covered here.

Critically, and contrary to widespread public belief, **auditors do not have a responsibility to detect and prevent fraud**. The responsibilities that auditors do have with regard to fraud and error are outlined here as well. Auditors are required to follow the guidance of ISA 240 *The Auditor's Responsibilities Relating to Fraud in an Audit of Financial Statements*.

Auditor liability is a key issue facing the profession globally, and is linked in with ongoing debate about the role of audit in the future. This area can be examined in topical **discussion** questions, or in **practical** scenarios considering whether an auditor may be held to have been negligent in specific circumstances. It can be tested in either Section A or Section B.

The extent of the auditor's responsibilities in relation to fraud and error is a critical element of the public's perception of the auditor's role. The requirements of ISA 240 in this respect are core knowledge for this exam and may have to be applied in practical scenarios.

Chapter overview

1 ISA 240 *The Auditor's Responsibilities Relating to Fraud in an Audit of Financial Statements*

1.1 Definitions

KEY
TERM

> **Fraud:** An **intentional** act by one or more individuals among management, those charged with governance (management fraud), employees (employee fraud) or third parties involving the use of deception to obtain an unjust or illegal advantage. (ISA 240: para. 11)
>
> Fraud may be perpetrated by an individual, or in collusion with people internal or external to the business.

Two types of **misstatements** caused by fraud are relevant to the auditor (ISA 240: paras. 3, A3, A5):

Misstatements resulting from **fraudulent financial reporting** (such as those used to **manipulate** financial results, artificially improving an entity's true position – revenue recognition is often tested as it is the most common form of this type of fraud)	Misstatements resulting from **misappropriation of assets** (such as **stealing cash** from fictitious payments or **inventory** for personal use or sale)

1.2 Responsibilities

The **primary responsibility** for the prevention and detection of fraud rests both with those charged with governance of the entity and with management. It is up to **management** to put a strong emphasis on fraud prevention within the company, putting in place **systems to prevent fraud** such as a **strong control environment and** a **culture** of honesty and ethical behaviour (ISA 240: para. 4).

However, the **auditor** should obtain **reasonable assurance** that the financial statements as a whole are free from **material misstatement**, whether caused by **fraud or error**. Specific objectives for achieving this assurance are:

- To **identify** and **assess** the **risks of material misstatement** due to fraud
- To obtain **sufficient appropriate evidence** regarding the assessed risks of material misstatement due to fraud, through designing and implementing appropriate responses; and
- To **respond** appropriately to fraud or suspected fraud identified during the audit

(ISA 240: para. 10)

1.3 Audit approach

Members of the engagement team should discuss the **susceptibility** of the entity's financial statements to material misstatement due to fraud. An overriding requirement of the ISA is that auditors are aware of the possibility of there being misstatements due to fraud. The mindset of **professional scepticism** is important here, with the auditor always being alert to the possibility that things may not be as they seem, and that the management who have always appeared honest may not really be (ISA 240: paras. 12–14).

The auditor should make **enquiries of management** regarding **management's assessment** of the risk that the financial statements may be materially misstated due to fraud and management's process for identifying and responding to the risks of fraud in the entity.

The auditor should also **determine management's process** for identifying and responding to the risks of fraud and how such a process is communicated, both to those charged with governance and to staff. The auditor should also enquire about any **actual, suspected or alleged fraud** affecting the entity, including discussions about fraud with Internal Audit.

The auditor should obtain an understanding of how those charged with governance exercise oversight of **management's processes for identifying and responding** to the risks of fraud and the internal control that management has established to mitigate these risks as part of its ongoing risk management procedures.

1.3.1 Examples of fraud risk factors

In determining an **approach** to fraud, auditors could consider the **conditions** that lead to fraud:

(a) An incentive or pressure to commit fraud (Motive)

(b) A perceived opportunity to commit fraud (Opportunity)

(c) An ability or attitude to rationalise the fraudulent action (Dishonesty)

(ISA 240: para. A1)

```
                        ┌─────────────────────────────────┐
                        │  Fraudulent financial reporting  │
                        └─────────────────────────────────┘
```

Incentives/pressures	Opportunities	Attitudes/rationalisations
• Financial stability/ profitability is threatened • Pressure on management to meet the expectations of third parties • Personal financial situation of management threatened by the entity's financial performance • Excessive pressure on management or operating personnel to meet financial targets	• Significant related-party transactions • Assets, liabilities, revenues or expenses based on significant estimates • Domination of management by a single person or small group • Complex or unstable organisational structure • Internal control components are deficient	• Ineffective communication or enforcement of the entity's values or ethical standards by management • Known history of violations of securities laws or other laws and regulations • A practice by management of committing to achieve aggressive or unrealistic forecasts • Low morale among senior management • Relationship between management and the current or predecessor auditor is strained

```
                        ┌─────────────────────────────────┐
                        │   Misappropriation of assets     │
                        └─────────────────────────────────┘
```

Incentives/pressures	Opportunities	Attitudes/rationalisations
• Personal financial obligations • Adverse relationships between the entity and employees with access to cash or other assets susceptible to theft	• Large amounts of cash on hand or processed • Inventory items that are small in size, of high value, or in high demand • Easily convertible assets, such as bearer bonds, diamonds, or computer chips • Inadequate internal control over assets	• Overriding existing controls • Failing to correct known internal control deficiencies • Behaviour indicating displeasure or dissatisfaction with the entity • Changes in behaviour or lifestyle

In accordance with ISA 330 (covered in Chapter 6) the auditor shall determine **overall responses** to address the **assessed risks of material misstatement due to fraud at the financial statement level** by performing the following:

(a) Consider the assignment and supervision of personnel

(b) Consider the selection and application of accounting policies used by the entity

(c) Incorporate an element of unpredictability in the selection of the nature, timing and extent of audit procedures

(ISA 240: paras. 28–29)

Similarly, the auditor may have to **amend** the **nature, timing or extent** of planned audit procedures to address assessed risks of material misstatement due to fraud at the **assertion level**.

Consequently, the auditor should also consider the following:

(ISA 240: paras. 30, A41–48)

1.3.2 Procedures when misstatements are discovered

The auditor **evaluates** the audit evidence obtained to ensure it is consistent and that it achieves its aim of answering the risks of fraud. This will include a consideration of results of analytical procedures and any misstatements found.

The auditor must obtain **written representations** that management accepts its responsibility for the prevention and detection of fraud and has made all relevant disclosures to the auditors. However, when there is a misstatement indicative of fraud, the auditor should consider its implications in relation to other aspects of the audit, particularly the reliability of those written representations.

The auditor must also document:

The significant decisions reached as a result of the team's discussion of fraud
The identified and assessed risks of material misstatement due to fraud
The overall responses to assessed risks
Results of specific audit tests
Any communications with management (ISA 240: paras. 44–46)

1.3.3 Communication

When the auditor identifies fraud or suspected fraud, they should communicate it to the **appropriate level of management** as soon as practicable.

Fraud should be communicated to **those charged with governance** where it involves:

(a) Management;

(b) Employees who have significant roles in internal control; and

(c) Others where the fraud results in a material misstatement in the financial statements.

The auditor should communicate to management, and those charged with governance, any material deficiencies in the design or implementation of internal control to prevent and detect fraud which have come to the auditor's attention. (ISA 240: paras. 40-41)

The auditor may have a **statutory duty** to report fraudulent behaviour to **regulators** outside the entity. If no such legal duty arises, the auditor must consider whether to do so would breach their **professional duty of confidence**. In either event, the auditor should take **legal advice**. (ISA 240: paras. A65–66)

1.3.4 Auditor's report

When the auditor confirms that, or is unable to conclude whether, the financial statements are materially misstated as a result of fraud, the auditor should consider the implications for the auditor's report:

1.3.5 Withdrawal from an engagement

The auditor should consider the need to withdraw from the engagement if they uncover **exceptional** circumstances with regard to fraud (ISA 240: para. 38).

If this becomes necessary, it will be necessary to discuss the reasons with management and those charged with governance, and it may be necessary to make a report to **regulators**. However, remember the **confidentiality** and **tipping-off issues** from earlier chapters: whenever you are considering whether to make a public interest disclosure, you should always bear this in mind.

2 Auditors' liability

2.1 Principles

Auditors could be found guilty of financial market abuse offences, such as **insider dealing**, since they are privy to inside information and may use this information for their own gain. Auditors could also be found guilty of a **criminal offence** if they knew or suspected a person was **laundering money** and they either 'tipped off' or failed to report their suspicions to the proper authority.

The auditor has a **contractual relationship** with their client. If they breach the contract, then they can be sued. In addition to this, auditors have a duty to carry out their work with reasonable skill and care. **Negligence** is a common law concept under English law. It seeks to provide compensation to a person who has suffered loss due to another person's wrongful neglect. To succeed in an action for negligence, **an injured party must prove four things**:

(a) A **duty of care** exists which is enforceable by law;

(b) This duty of care was **breached**;

(c) The breach caused the injured party **loss**. In the case of negligence in relation to financial advisers/auditors, this loss must be pecuniary (ie financial) loss; and

(d) The harm was **not too remote** a consequence of the breach.

2.2 The client

The **company** has a **contract** with the audit firm. In English law, a contract for the supply of a service such as an audit has a duty of reasonable care implied into it by statute.

Client	
Duty of care exists?	Automatic
Breached?	Must be proved

Client	
Loss arising?	Must be proved
Not too remote?	Must be proved

In order to prove whether a duty of care has been breached, the court has to give further consideration to what the duty of **reasonable care** means in practice. A number of judgements made in **case law** show how the auditor's duty of care has been gauged at various points in time because legislation often does not state clearly the manner in which the auditors should discharge their duty of care. It is also not likely that this would be clearly spelt out in any contract setting out the terms of an auditor's appointment.

As a basic rule though, demonstrating that the firm **followed auditing standards** would probably be seen as strong defence against claims of negligence from audit clients.

2.3 Third parties

'Third parties' in this context means **anyone other than the company (audit client) who wished to make a claim for negligence**. Clearly, this could be many people.

The key **difference** between third parties and the company is that third parties have **no contract** with the audit firm. There is therefore no implied duty of care, but the circumstances of the relationship between the audit firm and any third party might **create** a duty of care. The situation is therefore as follows.

Third parties	
Duty of care exists?	**Must be proved**
Breached?	Must be proved
Loss arising?	Must be proved
Not too remote?	Must be proved

Essential reading

See Chapter 3 of the Essential reading for more detail on the various cases that have been used to understand the extent of the auditor's professional liability. You are not expected to know all the precise details of the relevant cases for your exam, however; you will be tested on your ability to apply the basic principles to specific scenarios. It is vital that you use the right kind of **language** when answering questions in this area. Your correct use of such terms as **duty of care**, **liability**, **negligence**, **proximity** and **third party** can help to demonstrate to the marker that you are familiar with the subject matter, and that you are simply **applying** it to the circumstances in the question.

The Essential reading is available as an Appendix of the digital edition of the Workbook.

2.4 Disclaimers

The cases discussed suggest that a duty of care to a third party may arise when an accountant does not know that their work will be relied on by a third party, but only knows that it is work of a kind which is liable in the ordinary course of events to be relied on by a third party.

Conversely, an accountant may sometimes be informed or be aware, before they carry out certain work, that a third party will rely on the results. An example is a report on the business of a client which the accountant has been instructed to prepare for the purpose of being shown to a potential purchaser or potential creditor of that business. In such a case, an accountant should assume that they will be held to owe the same duty to the third party as to their client. The

Bannerman case suggests this will also be necessary for **audit work**. Since the Bannerman case, many audit firms have included a **disclaimer paragraph** in their auditor's report.

When ACCA's Council considered the use of such disclaimers, its view was that:

'Standard disclaimers are not an appropriate or proportionate response to the Bannerman decision. Their incorporation as a standard feature of the auditor's report could have the effect of devaluing that report.'

(ACCA, 2008: para. 20)

Activity 1: Moorland

Your firm of Certified Accountants, in common with many other firms of accountants and auditors, issues to its staff an audit manual which contains, amongst other matters, recommended procedures to be adopted in carrying out audits. A number of these recommended procedures relate to physical observation of inventory counts and review of inventory counting instructions. Owing to pressure of work, you neglected to arrange for the physical observation of inventories at the premises of Moorland, a limited liability company audit client, at 31 March 20X3, but your review of inventory counting instructions indicated that company procedures appeared to be in order. You decided to accept the amount at which inventories were stated in the financial statements at 31 March 20X3 on the grounds that:

(1)   The inventory counting instructions appeared to be satisfactory

(2)   No problems had arisen in determining physical inventory quantities in previous years

(3)   The figures in the financial statements generally 'made sense'

You issued your auditor's report with an unmodified opinion on 28 May 20X3 and unbeknown to you, Moorland used the financial statements and the auditor's report for the purpose of obtaining material additional finance from a third party in the form of an unsecured long-term loan. Unfortunately, in October 20X3, the company ran into financial difficulties and was forced into liquidation, as a result of which, the long-term loan holder lost the amount of their loan. During the liquidation proceedings, it became clear that inventory quantities at 31 March 20X3 had been considerably overstated.

Required

1   Explain the probable legal position (under English law) of your firm in respect of the above matter, commenting specifically on the following:

(a)   The possibility of demonstrating your firm was negligent.

(b)   The fact that the inventories figure in the financial statements apparently 'made sense'.

(c)   The fact that you were not informed that the financial statements and your auditor's report were to be used to obtain additional finance.

2   Describe the reasonable steps your firm should take to avoid a recurrence of a matter such as that described above.

(Total = 10 marks)

Solution

3 Limiting auditors' liability

The auditing profession is concerned about the extent of their liability to third parties. They argue that although they are required to have insurance, they are unable to get **sufficient** insurance cover to meet the potential level of claims. Also, even if other parties, such as directors, share an element of responsibility for misleading financial statements, audit firms argue that they still bear the burden of giving financial compensation while trying to act in good faith.

3.1 Insurance against losses

KEY
TERM

> **Professional indemnity insurance (PII):** Insurance against civil claims made by clients and third parties arising from work undertaken by the firm.
>
> **Fidelity guarantee insurance:** Insurance against liability arising through any acts of fraud or dishonesty by any partner, director or employee in respect of money or goods held in trust by the firm.

These types of insurance do not actually restrict the auditor's liability, but rather provide compensation to the auditor for liabilities that are incurred.

It is important that auditors have insurance so that if negligence occurs:

- The audit firm does not find itself with a liability that is **too big** for it to pay; and
- The client can be **compensated** for the error. An insurance policy would enable this to happen, even where the compensation is greater than the resources of the firm.

ACCA requires that all firms which hold practising and auditing certificates have PII with a reputable insurance company (ACCA Rulebook: s2.2.9(1)). If the firm has employees, it must also have fidelity guarantee insurance (ACCA Rulebook: s2.2.9(1)).

The insurance must cover 'all civil liability incurred in connection with the conduct of the firm's business by the partners, directors or employees' (ACCA Rulebook: s2.2.9(2)). The cover must continue to exist for **six years** after a member ceases to engage in public practice (ACCA Rulebook: s2.2.9(5)).

Remember that accountants usually trade as **partnerships,** so all the partners are jointly and severally liable to claims made against individual partners. However, insurance could be seen to encourage auditors to take **less care** than they should, knowing that they are covered for any potential liability, so it is not the only way of addressing auditors' liability.

3.2 Managing liability

Auditors may reduce the chances of litigation by ensuring they have good procedures over:

The following courses of action have been put forward as possible methods of reducing liability:

Incorporation

This would protect the partners from personal bankruptcy. However, the firm itself could be forced into liquidation. Further, there could be adverse tax implications and the firm would need to publish accounts and be subject to an audit, which might be unacceptable to partners. Despite these issues, many of the world's largest professional firms have incorporated in some way.

Limited Liability Partnerships (LLPs)

The Limited Liability Partnership Act 2000 enabled UK firms to establish limited liability partnerships as separate legal entities. These combine the flexibility and tax status of a partnership with limited liability for members.

The effect of this is that **the partnership, but not its members, will be liable to third parties.** However, the personal assets of **negligent** partners will still be at risk.

Several prominent professional partnerships are incorporated as LLPs.

Limited liability partnerships are set up by similar procedures to those for incorporating a company. An incorporation document is sent to the Registrar of Companies. The Registrar will issue a certificate of incorporation to confirm that all statutory requirements have been fulfilled.

In a similar way to traditional partnerships, relations between partners will be governed by internal partner agreements, or by future statutory regulations. Each member of the partnership will still be an agent of the partnership, unless they have no authority to act and an outside party is aware of this lack of authority.

Liability limitations

Even with PII and other means of restricting liability, there has been great concern throughout the audit profession globally about the remaining risks to firms' survival in the face of claims which still might exceed their insurance cover. One protection against these is to control the liability itself via agreements between auditors and their clients.

Proportionate liability: Allows claims arising from successful negligence claims to be split between the auditors and the directors of the client company, the split being determined by a judge on the basis of where the fault was seen to lie. This would require the approval of shareholders.

Capping liability: Sets a maximum limit on the amount that the auditor would have to pay out under any claim.

Essential reading

See Chapter 3 of the Essential reading for more detail on the advantages and disadvantages of different structures for firms to adopt.

The Essential reading is available as an Appendix of the digital edition of the Workbook.

4 The expectation gap

Expectation gap: This term is used to describe the difference between the expectations of those who rely upon auditor's reports concerning audit work performed and the actual work performed.

The expectation gap arises due to a general **misunderstanding** by the **public** of the respective **responsibilities of both management** and the auditor, and a **misunderstanding** of the **scope of an audit**. Such misunderstandings might include the following perceptions:

That it is the auditor's duty to prevent and detect fraud	That the auditor is liable for any errors in the financial statements

Clearly, there is still a **debate** to be had and the continuing occurrence of financial **scandals** where fraud was present, despite an audit being conducted, means that this debate is not about to go away. Logically, the expectations gap could be narrowed in two ways.

(a) **Educating users**

The auditor's report, as outlined in ISA 700 *Forming an Opinion and Reporting on Financial Statements*, now includes an explanation of both the auditor's and management's responsibilities, but also quite extensive discussions of the key matters arising from the audit.

Additionally, the audit firm will reiterate the respective responsibilities of management and the auditor, and the nature, scope and purpose of an audit, in the **engagement letter.**

(b) **Extending the auditor's responsibilities**

Research indicates that extra work by auditors, with the inevitable extra costs, is **likely to make little difference to the detection of fraud** because:

- Most material frauds involve management

- More than half of frauds involve misstated financial reporting but do not include diversion of funds from the company
- Management fraud is unlikely to be found in a financial statement audit
- Far more is spent on investigating and prosecuting fraud in a company than on its audit

Suggestions for expanding the auditor's role have included:

- Requiring auditors to **report** to boards and audit committees on the adequacy of controls to prevent and detect **fraud**
- Encouraging the use of **targeted forensic fraud** reviews (see Chapter 14)
- **Increasing** the requirement to report **suspected frauds**

However, the adoption (in the UK for example) of **caps on auditors' liability** has been seen as a **retrograde step in 'building bridges'** between the audit profession and those members of the public who remain sceptical of the auditor's benefits to society and their apparent reluctance to stop future Enron-style scandals.

In an attempt to redress the balance following audit firm **Andersen's** involvement in the **Enron** collapse, the **UK Companies Act 2006** includes an **offence** aimed at punishing audit firms that knowingly or recklessly cause an auditor's report to be misleading, false or deceptive. Committing such an offence would lead to a fine.

The many different forms of assurance report that we will see in AAA all seem full of **disclaimers** that appear to protect the auditor and reduce the amount of reliance that users can place on these reports. However, without any protection from **potentially unscrupulous clients**, auditors are continually exposed to the threat of liability and without protection, auditors would not consider accepting any such engagement. If this were to happen, who would perform the audit?

BPP
LEARNING
MEDIA

University
of Ulster
LIBRARY

Chapter summary

Fraud and professional liability

ISA 240 The Auditor's Responsibilities Relating to Fraud in an Audit of Financial Statements

Definitions
- An intentional act involving the use of deception to obtain an unjust or illegal advantage
- Two main types:
  - Fraudulent financial reporting (eg Enron)
  - Misappropriation of assets (eg security guard stealing from warehouse)

Responsibilities
- **Primary responsibility for prevention and detection** rests with management
- Auditor should obtain **reasonable assurance** that the F/S are free from material misstatement whether caused by fraud or error

Audit approach
- Act with professional scepticism
- Assess risks due to fraud
- Fraud risk factors
  - An incentive or pressure to commit fraud (motive)
  - Opportunity to commit fraud
  - Ability to rationalise such actions (dishonesty)
- Respond to risk at F/S level (assignment and supervision; accounting policies; introduce unpredictability; reviewing nature, timing and extent of audit procedures)
- Respond to risk at assertion level (sensitive controls; journals; estimates; significant transactions)
- Reporting or withdrawing if necessary

Auditors' liability

Principles
- Duty of care exists
- Duty of care was breached
- Loss arose from that breach
- Not too remote

The client

Following auditing standards will support automatic duty of reasonable care to clients

Third parties

Not guaranteed but may be present from situations in the scenario – need to know case law

Disclaimers
- Bannerman connection
- Need to be used if felt it will protect auditor's liability
- Discouraged by ACCA as seen to devalue the auditor's report

Limiting auditors' liability

Insurance against losses
- Professional indemnity insurance (PII) for civil claims from clients and third parties
- Fidelity guarantee insurance (FGI) for losses due to fraud by firm employees

Managing liability
- Avoid litigation by performing quality audits
- Incorporation
- Limited liability Partnerships (LLPs)
- Proportionate and capping liability (UK CA 2006)

The expectation gap
- Due to misunderstanding of auditor's responsibilities
- Educate users – auditor's report wording seeks to close the expectation gap
- Extend auditor's responsibilities
- Caps vs 'reckless knowledge' offence

BPP LEARNING MEDIA

Knowledge diagnostic

1. Fraud

Fraud is a risk that auditors must be aware of. However, the primary **responsibility** for prevention and detection lies with the **directors** of the entity. Auditors have a variety of issues to consider when fraud is either discovered or suspected and should act appropriately.

2. Negligence

Auditors take a considerable risk when signing the auditor's report, since many third parties rely on the opinion given. If the opinion is proven to have been negligently provided, the **auditor** may be **liable** for financial losses suffered. This leads to the risk of **litigation**.

3. Case law

Case history has determined that auditors are currently only likely to be **liable** to the **client** itself and the **shareholders as a body**. Any other third party would have to demonstrate sufficient **proximity**, and therefore a **duty of care**, to be successful in a claim of negligence.

4. Liability limitation

The profession has taken many steps recently to try to **limit liability** to third parties via **caps**; many major firms have changed their **legal structure** as a result (eg **LLPs** or **limited companies**). All firms hold insurance as part of the requirements for holding a practising certificate: **PII** is mandatory for all ACCA firms alongside **FGI**.

5. Expectation gap

The expectation gap refers to the difference between what the **public perceives** the role of the audit to be and the **actual responsibilities** that the auditor is prepared to accept. This is very contentious.

Further study guidance

Question practice

Now try the following from the Further question practice bank (available in the digital edition of the Workbook):

- Question 4 'Professional responsibilities' is an opportunity to display your overall knowledge of the auditor's responsibilities in the areas covered by this chapter.
- Question 5 'Mobile Sales' is approaching exam standard and tests how well you can apply this knowledge to a scenario.

Further reading

There are technical articles on the ACCA website written by members of the AAA examining team which are relevant to some of the topics covered in this chapter that you should read:

- *Auditor liability*
- *ISA 240 (redrafted), auditors and fraud*

Own research

Consider your own organisation or one that you are familiar with – what can you learn from the following to help you with topics from this chapter?

- Consider the current 'width' that you believe the expectations gap is currently at – is it getting wider or narrower? Do you think recent corporate failures (for example, such as BHS and Carillion in the UK) are helping the auditor's case that they are doing as much as they can?
- Can you find an example of an auditor's report that includes a disclaimer paragraph?
- Find some examples of frauds online and see if you can determine what caused them – if you had been the external auditor in each case, what might you have done to try and uncover the fraud yourself?

Activity answers

Activity 1: Moorland

> **Approach**
>
> While based on an exam-standard question, this activity is really all about seeing how well you can apply your knowledge of liability issues to a specific set of circumstances. Use the Essential reading (available in the digital edition of the Workbook) to refresh your knowledge if required and consider how each requirement is testing the various factors associated with liability.

1 Suggested solution

There were a number of interesting developments in the area of auditors' liability to third parties in the 1980s and 1990s. The most significant recent case decision is the *Caparo* case (1990).

Prior to the *Caparo* case, the position was that auditors' liability depended on a qualified test of reasonable foresight, that is to say, liability depended on a principle whereby negligent accountants owed a duty of care to those who can be foreseen as likely to sustain damage if carelessness exists. However, this came with the important qualification that any prospective plaintiff, to succeed in their action, must establish that it was reasonable in the circumstances for them to rely on the audited accounts.

However, the *Caparo* case narrowed those who can successfully sue the auditors for negligence to the company or the shareholders as a group. It is unlikely that an individual shareholder will be able to successfully sue an auditor. However, the case has not yet been tested in the UK courts.

(a) *The possibility of demonstrating negligence*

The *Littlejohn* case demonstrated the principle that following auditing standards and documenting the approach is a good defence against possible third-party action related to negligence.

In the case of Moorland, the auditors seem to have laid themselves open to a possible charge of negligence in that they did not attend to observe the company's physical inventory counting procedures as recommended by ISA 501 *Audit Evidence – Specific Considerations for Selected Items*. Much would depend on whether or not the auditors could satisfy the court as to whether there were good practical reasons for non-attendance and the other audit work which they carried out in relation to inventories provided sufficient, relevant and reliable audit evidence on which to base the audit opinion.

(b) *The fact that the inventories figure in the financial statements apparently 'made sense'*

This seems to suggest that the main audit evidence on which the auditors based their opinion, in relation to the inventories figure, was the result of his analytical review work in this area. As the auditors seem, through pressure of work, to have neglected to attend the inventory count, then one would expect them to have carried out more extensive analytical review procedures than would perhaps normally have been the case for that client. If it appeared that the auditors had only carried out a minimal amount of review tests, then they would be very likely to be open to a charge of negligence.

(c) *The fact that the auditor was not informed that the financial statements and auditor's report were to be used to obtain additional finance*

If the person who provided the unsecured long-term loan to Moorland were to be able to recover damages against the auditors, then the court would need to be satisfied, on the evidence before it, that:

(1) The auditors had been negligent;

(2) The third party had suffered loss in consequence of that negligence on the part of the auditors; and

(3) The auditors should reasonably have foreseen that the third party might wish to place reliance on the audited accounts.

As a result of the *Caparo* case, it would appear that the third party would not succeed in an action against the company: the plaintiff would need to prove that the auditors knew that the financial statements would be used specifically to obtain finance from this third party, which is not the case here.

However, this can only be decided by the courts.

2   From the above it may be seen that the issue of auditors' liability will always be dependent on the facts of an individual case. However, there are steps that any firm of auditors/accountants should take to minimise the risk of successful litigation against them on the part of clients and/or third parties. Such steps would include:

(1) Adhering at all times to International Standards on Auditing relevant to the client

(2) Adequate training of all audit staff to ensure that they are fully aware of how the audit procedures considered necessary by the firm are to be carried out

(3) Ensuring that there are adequate review procedures which are constantly applied within the firm to see that laid-down standards are being properly applied in practice

Skills checkpoint 1

Legal and ethical responsibilities

Chapter overview

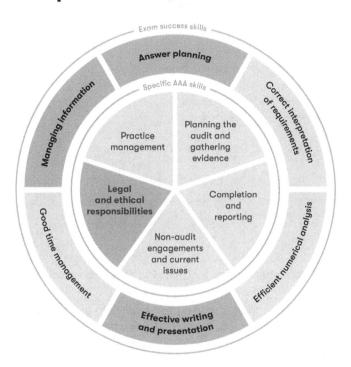

Introduction

The AAA exam will always test the application of your knowledge of this area. Candidates tend to remember enough to be able to identify when something's not right in a scenario – however, explaining **why** something is not right and **how** the firm should **respond** appears to be more challenging. You therefore need to be able to develop an approach that will assist you, both in advance of the exam and on the day itself.

While the context and complexity of scenarios testing legal and ethical responsibilities may be different to those you would have seen in the Audit and Assurance exam, the knowledge that you require for AAA should not be new to you – it is therefore important that you refresh your memory using the **technical knowledge** presented in this workbook before you attempt more exam-standard questions.

AAA Skill: Legal and ethical responsibilities

A step by step technique for approaching questions testing this part of the syllabus now follows (you may find that some of these techniques are suitable for other parts of the syllabus as well – why not start practising them now?)

> **STEP 1:**
> Think about the requirement and consider all the tasks that you are being asked to undertake.

> **STEP 2:**
> Read the scenario and identify all the areas of legal and/or ethical concern that you can.

> **STEP 3:**
> For each of the areas you have identified, list the reasons why you think they may be of concern to you.

> **STEP 4:**
> Add suitable responses to each of the matters listed and their reasons.

> **STEP 5:**
> Write your answer.

Exam success skills

There are some key exam skills that will help you when answering this kind of question, which are summarised below:

- **Managing information.** Actively reading the scenario for the key facts will help you create a good answer – in the case of legal and ethical issues, you need to identify the information that clarifies the issues presented, as there may be more than one response to an issue but a specific fact might help point you in the right direction.

- **Answer planning.** It sounds obvious, but in most cases, requirements to questions testing this part of the syllabus will be phrased along the following lines of: (1) 'What are the issues?'; and (2) 'How should the firm respond?'. Answers need to do more than this though – answering the first point needs you to say something along these lines: '... the scenario says this, which is wrong because ...' while the second should feature some form of logic: '... because of ... the firm should therefore do ...'.

- **Effective writing and presentation.** Having mined the scenario for all the relevant information and then planned your answer, you are then faced with the most straightforward task – writing what you want to say. This can be a challenge though, especially if you do not practise how to lay out your answer and how your plan will be expanded in full. This will only come from practice and asking a peer to read through what you've written to make sure it gets the message across effectively.

Skill activity

STEP 1 Consider the following requirement and write a short list of the tasks you are going to need to complete in order to satisfactorily answer it.

Required

Comment on the ethical and other professional issues raised by the above matters and recommend suitable responses.

There are two verbs here – 'comment' and 'recommend' – so you will need to make sure that you connect the two by some sound **logic**. This is based on being able to identify the ethical and professional issues, explain why they require action and then describe what that action should be. Your task list should therefore include the following:

(a) Read the scenario, identifying the areas of ethical or professional concern

(b) List these matters with reasons why they might be a problem

(c) Add suitable responses to each matter listed

(d) Write your answer

STEP 2 Read the scenario, identifying the areas of ethical and professional concern.

You are the Ethics Partner[1] at SB & Co, a firm of Chartered Certified Accountants. The following situations exist.

> [1] So you should be able to answer this without help from any of the other partners

Tammy is the audit manager[2] assigned to the audit of Recreate Co ('Recreate'), a large quoted company[3]. The audit has been ongoing for several weeks. Yesterday, Tammy's husband inherited 1,000 shares in Recreate. Tammy's husband wants to hold on to the shares as an investment.[4]

> [2] Not the partner but still significant, so it does matter

> [3] Threats may be more significant as it is quoted

> [4] Creates a self-interest threat...

The SB & Co pension scheme, which is administered by Friends Benevolent, an unconnected company[5], owns shares in Tadpole Group, a listed company with a number of subsidiaries. SB & Co has recently been invited to tender for the audit of one of its subsidiary companies, Frog Co[6].

> [5] ...but is it material and does it matter if a 3rd party is in control?

> [6] Another self-interest threat but only if material?

SB & Co has been the auditor of Kripps Bros, a limited liability company, for a number of years. It is a requirement of Kripps Bros' constitution that the auditor owns a token $1 share in the company[7].

> [7] Creates a self-interest threat

STEP 3 Now list these matters with reasons why they might be a problem.

* Audit manager's husband owns shares in a current, quoted audit client = self-interest threat

* The SB & Co pension fund would benefit from the results of Frog Co being as good as possible – as the prospective auditor of Frog, this also creates a self-interest threat

* Is the investment in Kripps Bros material? Is it essential to have it – why does it help to have the auditor as a shareholder?

STEP 4 Add suitable responses to each matter listed.

* Self-interest threat from shares = either dispose of shares or rotate audit manager?

* Self-interest threat from indirect investment in the pension fund = if both material and there is some form of control over this investment (unlikely as controlled by broker) a financial self-interest threat exists, so need to establish these facts – material?

* Confirm materiality of $1 share plus consider whether disposal is possible?

STEP 5 Write your answer.

Shares

Tammy is at present a member of the assurance team and a member of her immediate family owns a direct financial interest in the audit client. This creates a self-interest threat (IESBA Code para. R510. A1–4) due to the possible influence that a favourable auditor's report could deliver.

In order to mitigate the risk to independence that this poses on the audit, SB & Co needs to apply one of two safeguards.

• Ensure that the connected person disposes of the shares

• Remove Tammy from the engagement team

Tammy should be told that these are the options and removed from the team while a decision is taken regarding whether or not to sell the shares. Tammy's husband appears to want to keep the shares, in which case Tammy should be removed from the team immediately (IESBA Code: para. 510.10.A1–4).

SB & Co should inform the audit committee of Recreate of what has happened and the actions they have taken. The partners should consider whether it is necessary to bring in an independent partner to review any audit work that Tammy could have influenced. However, given Tammy's involvement is subject to the review of the existing engagement partner and she was not connected with the shares while she was carrying out the work, a second partner review is unlikely to be necessary in this case.

Pension fund

The audit firm has an indirect interest in the parent company of a company it has been invited to tender for, by virtue of its pension scheme having invested in Tadpole Group (IESBA Code: para. 510.10 A13).

This is no barrier to the audit firm tendering for the audit of Frog Co. Should the audit firm win the tender and become the auditors of Frog Co, it should consider whether it is necessary to apply safeguards to mitigate against the risk to independence on the audit as a result of the indirect financial interest.

The factors that the partners will need to consider are the materiality of the interest to either party and the degree of control that the firm actually has over the financial interest (IESBA Code: para. R510.6).

In this case, the audit firm has no control over the financial interest. An independent pension scheme administrator is in control of the financial interest. In addition, the interest is unlikely to be substantial and is therefore immaterial to both parties. Only if the threat is significant should the interest be sold.

It is likely that this risk is already sufficiently minimal so as not to require safeguards. However, if the audit firm felt that it was necessary to apply safeguards, it could consider the following.

• Notifying the audit committee of the interest

• Requiring Friends Benevolent to dispose of the shares in Tadpole Group.

Kripps Bros

In this case, SB & Co has a direct financial interest in the audit client, which is technically prohibited by the IESBA Code. However, it is a requirement of any firm auditing the company that the share be owned by the auditors.

The interest is not material. The audit firm should safeguard against the risk by not voting on its own re-election as auditor. The firm could also recommend to the company that it removes this requirement from its constitution, as it is at odds with ethical requirements for auditors.

Exam success skill diagnostic

Every time you complete a question, use the diagnostic below to assess how effectively you demonstrated the exam success skills in answering the question. The table has been completed below for SB & Co to give you an idea of how to complete the diagnostic.

Exam success skills	Your reflections/observations
Good time management	This was not explicitly tested here but remember to consider the total time to answer the question (up to 1.95 minutes per mark) and the split between reading/thinking/planning time and writing time (something like ¼ to ¾ respectively of the total time)?
Managing information	Did you pick up on all the information you needed to satisfactorily answer the question?
Correct interpretation of requirements	Do you think you were able to 'comment' and 'recommend' effectively?
Answer planning	Was your logic sound when drawing conclusions about points raised and the consequent impact on the firm in each case? Note that in some cases, the IESBA Code only identifies issues and the responses will still require some form of judgement on your behalf in response to the specific factors in the scenario.
Effective writing and presentation	Did you manage to carry all the points from your plan through into your final answer?
Efficient numerical analysis	Not applicable for this question
Most important action points to apply to your next question	

Summary

Legal and ethical responsibilities provide a very specific challenge when presented with a series of events and circumstances and the requirement to comment on them in line with the IESBA Code and any other regulatory framework. Some of them may be perfectly acceptable; some might be clearly prohibited; however, some (and these are likely to be the majority) you can't answer right now, as there is some further information that you need to uncover. Success comes from technical knowledge and experience in how to explain your thought process.

4 Quality control

Learning objectives

On completion of this chapter, you should be able to:

	Syllabus reference no.
Explain the principles and purpose of quality control of audit and other assurance engagements.	C1(a)
Describe the elements of a system of quality control relevant to a given firm.	C1(b)
Evaluate the quality control procedures which are in place for a given firm and assess if they have been appropriately applied in a given engagement.	C1(c)

Business and exam context

The role performed by auditors represents an activity of significant public interest. Quality independent audit is crucial, both to users and to the audit profession as a whole. Poor audit quality damages the reputation of the firm and may lead to loss of clients and thus fees, as well as an increased risk of litigation and associated professional insurance costs.

Although there are specific standards giving guidance on how auditors should perform their work with satisfactory quality, these can never cater for every situation. Quality at a general level is dealt with by ISQC 1 *Quality Control for Firms that Perform Audits and Reviews of Financial Statements, and Other Assurance and Related Services Engagements.*

Issues relating to firm-wide quality control link best with professional and ethical considerations, and should be distinguished from quality control issues on an individual audit, which are likely to be examined at the completion stage (Chapter 10).

You could be asked to suggest quality control procedures that a firm should implement in specific circumstances, or to review a firm's procedures and assess their adequacy. Firm-wide quality control can be tested in either Section A or Section B.

Chapter overview

Quality control

ISQC 1 *Quality Control for Firms that Perform Audits and Reviews of Financial Statements, and Other Assurance and Related Services Engagements*

Elements of a system of quality control

Leadership responsibilities for quality within the firm

Relevant ethical requirements

Acceptance and continuance of client relationships and specific engagements

Human resources

Engagement performance

Monitoring

BPP
LEARNING
MEDIA

1 ISQC 1 *Quality Control for Firms that Perform Audits and Reviews of Financial Statements, and Other Assurance and Related Services Engagements*

Activity 1: Does quality matter?

Quality control is a key issue for all audit firms. Why do firms want or need good quality control?

Solution

2 Elements of a system of quality control

The firm's system of quality control shall include policies and procedures addressing each of the following elements:

(a) Leadership responsibilities for quality within the firm

(b) Relevant ethical requirements

(c) Acceptance and continuance of client relationships and specific engagements

(d) Human resources

(e) Engagement performance

(f) Monitoring

(ISQC 1: para. 16)

2.1 Leadership responsibilities for quality within the firm

The firm shall establish policies and procedures designed to promote an internal culture recognising that quality is essential in performing engagements.

This is achieved in the following ways:

(a) The firm assigns its management responsibilities so that commercial considerations do not override the quality of work performed.

(b) The firm's policies and procedures addressing performance evaluation, compensation and promotion are designed to demonstrate the firm's overriding commitment to quality.

(c) The firm devotes sufficient resources for the development, documentation and support of its quality control policies and procedures.

The firm shall ensure that whoever assumes ultimate responsibility for quality within the firm (which could be a chief executive officer, the managing board of partners or equivalent) has the sufficient experience, ability and authority to fulfil this role.

(ISQC 1: paras. 18, 19, A5)

2.2 Relevant ethical requirements

The firm shall establish policies and procedures designed to provide it with reasonable assurance that the firm and its personnel comply with relevant ethical requirements (as covered in Chapter 2).

The firm's policies and procedures should emphasise the fundamental principles of the IESBA Code of Ethics (or others, such as the FRC's Revised Ethical Standard in the UK for example) and reinforce them through:

(a) The leadership of the firm

(b) Education and training

(c) Monitoring

(d) A process for dealing with non-compliance

The firm shall establish policies and procedures designed to provide it with reasonable assurance that the firm, its personnel and, where applicable, others subject to **independence** requirements (including network firm personnel) maintain independence where required by relevant ethical requirements.

At least annually, the firm should obtain written confirmation of compliance with its policies and procedures on independence from all firm personnel required to be independent by the IESBA Code and national ethical requirements.

(ISQC 1: paras. 20–25)

2.3 Acceptance and continuance of client relationships and specific engagements

The firm shall establish policies and procedures for the acceptance and continuance of client relationships and specific engagements, designed to provide the firm with reasonable assurance that it will only undertake or continue relationships and engagements where the firm:

(a) Is competent to perform the engagement and has the capabilities, including time and resources, to do so;

(b) Can comply with relevant ethical requirements; and

(c) Has considered the integrity of the client and does not have information that would lead it to conclude that the client lacks integrity.

(ISQC 1: paras. 26–28)

2.4 Human resources

The firm shall establish policies and procedures designed to provide it with reasonable assurance that it has sufficient personnel with the capabilities, competence and commitment to ethical principles necessary to perform engagements in accordance with professional standards and regulatory and legal requirements, and to enable the firm or engagement partners to issue reports that are appropriate in the circumstances. *(ISQC 1: para. 29)*

Such policies and procedures address the following personnel issues:

*   Recruitment
*   Performance evaluation
*   Capabilities and competence
*   Career development
*   Promotion
*   Compensation
*   The estimation of personnel needs

 (ISQC 1: para. A24)

Activity 2: Capabilities and competence

List examples of appropriate control procedures to ensure the firm's staff have the necessary capabilities and competence.

Solution

2.4.1 Assignment of personnel to engagements

Audit work is to be assigned to personnel who have the degree of technical training and proficiency required in the circumstances.

Activity 3: Assignment of teams

What matters would you consider when assigning personnel to a particular audit?

Solution

2.5 Engagement performance

The firm shall establish policies and procedures designed to provide it with reasonable assurance that engagements are performed in accordance with professional standards and applicable legal and regulatory requirements, and that the firm or the engagement partner issue reports that are appropriate in the circumstances (ISQC 1: para. 32).

Matters to be addressed in the firm's guidance materials include the following:

- How engagement teams are briefed on the engagement to obtain an understanding of the objectives of their work
- Processes for complying with applicable engagement standards
- Processes of engagement supervision, staff training and coaching
- Methods of reviewing the work performed, the significant judgements made and the form of report being issued
- Appropriate documentation of the work performed and of the timing and extent of the review
- Processes to keep all policies and procedures current

The engagement process should include both:

- **Supervision** of the work as it is undertaken (including tracking progress to ensure there is sufficient skill and time to complete the work and to address matters effectively as they arise); and

- **Review** that it has been performed in accordance with professional and legal requirements, achieving the objectives of the engagement, and that the evidence obtained is sufficient and appropriate to support the conclusions drawn and the required report *(ISQC 1: paras. A34–35)*.

2.5.1 Consultation

The firm shall establish policies and procedures designed to provide it with reasonable assurance that:

(a) Appropriate consultation takes place on difficult or contentious matters;

(b) Sufficient resources are available to enable appropriate consultation to take place;

(c) The nature and scope of such consultations are documented; and

(d) Conclusions resulting from consultations are documented and implemented (ISQC 1: para. 34).

Consultation includes discussion, at the appropriate professional level, with individuals within or outside the firm who have specialised expertise, to resolve a difficult or contentious matter.

Effective consultation with other professionals requires that those consulted be given all the relevant facts that will enable them to provide informed advice on technical, ethical or other matters in order to maintain suitable quality standards for the engagement.

2.5.2 Engagement quality control reviews

An engagement quality control review is an objective evaluation of the significant judgements made by the engagement team and the conclusions reached in formulating the report.

Engagement quality control reviews are **required** for:

(a) All audits of financial statements of listed entities

(b) Other audit, assurance and related services engagements meeting appropriate criteria set by the firm (such as the nature of the engagement and whether it involves a matter of public interest, any unusual circumstances or risks or whether any laws and regulations require such a review to be carried out) (ISQC 1: paras. 35 and A41)

This review is performed **prior** to signing the opinion and is often referred to as a **pre-issuance review** or 'hot' review. The firm must also have standards regarding what constitutes a **suitable** quality control review (the nature, timing and extent of such a review, the criteria for eligibility of reviewers and documentation requirements).

Quality control reviews	
Nature, timing and extent (ISQC 1: paras. 37–8)	It ordinarily includes discussion with the engagement partner, review of the financial statements/other subject matter information and the report, and consideration of whether the report is appropriate. It will also involve a selective review of working papers relating to significant judgements made.
Eligibility (ISQC 1: paras. 39–41)	The reviewer must have sufficient technical expertise and be objective towards the assignment.
Documentation (ISQC 1: para. 42)	Documentation showing that the firm's requirements for a review have been met, that the review was completed before the report was issued and a conclusion that the reviewer is not aware of any unresolved issues (especially in respect of significant judgements).
Listed companies (ISQC 1: paras. 38; A45)	The review should include: • The engagement team's evaluation of the firm's independence in relation to the specific engagement

	• Significant risks identified during the engagement and the responses to those risks
	• Judgements made, particularly with respect to materiality and significant risks
	• Whether appropriate consultation has taken place on matters involving differences of opinion or other difficult or contentious matters, and the conclusions arising from those consultations
	• The significance and disposition of corrected and uncorrected misstatements identified during the engagement
	• The matters to be communicated to management and those charged with governance and, where applicable, other parties such as regulatory bodies
	• Whether working papers selected for review reflect the work performed in relation to the significant judgements and support the conclusions reached
	• The appropriateness of the report to be issued

2.6 Monitoring

The firm shall establish a monitoring process designed to provide it with reasonable assurance that the policies and procedures relating to the system of quality control are relevant, adequate, operating effectively.

Such policies and procedures shall include an ongoing consideration and evaluation of the firm's system of quality control including, on a cyclical basis, inspection of at least one completed engagement for each engagement partner.

The purpose of monitoring compliance with quality control policies and procedures is to provide an evaluation of:

(a) Adherence to professional standards and regulatory and legal requirements;

(b) Whether the quality control system has been appropriately designed and effectively implemented; and

(c) Whether the firm's quality control policies and procedures have been appropriately applied, so that reports that are issued by the firm or engagement partners are appropriate in the circumstances.

The firm entrusts responsibility for the monitoring process to a partner or partners or other persons with sufficient and appropriate experience and authority in the firm to assume that responsibility (and obviously, to those who have not performed the engagement itself!). (ISQC 1: paras. 48 and A64)

The monitoring process is focused on completed engagements where the auditor's report has **already been signed** and is often referred to as a **post-issuance review** or **'cold' review**.

Activity 4: VBMC

Varley, Bell, Murphy and Cobbitt (VBMC) is a small four-partner independent audit firm with a single office in a regional location. Clients include businesses and companies mainly in the retail and financial services industries. Two of the firm's biggest clients are listed. VBMC operates in a regime which has adopted IAASB audit, assurance, quality control and ethical standards as its national standards.

Leadership for quality within the firm

The firm considers quality control very important and endeavours to comply with international guidance. Mickey Murphy is the partner in charge of quality. He is also Marketing Partner of the firm due to his commercial awareness. There is no specific quality control department, but Mickey gives an annual update on the firm's quality control procedures in August when he is not busy.

Annual quality control reviews of audits are not undertaken due to the firm's size: the partners are in daily contact and discuss quality at their monthly meetings. However, as part of Mickey's annual marketing review of clients, he identifies any clients perceived as risky due to their size or the firm's dependence on them.

Human resources

New joiners to the firm are generally accounting graduates from the local university to minimise training costs. They all attend final interviews with the Senior Partner, Roger Varley. Selection is based on their exam marks, the ability to speak fluent English, presentation and confidence. Annual appraisals of all professional staff are conducted by the Senior Partner. He feels that the firm which, although growing, is still small enough to appraise staff personally.

Promotion is based on a 'balanced scorecard' of four criteria:

- Marketing events attended
- Completion of audit work on time
- Feedback from clients (based on an assessment after each audit)
- Punctuality of arrival in the mornings (staff should arrive by 8am, but can leave once their work is complete)

Audit process

All audit work is reviewed by the auditor in charge (AIC) before presentation of the files to the engagement partner. The AIC highlights the key risk areas for the partner to perform a second review on. Files are created and delivered for review entirely electronically. Due to the firm's scanning facility being oversubscribed, less important physical evidence is discarded at the end of the audit. The firm is too small to have industry units, so clients are spread across the four partners based on their location.

Technical matters

An ethical helpdesk is staffed by one of the partners, Janine Bell (when she's in the office), who is respected in the firm for her technical knowledge. Staff are encouraged to seek help where they consider it appropriate. All audit staff are provided annually with a memory stick containing PDFs of the latest IFAC Pronouncements for reference while conducting audits. Any necessary 'library' data – exchange rates, share prices etc – are obtained directly by audit staff from the internet. Technical issues are resolved by the engagement partner on the relevant audit.

Required

Identify and comment on the quality control issues arising from the scenario. **(10 marks)**

Solution

Chapter summary

```
┌─────────────────────────┐
│     Quality control     │
└─────────────────────────┘
```

```
┌──────────────────────────────────────────────┐
│  ISQC 1 Quality Control for Firms that Perform │
│  Audits and Reviews of Financial Statements,   │
│  and Other Assurance and Related Services      │
│  Engagements                                   │
└──────────────────────────────────────────────┘
```

```
┌──────────────────────────────────────────┐
│   Elements of a system of quality control  │
└──────────────────────────────────────────┘
```

Leadership responsibilities for quality within the firm

- Assign management responsibility so that commercial considerations do not override quality
- Overriding commitment to quality from senior management down

Relevant ethical requirements

- Firm's policy shall emphasise the fundamental principles:
  - Leadership
  - Education & Training
  - Monitoring
  - Dealing with non-compliance
- Annual confirmation by staff of independence compliance

Acceptance and continuance of client relationships and specific engagements

- Consider:
  - Integrity of client
  - Firm's competence
  - Firm's ethical compliance

Human resources

- Firms shall ensure they have sufficient personnel with the capabilities, competence and commitment to ethical principles
- Appropriate staff (skills and experience) shall be assigned to each engagement

Engagement performance

- Consultation
  - Internal or external
- Engagement quality control reviews
  - 'Hot ("pre-issuance") reviews' carried out during the engagement and BEFORE the audit opinion is signed (required for listed clients and unusual or high risk audits)

Monitoring

- Aim is to ensure that professional standards have been adhered to and that QC systems have worked
- 'Cold ("post-issuance") reviews' carried out after the audit opinion is signed and the audit is completed

Knowledge diagnostic

1. Principles of quality for firms

Quality control is a **fundamental issue** for all audit firms. The main source of guidance for firms in relation to quality control comes from **ISQC 1** which details the specific elements of a system of quality control for a **professional firm** to adopt.

2. Quality control elements

Sound systems of quality include the following:

- **Leadership responsibilities** for quality within the firm;
- **Ethical requirements** including any independence issues;
- **Acceptance and continuance** of client relationships and specific engagements;
- **Human resources** including the assignment of personnel to engagements;
- **Engagement performance** including procedures over adequate consultation if required and specific quality control reviews; and
- **Monitoring** to ensure compliance with the standard.

Further study guidance

Question practice

Now try the following from the Further question practice bank (available in the digital edition of the Workbook):

- Question 6 'Osbourne Co' tests how well you have remembered quality control from AA and that you can apply the theory to an applied scenario.

Further reading

There is one technical article on the ACCA website written by members of the AAA examining team which is relevant to some of the topics covered in this chapter that you should read:

- *Audit quality – a perpetual current issue*

You may find it helpful to read alongside the article on 'Professional scepticism' as they both support the importance of quality auditing.

Own research

If you want to understand the way that regulators are attempting to enhance the quality of audit, you could research this using resources available where you are studying – for example:

- In the UK, the FRC undertakes a series of quality inspections which you may find of use: www.frc.org.uk/auditors/audit-quality-review/thematic-inspections
- The IAASB also regularly consults on quality issues: www.iaasb.org/focus-audit-quality

Activity answers

Activity 1: Does quality matter?

Approach

This is a brief discussion question – remember that you could always be asked for something like this in the exam, so you need to have something to say about everything!

Suggested solution

- To provide reasonable assurance that the firm and its personnel comply with professional standards and applicable legal and regulatory requirements (ISQC 1: para. 11a)
- To ensure that reports issued by the firm or engagement partners are appropriate in the circumstances (ISQC 1: para. 11b)
- To protect the reputation of the firm
- To protect the reputation of the profession (ie to narrow the expectation gap)
- To reduce the risk of legal action against the firm for negligence

Activity 2: Capabilities and competence

Approach

Sometimes the answer is just what the standard says – get used to being able to summarise some of the key elements of each one – fortunately in this case, much of this is common sense.

Suggested solution

(1) Professional education requirements, eg passing ACCA exams before promotion;

(2) Establishing a system of continuing professional development and training within the firm;

(3) Work experience;

(4) Coaching by more experienced staff, eg other members of the engagement team; and

(5) Independence education for personnel who are required to be independent.

(ISQC 1: para. A25)

Activity 3: Assignment of teams

Approach

Again, this is a direct lift from the standard, although in the real exam, it's likely that you will have been given more to work with. For example, the scenario may state that a newly appointed audit trainee has been asked to audit complex and subjective balances such as financial instruments and accounting estimates: here you should be able to explain that unless they have come to the firm with significant skills and experience, it is unlikely that they can cope with this and should not have been assigned to such tasks.

Suggested solution

(1) Understanding of, and practical experience with, engagements of a similar nature and complexity through appropriate training and participation;

(2) Understanding of professional standards and applicable legal and regulatory requirements;

(3) Technical knowledge and expertise, including knowledge of relevant information technology;

(4) Knowledge of relevant industries in which the clients operate;

(5) Ability to apply professional judgement; and

(6)   Understanding of the firm's control policies and procedures.

(ISQC 1: para. A31)

Activity 4: VBMC

> **Approach**
>
> From a quick read of the scenario, it appears that VBMC do not take quality as seriously as ISQC 1 requires, so you have plenty to write about here! The good news is that when this is tested in the exam, quality control and other professional issues frequently appear as described here (clearly wrong). However, the challenge is to present your assessment by explaining why they are wrong in the context of ISQC 1. You can assume at least one mark for each well-explained point, so you should have come up with at least ten points – fortunately, that would not have been a struggle here!

Suggested solution

- Mickey's role as Marketing Partner, managing the growth of the business, is in direct conflict with his role as Quality Partner – it should be allocated to one of the other partners. This goes against the **leadership** aspects of ISQC 1.

- It is also possible that this conflict of interests between Mickey's commercial and ethical roles might obstruct the necessary **acceptance and continuance** procedures that the firm should have in place – there is no mention of any screening procedures for determining client integrity or to ascertain the availability of time and resources for any of the firm's engagements.

- The approach to quality control updates is inadequate to meet ISQC 1's **human resources** (HR) requirements; a more formalised programme is needed. Training should be conducted at a time when staff are not likely to be on holiday (or on alternative dates).

- Ongoing **monitoring** of compliance with the firm's quality control, professional and ethical procedures is required but the necessary inspections do not appear to be present. The partner cannot argue that the firm is too small if working under IAASB standards. Indeed, an engagement quality control review for the firm's two listed clients is required before the auditor's report can be issued.

- New joiners should be trained in the firm's **HR** principles and methodology. The firm cannot rely on their university degree. It is not sufficient to provide staff with standards on a memory stick. Typically, a staff manual would be produced, backed up by training and updates.

- In addition to **HR**, the appraisal criteria are not consistent with quality control objectives; for example, a 'quality' audit may overrun due to investigation of emerging issues.

- The review process undertaken as part of **engagement performance** is inadequate to ensure quality. Areas undertaken by the AIC not highlighted as important would not be reviewed by anyone. Typically, a manager review would cover the AIC's work and a second review of work undertaken by more junior staff.

- Documentation is key to quality when assessing **engagement performance**. Audit evidence required to support the file should not be destroyed.

- Allocation of audits to partners based on location does not foster quality. Industry units may not be practical in a small firm, but the retail and financial clients could be divided between the partners to develop specialisms (and foster efficiency). This approach to **HR** is a particular concern for the financial services clients which are subject to complex regulation, which could open up VBMC to liability if not suitably competent and experienced with the requirements of such work.

- Facilities should be available for technical consultation when assessing **engagement performance** (beyond simply ethical issues) both within and outside the firm. A facility for second opinions should be put into place between the partners. Consultation would be better allocated to a technical manager (or group of staff) to make them more accessible to audit team members.

- Additionally, **ethical** compliance should not be left to members of staff. At least annually, written confirmation of independence is required from professional staff by ISQC 1 to ensure there are no individual conflicts of interest (such as shareholdings or other connections).
- Data can be obtained from the internet, but staff should be provided with guidance as to where to source data from, to ensure accuracy and consistency of approach during **engagement performance**.

5

Obtaining and accepting professional appointments

Learning objectives

On completion of this chapter, you should be able to:

	Syllabus reference no.
Evaluate the appropriateness of publicity material including the use of the ACCA logo and reference to fees.	C2(a)
Outline the determinants of fee-setting and justify the bases on which fees and commissions may and may not be charged for services.	C2(b)
Discuss the ethical and other professional problems, for example, lowballing, involved in establishing and negotiating fees for a specified assignment.	C2(c)
Recognise and explain the matters to be considered prior to tendering for an audit or other professional engagement and explain the information to be included in the proposal.	C2(d)
Explain the matters to be considered and the procedures that an audit firm/professional accountant should carry out before accepting a specified new client/engagement or continuing with an existing engagement, including: (a) Client acceptance (b) Engagement acceptance (new and existing engagements) (c) Establish whether the preconditions for an audit are present (d) Agreeing the terms of engagement	C3(a)
Recognise the key issues that underlie the agreement of the scope and terms of an engagement with a client.	C3(b)

Business and exam context

It is a commercial fact that companies change their auditors. The question that firms of auditors need to understand the answer to is 'Why do companies change their auditors?' We shall examine some of the common reasons here.

Related to the fact that entities change their auditors is the fact that many auditing firms advertise their services. ACCA has set out rules for professional accountants who advertise their services which we shall also examine.

The audit fee can be a key consideration for an entity when it makes decisions about its auditors. Determining the price to offer to potential clients can be difficult, but it is just one part of the whole process that is tendering. Audits are often put out to tender by companies. We shall examine all the matters firms consider when tendering for an audit.

Linked in with tendering is the process of determining whether to accept the audit engagement if it is offered. ISQC 1 *Quality Control for Firms that Perform Audits and Reviews of Financial Statements, and Other Assurance and Related Services Engagements* sets out some basic requirements for all audit firms accepting engagements. Finally, ISA 210 *Agreeing the Terms of Audit Engagements* sets out the agreement necessary when an audit is accepted.

Many of the issues in this chapter are ethical. You could be faced with a change in auditor scenario in the exam. The issues surrounding a change in auditor have often been examined in the past, with scenarios featuring tendering and practical issues around audit planning. This area could be examined in either Section A or Section B.

Chapter overview

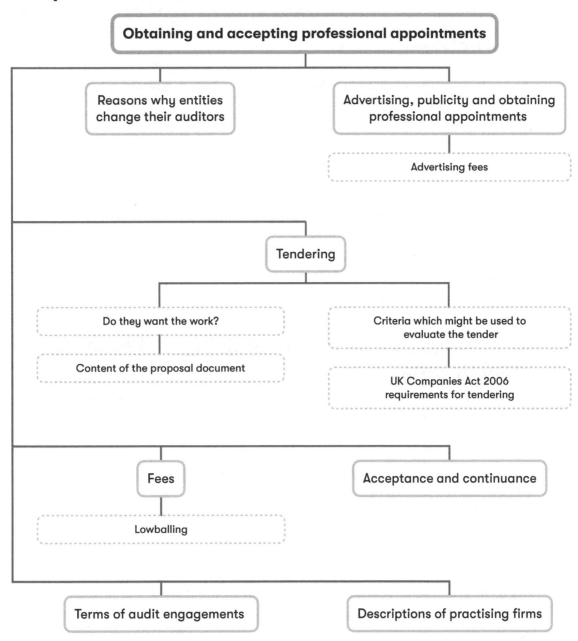

Obtaining and accepting professional appointments

- Reasons why entities change their auditors
- Advertising, publicity and obtaining professional appointments
  - Advertising fees

Tendering
- Do they want the work?
  - Content of the proposal document
- Criteria which might be used to evaluate the tender
  - UK Companies Act 2006 requirements for tendering

Fees
- Lowballing

Acceptance and continuance

Terms of audit engagements

Descriptions of practising firms

1 Reasons why entities change their auditors

The focus of this topic is on issues surrounding the change of auditors by an entity. It is important that you are aware of the circumstances that may lead to a need for the auditors to be replaced.

Activity 1: Changing auditors

Can you think of reasons why an entity may need to replace its auditors?

Solution

2 Advertising, publicity and obtaining professional appointments

Audit firms are allowed to advertise. The ACCA Code states that any advertisements or promotional material shall not reflect adversely on the professional accountant, ACCA or the accountancy profession (ACCA Code: Section B13 para. 1).

Advertisements and promotional material should not:

- Bring ACCA into **disrepute** or bring **discredit** to the professional accountant, firm or the accountancy profession;
- **Discredit** the **services** offered by others whether by claiming superiority for the professional accountant's or firm's own services or otherwise;
- Be **misleading**, either directly or by implication; and
- **Fall short of any local regulatory or legislative requirements**, such as the requirements of the United Kingdom Advertising Standards Authority's Code of Advertising and Sales Promotion, notably as to legality, decency, clarity, honesty and truthfulness

(ACCA Code: Section B13 para. 2)

2.1 Advertising fees

It is difficult to explain the service represented by a single fee in the context of an advertisement and **confusion may arise as to what a potential client might expect to receive in return for that fee** (ACCA Code: Section B13 para. 5). This means that it is risky for an accountant to refer to fees in advertising.

In longer advertisements, where reference is made to fees in promotional material, the **basis** on which those fees are calculated (hourly and other charging rates etc) **should be clearly stated** (ACCA Code: Section B13 para. 4).

The key issue to remember with regard to advertising fees is that the **greatest care should be taken not to mislead potential clients, particularly if comparing fees with those of competitors** (ACCA Code: Section B13). Any reference to fees must be **factual**, and the accountant **must be able to justify it**. It should not make 'unflattering' references to competitors (ACCA Code: Section B13 para. 10). It is appropriate to advertise free consultations to discuss fee issues (ACCA Code: Section B13 para. 9). This free consultation will allow fees to be explained, thus avoiding the risk of confusion.

We will look at how firms should set their fees in Section 4.

3 Tendering

A firm puts together a tender either in response to an **open invitation to tender** or if it has been **approached** by a prospective client and the partners have decided that they are capable of doing the work for a reasonable fee.

When an audit firm is approached by a prospective client, the first question it has to ask itself is whether or not it wants the work.

3.1 Do they want the work?

The **risk** attaching to the client must be considered. The audit firm would wish to consider the following:

Why has the approach arisen – first year of audit or a desire to change auditors?	What the future plans of the entity are – growth, survival, change etc?	What the client requires from the audit firm (for example, audit, number of visits, tax work?)
Can the firm afford to spend time on the proposal?	Does the proposed timetable for the work fit with the current work plan?	Does the firm have suitable personnel available?
Where will the work be performed and is it accessible/cost effective?	Are (non-accounting) specialist skills necessary?	Will staff need further training to do the work and if so, what is the cost of that further training?

Activity 2: Risks from prospective clients

What work would you perform in order to assess the risk attached to a prospective client?

Solution

3.2 Content of the proposal document

Assuming a firm is happy that it can manage the risks discussed above, the basic format of the tender proposal will depend on the **circumstances** and the **prospective client's requirements**. The principal objective is to convince the client to appoint the audit firm. The firm will therefore want to demonstrate that it has **understood** the **unique** features and requirements of the business and has considered how best it can **meet** those.

The following matters will usually need to be covered:

- The fee and details of how it has been calculated (discussed in Section 4)
- An assessment of the requirements of the prospective client
- An outline of how the firm proposes to address those requirements for the fee
- The assumptions made, for example, regarding deadlines or availability of information
- The proposed approach to the engagement
- An outline of the firm and the staff involved

If the tender is being submitted to an **existing client**, some of those details will be unnecessary. However, if it is a competitive tender, the firm should ensure they submit a comparable tender, even if some of the details are already known to the client. This is because the tender must be **comparable** to competitors and must appear professional.

3.3 Criteria which might be used to evaluate the tender

Academic research has shown that proposals are often won on the quality of service offered, value for money and the chemistry with the client, rather than simply on fees. The following criteria are likely to be used by prospective clients to evaluate the tender:

- Location
- Personal knowledge of the partners and staff
- Prior experience of the industry or of a similar sized business
- Matching the service offered to the specific needs of the business
- Communication, including prior agreement of the impact on fees before any additional work is undertaken
- The development of an effective relationship between the client and the key members of the audit teams

3.4 UK Companies Act 2006 requirements for tendering

As an **example**, the UK Companies Act 2006 requires some companies to put the audit out to tender after 10 years, with mandatory rotation after 20 years.

The tender will not always result in a change in auditor – it is possible that the current auditor will win the tender. But it means that management will have to consider whether the audit meets its needs, as discussed above.

Under the UK Companies Act 2006, for a quoted (listed) company, an auditor must always submit a **statement of circumstances** when they cease to be auditor, even where there are no matters which the auditor believes should be brought to the attention of members or creditors (Companies Act 2006: s.519).

In the case of a **private company** (or an **unlisted** public company), the auditor does not need to submit a statement if they are leaving because their term of office has come to an end. If they are leaving before this, then a statement must be submitted, unless the reasons for leaving are 'exempt reasons' (eg the auditor is ceasing to practise as an auditor, or the company is now exempt from audit), and there is nothing that needs to be communicated (*Companies Act 2006*: s. 519(1)–(3)).

4 Fees

The ACCA Code of Ethics and Conduct states that fees should be '**fair and reasonable**'. They recommend that the basis of charging fees should be mentioned in the engagement letter (ACCA Code: para. 330.3 A7).

Fees should not be charged on a **contingency, percentage** or similar basis, save where that course of action is generally accepted practice for certain specialised work (ACCA Code: para. 330.4 A5). **Commission paid and received** as a result of recommendations from and to clients respectively can be accepted, as long as adequate safeguards exist (usually full disclosure will suffice) (ACCA Code: para. 330.5 A2).

Fee disputes may arise when the client believes that the fee charged is excessive. If a firm is about to issue a fee note which is higher than previous fees, it is good practice to explain the reasons for the variation to the client concerned (ACCA Code: para. 330.7).

Assuming there is **no dramatic change** in the size or complexity of an audit client, it is reasonable to expect that the **audit fee should fall over time**. Some reasons why this would be the case are as follows:

(a) Time spent on the audit should reduce as the **auditors' knowledge** of the business improves over time, allowing the work to be completed **more efficiently**.

(b) The **client's systems and procedures** should be **fully documented** in the first year. This is very time consuming; in subsequent years, this information only needs updating if there have been any major changes.

(c) The **first year** of an audit is generally **high risk** due to a lack of knowledge of the business; the firm is likely to respond to this risk by assigning more senior staff to the audit, which will drive the fee up. In **subsequent years**, this **risk should fall** and more junior, and therefore cheaper, staff can be assigned to the audit.

4.1 Lowballing

> **Lowballing:** This refers to the practice of setting the initial audit fee low in order to win the client.

The ACCA's guidance on quotations states that it is **not improper** to secure work by **quoting a lower fee**, so long as the **client has not been misled** about the level of work that the fee represents, and as long as audit quality is not compromised (ACCA 2012: p4 'Fees').

Section 410 of the ACCA Code also discusses fee levels. The **ethical implications** of this practice are:

(a) Because the fee is set low, the audit firm needs to **retain** the client for a number of years in order to recover its initial losses; therefore, independence will be impaired via a **self-interest threat** as the audit firm will not wish to lose the client in the short term.

(b) **Professional competenceanddue care** may not be applied if the fee is so low that adequate levels of quality control cannot be displayed on the engagement.

(c) This can be seen as unprofessional because it means that **smaller practices** cannot compete.

5 Acceptance and continuance

There are a number of **issues** that auditors should consider when their tender proposal has been accepted by a prospective client:

- Does the firm have the necessary **technical competence** to perform the work?
- Does the firm have **sufficient resources** to perform the work?
- Are there any **ethical or independence issues** if the firm decides to proceed with the work?
- Has the firm considered the risks associated with **new clients**, such as **money laundering** or the potential for them becoming a **Politically Exposed Person**? Such people (known as PEPs) are usually in the public eye and as such become a target for extortion, blackmail or simple

human frailties such as corruption – this makes any association with them a possible threat to a firm's reputation.

- Has the auditor obtained **references** for the entity's directors?
- Has the auditor obtained **professional clearance** from the **outgoing auditors**?
- Have the **terms of engagement** (covered in Section 6) been discussed and agreed prior to accepting the appointment?

Note. This list is not exhaustive and that many of these relate to questions asked at the tendering stage.

Why might the firm be offered an engagement that it has submitted a tender for, but then choose not to proceed with the engagement?

Consider this in the context of a **graduate** looking for work – they may submit a number of job applications (like tender proposals) and some of them may lead to interviews and even job offers from prospective employers (like offers of acceptance by the client). However, in the **time** between submission and job offer, **factors may have emerged** that might mean the graduate is less keen to work at this particular employer and if they have a number of options available, the graduate may decide to go with the best one that fits their circumstances at that time.

Essential reading

See Chapter 5 of the Essential reading for more detail on acceptance and continuance procedures. This includes an awareness of the ethical and professional matters required for consideration and the requirements of ISQC 1.

The Essential reading is available as an Appendix of the digital edition of the Workbook.

Activity 3: Albion and Baggie

Albert Albion and Chris Baggie are partners in a successful firm of certified accountants. Total fee income for the firm is $5 million.

Last year, a branch of the large national firm Anders Arthurson opened up in the same town and since that time, Albion & Baggie Certified Accountants have been losing business.

Albert has therefore launched an advertising campaign, of which he is very proud, to try to win clients away from Anders Arthurson. The campaign has consisted of the following quarter-page advert being placed in the local newspaper every day for three weeks:

Albert has also organised a door to door leaflet drop, paying his nephew $3.00 to deliver 500 leaflets to local businesses and personal addresses.

Chris has been reviewing outstanding fee income. He has noticed that one of the partnership's clients, Virgo, owned by Dick Branston, has still not paid the previous year's audit fee. Virgo has tendered for a contract to run the National Lottery which has left the company with cash flow problems. Dick and Chris are very good friends; Chris is sure that Dick would not default on the fee.

In reply to the advertising campaign, a lottery company called Rolling Balls has approached Albion & Baggie, requesting the firm to act as its auditor. Rolling Balls is a large company which currently runs the Florida lottery and is also tendering for the National Lottery contract. Albert is immensely excited about this opportunity, as the audit fee is likely to be in the region of $500,000. As well as the audit, Rolling Balls would like Albion & Baggie to supply other services including accounts preparation and compliance monitoring (which would involve ensuring that Rolling Balls is complying with all lottery regulations).

Chris Baggie has two adult daughters, who both work for Albion & Baggie. Sophie, who has worked for the partnership for seven years, has recently taken out a $500,000 mortgage with Midwest bank, which is an audit client of the partnership.

Maggie, Chris's other daughter, has only recently joined the partnership. Up until three months ago, she was the financial accountant at Nibbles Pet Foods, which is also an audit client. Chris feels that Maggie's knowledge of this client will be a great help and is intending to use her as the manager on this year's audit of Nibbles. Maggie's husband Sid owns $100,000 worth of shares in this company.

Required

Comment on the practice management and ethical issues presented by the above scenario.

Solution

6 Terms of audit engagements

ISA 210 *Agreeing the Terms of Audit Engagements* sets out best practice concerning this issue.

The objective of the auditor is to accept or continue an audit engagement only when the basis on which it is to be performed has been agreed, through:

(a) Establishing whether the **preconditions for an audit** are present, and

(b) Confirming that there is a **common understanding** between the auditor and management and, where appropriate, those charged with governance of the terms of the audit engagement. (ISA 210: para. 7)

> **Preconditions for an audit:** The use by management of an acceptable financial reporting framework in the preparation of the financial statements and the agreement of management and, where appropriate, those charged with governance to the premise on which an audit is conducted.
>
> To determine if these preconditions exist, the auditor will assess whether the applicable financial reporting framework is acceptable, ensuring fair presentation of the financial statements, sufficient internal control to address material misstatements due to fraud or error and that the auditor has been provided with access to all the evidence they require for their opinion.
>
> (ISA 210: paras. 4–6)

This will all be confirmed in the **engagement letter**.

Essential reading

See Chapter 5 of the Essential reading for a reminder of the contents of an engagement letter.

The Essential reading is available as an Appendix of the digital edition of the Workbook.

If any of these conditions do not exist (eg the framework used is unacceptable or management does not acknowledge its responsibilities) or those charged with governance impose **a limitation on the scope of the auditor's work** which is likely to result in a disclaimer of opinion, then the auditor should **not accept the engagement**, unless legally required to do so (ISA 210: para. 7).

In a **recurring or continuing audit**, the auditor must assess whether circumstances have changed so that the engagement terms need to be changed. The auditor must also assess whether the entity needs to be reminded of the existing terms (ISA 210: para. 13). There is no need to send a new letter for each audit unless there is evidence of misunderstanding by the client.

7 Descriptions of practising firms

Members of the ACCA may be either associates or fellows, in which case they are allowed to use the designatory letters ACCA or FCCA after their names (ACCA Code: Section B4 paras. 5–6).

A firm may describe itself as a firm of 'Chartered Certified Accountants' where:

- At least half the partners are ACCA members
- Those partners hold at least 51% of voting rights under the partnership agreement

(ACCA Code: Section B4 para. 15)

Such a firm may use the ACCA logo on its stationery and website.

A firm which holds a firm's auditing certificate from ACCA may **describe** itself as 'Registered Auditors' and a firm in which all the partners are Chartered Certified Accountants may use the description 'Members of the Association of Chartered Certified Accountants'.

However, a firm must not use this term as part of its **registered practice name** (ACCA Code: Section B4 para. 19) which should be consistent with the dignity of the profession in the sense that it should not project an image inconsistent with that of a professional bound by high ethical and technical standards (ACCA Code: Section B4 para. 32).

Chapter summary

Obtaining and accepting professional appointments

Reasons why entities change their auditors

- Fee is too high or audit is no longer value for money
- Auditor no longer large enough to service a growing client
- Auditor may resign due to not making enough profit or independence issues
- Breakdown in relationship

Advertising, publicity and obtaining professional appointments

- Firms are allowed to advertise...
- ...but should comply with advertising standards and not discredit the work of another member, firm or the profession
- Fees must not be misleading

Advertising fees

Needs to explain fees clearly and what clients will get in return

Tendering

Do they want the work?

- Risks – what could change?
- Enough time and staffing?
- Logistics and expertise?
- Nature of work?
- Why approached?
- Cost effective and deadlines?

Content of the proposal document

- Fee
- Client requirements
- How firm will address requirements
- Assumptions
- Proposed approach
- Outline of firm and staff

Criteria which might be used to evaluate the tender

- Location
- Knowledge of partners and staff
- Prior experience of industry
- Matching service offered to needs of business
- Communication
- Development of effective relationship

UK Companies Act 2006 requirements for tendering

Statement of circumstances

Fees

- Should be fair and reasonable
- Commission OK only if disclosed
- No contingent fees for audits

Lowballing

- Practice of setting the initial fee low in order to win the client
- Not unethical but may affect quality and competition
- Auditor may need to retain the client in subsequent years in order to recover initial losses (self-interest threat)

Acceptance and continuance

- Necessary technical competence?
- Sufficient resources to complete the work?
- Ethical or independence issues?
- Obtained references for entity directors (PEPs?)
- Obtained clearance from outgoing auditors?
- Agreed and discussed the terms of the engagement prior to acceptance?

ISQC 1 has further details (Essential reading found in the digital edition of this Workbook)

Terms of audit engagements

- Contractual terms and conditions in engagement letter (ISA 210)
- Pre-conditions for an audit present?

Descriptions of practising firms

At least 50% of partners are ACCA and have at least 51% of voting rights

Knowledge diagnostic

1. Changing auditors

There is nothing unusual about an entity **changing** its **auditors** and there are a number of reasons why it would wish to do so: fees; client fit; rotation due to independence issues; disputes etc.

2. Advertisements

Advertising by audit firms is perfectly acceptable; however, firms should be aware of their responsibility to the profession and do nothing to bring it into disrepute.

3. Tendering

Tendering is a very common way for businesses to select auditors and requires the following questions to be considered: do we want the work and can we do it profitably? If so, the content of the tender and how it is likely to be assessed is considered.

4. Fees

Auditors have a professional responsibility to charge **fees** that are fair and reasonable: all things being equal, we can expect audit fees for a client to fall over time. Fees must not be so low to adversely affect audit quality though – this is the practice known as **'lowballing'**.

5. Acceptance issues

There are a number of considerations the auditor needs to assess before officially **accepting** a new engagement: quality control and professional issues are often the most important.

6. Engagement letters

The terms of audit engagements are agreed and recorded in the **engagement letter** and act as defined terms of reference for both client and auditor, provided the pre-conditions for an audit are present.

7. Other factors

A firm may only call itself 'certified' if it has **at least half its partners as ACCA members** and those partners own **at least 51%** of the **voting rights** in the firm.

Further study guidance

Question practice

Now try the following from the Further question practice bank (available in the digital edition of the Workbook):

- Question 7 'PLD Associates'
- Question 8 'Scenarios'

Both are excellent practice for applying this knowledge about acceptance and continuance in a scenario-based question – remember to justify your answer with reasons if asked to discuss or comment on anything.

Further reading

There is one technical article on the ACCA website written by members of the AAA examining team which is relevant to some of the topics covered in this chapter that you should read:

- *Acceptance decisions for audit and assurance engagements*

Own research

- In the UK, the FRC has conducted research into the current state of the audit market – as an example, you can see how issues you have studied so far interact in the real world by accessing their reports:

  www.frc.org.uk/auditors/report-on-developments-in-audit

Activity answers

Activity 1: Changing auditors

> **Approach**
>
> As this is just an idea generation exercise, you should only spend a few minutes thinking about the various reasons that an entity might change its auditor:
>
> - Who might be keen to make this happen?
> - Why might this be?
> - Is it a choice or an obligation?

Suggested solution

- The client may perceive the audit fee to be too high or poor value for money.
- The 'fit' between the auditor and the client may no longer be appropriate. For example, a company experiencing rapid growth may become too large and complex relative to the capabilities of its auditors.
- The audit firm may not seek re-election or resign. This could be for a number of reasons. For example, the auditor may have independence issues with the client or the auditor may have doubts about the integrity of the client staff. There may also be an insurmountable conflict of interest with another client. There may also just be a routine need to rotate or re-tender the audit due to the legal and regulatory framework in place.
- The reason could be due to a breakdown in the working relationship between the auditor and the client; this is especially likely with small clients who value a fairly close relationship with their auditors.

Activity 2: Risks from prospective clients

> **Approach**
>
> This is getting closer to an exam-standard question as it requires some lateral thinking. However, in the exam, you will have to consider this kind of request in the context of a scenario, so consideration of the factors presented will help you generate ideas.

Suggested solution

The following work would be performed in order to assess the risk attached to a prospective client:

- Perform a company search to ascertain shareholders, directors, security granted and whether or not annual returns are filed on a timely basis.
- Consult a credit reference agency to review solvency and consider whether the firm's fees are likely to be paid promptly.
- Review the most recent published financial statements for solvency, adequacy of disclosure and to determine whether or not the accounting policies adopted are acceptable to the firm.
- Examine background information to identify industry-specific problems, issues, legislation and trends.
- Less 'technical' methods such as looking at business and other media or finding out about the company's location and reputation in that area may also be productive.
- The firm may make use of contacts with knowledge of the company to assess its reputation and that of its owners and managers. Useful sources of information may include trade associations and local chambers of commerce.

Activity 3: Albion and Baggie

> ### Approach
>
> You could view this as a progress test, as it covers material from previous chapters as well as content on fees and advertising. This is very much exam-standard, and so you can start to get into good habits right now:
>
> - Always start with the issue, explaining why it is an issue.
> - Justify the issue using the ACCA or IESBA Code if possible.
> - Recommend suitable responses, acknowledging that there may be outstanding information which is required before you can respond.
> - Consider the 'bigger picture' of events that could change from what's presented in the scenario, as these may be relevant to the firm's consideration.
> - Format your answer using sub-headings and separate paragraphs.

Suggested solution

Advertisement

Albion & Baggie has clearly broken the ACCA's ethical guidance on 'Marketing professional services' (ACCA Code: Section B13 para. 2) by **discrediting** the services offered by another firm.

The **leaflet drop** itself is acceptable as long as it abides by advertising rules – Section B13 paragraph 11 of the ACCA Code states:

Professional accountants in public practice are reminded that any promotional activity shall be carried out in accordance with any relevant legislation. For example, a professional accountant in public practice shall comply with legislation relating to the making of unsolicited telephone calls or other communication to a non-client with a view to obtaining professional work.

The **fixed fee** is acceptable. However, fixed fees are not generally wise as the auditor is unable to assess the amount of work required until discussion with the client has taken place – fixed fees may reduce service and quality, if insufficient time can be devoted to the audit and losses may be made if problems occur that cannot be covered by increasing fees. An alternative basis may need to be considered by the firm to maintain quality and manage clients' expectations.

Outstanding fee income from Virgo

The outstanding fee income is similar to **making a loan to a client** – it may create a **self-interest threat** as the firm may choose to ignore issues relevant to the audit until it has received its own overdue fees. IESBA Code para. 410.7 A1 says that you would expect the fee to be settled before the auditor's report is issued, and if fees are overdue the firm should consider whether to continue, therefore prompt payment should be encouraged.

There is an implied **familiarity threat** to objectivity presented by the friendship between Dick and Chris. However, this is neither immediate or close family, so could be addressed by applying safeguards such as an independent review of the Virgo audit.

Virgo and Rolling balls

The lottery company tendering for the same contract as Virgo would constitute a **conflict of interest** for the firm if it wishes to act for both clients, as this is a major contract and they are competitors. This could also present confidentiality issues regarding any sensitive information about tenders for either client.

The Rolling Balls appointment could be accepted providing:

- Both parties are informed that you are acting for the other;
- Both parties are in agreement that this situation is acceptable;
- Different audit teams should be used on each audit and information should not be transferred between teams (safeguards such as the use of confidentiality agreements and information barriers would be required); and
- Reviews are carried out by different partners to those involved in each audit.

Rolling balls fee income

The ACCA and IESBA only set fee thresholds for public interest entities (PIEs) and in this case, the threshold is 15% of the firm's total fees for two consecutive years (IESBA Code: para. R410.4–6) before a **self-interest threat** starts to emerge (guidance in the UK is that the maximum fee income from one client should not exceed 15% of gross recurring practice income, but this is reduced to 10% if the company is a listed or other public interest client).

The Rolling Balls fee currently only represents 10% of recurring income. However, two issues arise:

(1)   We need to determine whether Rolling Balls is a PIE due to being a lottery company and not just because of its size or status; **and**

(2)   Other services are required (presumably on a regular basis) which are likely to push the fee percentage closer to 15% for future years.

Although there is no imminent self-interest threat, it is necessary to take extra precautions, such as disclosing this issue to those charged with governance at Rolling Balls and performing an external review of the engagement.

Additional services for Rolling Balls

In addition to the fee limit issue, the auditor should consider:

•   The amount of fee generated from Rolling Balls compared to the audit fee could create a **self-interest threat** (ie would Albion & Baggie be inclined to not modify the auditor's report in order to 'please' the client and retain lucrative other services?).

•   Whether Albion & Baggie have adequate **resources** and **expertise** required to perform the additional services (for example, do they know enough about lottery regulations?). The fundamental principle of **professionalcompetence and due care** is the key issue here.

Sophie and Maggie

The issue here is close, but not immediate, family connections that could create a **familiarity threat**. The risk is that the auditor may not be willing to issue a modified audit opinion to someone they are closely attached to, either in business or personally.

The issue is **perceived independence** – whether the public would perceive that the auditor has done a 'proper audit' on the financial statements of a party where such a connection exists or whether independence and objectivity have been compromised.

Under the ACCA Code (para. R511.5) there appears to be **no self-interest threat** regarding Sophie's **$500,000 mortgage**, as long as the loan from Midwest is on normal commercial terms.

Maggie cannot be manager on the audit of **Nibbles** until two years have elapsed since leaving the company, otherwise she may be auditing her own work and **no safeguards** could reduce the familiarity, self-interest and self-review threats to acceptable levels.

Despite Sid and Maggie being immediate family members, **Sid's shares** should not present a **self-interest threat** and do not require disposal because she is not to be involved in the audit. However, should Maggie subsequently be involved in the Nibbles audit, then Sid should **dispose** of his shares.

Skills checkpoint 2

Practice management

Chapter overview

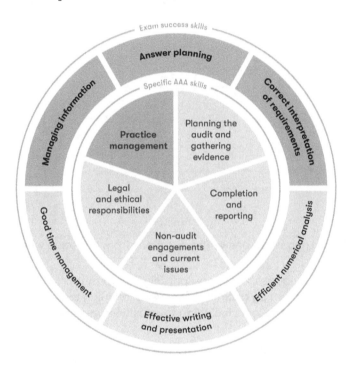

Introduction

This area of the syllabus could either be tested in a discrete, stand-alone way or as part of a larger question testing professional issues in general – practice management includes both quality control as well as tendering, fees and acceptance, so these could be combined too. There is sometimes even a cross-over with ethical issues as well, so questions on this topic could vary and you need to be prepared.

Answering questions related to practice management do require some learned theory to inform your approach – this will also help you identify areas of the scenario that may not look quite right and which will need some further investigation. The AAA skills and exam success skills in this checkpoint will help you to develop an approach that you can apply throughout the rest of your studies.

AAA Skill: Practice management

A step by step technique for approaching questions testing this part of the syllabus now follows (you may find that some of these techniques are suitable for other parts of the syllabus as well – why not start practising them now?)

> **STEP 1:**
> Isolate the verbs and confirm what the requirement is looking for.

> **STEP 2:**
> For theory-based requirements, consider whether there is a list that can be used to help you create an answer.

> **STEP 3:**
> For application-based requirements, what information do you need to focus on?

> **STEP 4:**
> Create an approach that takes steps 1, 2 and 3 into account.

> **STEP 5:**
> Write your answer.

Exam success skills

There are some key exam skills that will help you when answering questions from this topic which are summarised below:

- **Managing information**. It is important that you respond appropriately to information presented in the scenario as it is not put in there by accident! The AAA examining team will have considered how they want each question to look, including the positioning of certain pieces of information.

  In the Audit and Assurance (AA) exam, for example, you are presented with a scenario and each issue is documented logically and sequentially, with very little in the way of 'interference' to confuse you. In the AAA exam, you will need to look around the scenario more carefully – although there should not be any 'interference' you may need to piece together the facts a little more to see the whole picture – the question below is a good example of how to piece information together.

- **Answer planning**. Making use of lists can be a great way to start planning your answer. While we do not support the use of 'rote learned' generic lists of procedures or tasks that could be applied in every situation, a framework can be used in certain situations as a starting point for generating ideas.

  It is especially helpful in questions where there is more than one requirement, as a list can help you with a more factual or theory-based task, as well as when you need to apply the theory from that list to the scenario. The question below will show you an example of how this can work.

- **Correct interpretation of requirements**. Whenever you attempt any AAA question (both as part of your revision and in the real exam) you will usually start with the requirement, so you know what you are being asked to do. When reading through the requirement, you need to be sure that you have fully understood what you are being asked to do.

  In the case of the question that follows, you need to understand what stage of the process you are at (post tender, pre-acceptance) so your answer does not discuss things from the wrong perspective: for example, asking about the previous year's financial statements and the prior year auditor may be on your generic list of final acceptance procedures, but as the question has already addressed these, that will score no marks and will waste valuable time.

Skill activity

STEP 1 Isolate the verbs and confirm what the requirement is really looking for. Is there anything in the requirement that you need to take account of?

You are a partner in Hamlyn, Jones and Co, a firm of Chartered Certified Accountants. You have just successfully tendered for the audit of Lunch Co, a chain of sandwich shops across west London. The invitation to tender was received 'cold', which means that the company and its officers are not known to your firm. The company has just been incorporated and has not previously had an audit. You are almost ready to accept nomination but still have some outstanding tasks to perform.

In the course of your acceptance procedures, you received a reference from a business contact of yours concerning one of the five directors of Lunch Co, Mr V. Loud. It stated that your business contact had done some personal tax work for Mr Loud ten years previously, when he had found Mr Loud to be difficult to keep in contact with and slow to provide information and he had suspected Mr Loud of being less than entirely truthful when it came to his tax affairs. As a result of this distrust, he had ceased to carry out work for him.

Required

(a) Explain the procedures your firm should carry out prior to accepting nomination as auditor of Lunch Co. **(3 marks)**

(b) Comment on the matters to be considered as part of your firm's acceptance procedures from the reference received regarding Mr Loud. **(6 marks)**

(Total = 9 marks)

There are two verbs here – 'explain' and 'comment': the first is likely to require some theory to help you generate a series of points; the second is more challenging – commenting requires judgement and an assessment of what's presented in the scenario. You will therefore need to write more for this to justify your comments.

The mark scheme is different too – part (b) is worth double the marks compared to part (a), so you will need to establish how many points each will require to score well.

STEP 2 For theory-based requirements, consider whether there is a list that can be used to help you create an answer.

We have already explained that rote-learned lists are bad, so why are we recommending the use of one here?

Basically, all a list does is provide you with a selection of ideas that might be helpful when creating an answer – later in this workbook, we will look at how mnemonics can help here too. For now, let's look at the questions that you could ask as part of your decision to accept a prospective engagement:

- Do we have the right skills and experience to undertake this engagement?
- Do we have the resources available at the time required to undertake this engagement?
- Are there any ethical reasons why we may not be able to undertake this engagement?
- Is there anything about the client that might mean we don't want this engagement?
- Have we spoken to the outgoing auditors to see if they can tell us anything about this engagement?

STEP 3 For application-based requirements, what information do you need to focus on?

The application is required in part (b) – the part of the scenario that deals with the reference is shown below – so let's highlight the question as we would in an exam with the points that we need to develop:

In the course of your acceptance procedures, you received a reference from a business contact of yours concerning one of the five directors of Lunch Co, Mr V. Loud. It stated that your business contact had done some personal tax work for Mr Loud ten years previously, when he had found Mr Loud to be difficult to keep in contact with[8] and slow to provide information[9] and he had suspected Mr Loud of being less than entirely truthful[10] when it came to his tax affairs. As a result of this distrust, he had ceased to carry out work for him.

[8] May not be a problem but could affect the efficiency of the audit – why did he not stay in touch though?

[9] This could also affect the efficiency of the audit, especially if this is the finance director – possible that the directors don't know how an audit works?

STEP 4 Create an approach that takes steps 1, 2 and 3 into account.

For part (a) how many points from our list can we use and how can we tailor it to the specific circumstances in the scenario?

[10] This is not good – concerns over management integrity may mean we are unable to accept this engagement – might he have changed in the last ten years though?

Do we have the right skills and experience to undertake this engagement?	Should have been established at the tender stage, but greater client knowledge should exist now, so worth checking to see if anything has changed.
Do we have the resources available at the time required to undertake this engagement?	Again, should have already been asked at the tender stage, but we may have a better idea now if anything's changed – this would include any logistical issues of travel and evidence availability.
Are there any ethical reasons why we may not be able to undertake this engagement?	There are many issues here – the firm should already have known if there were any reasons why this engagement could not be taken on at the tender stage (eg conflicts of interest with competing clients; staff with financial interests in Lunch Co etc). However, the engagement partner may not have been allocated, so any ethical issues related to you as the partner should be explored.
Is there anything about the client that might mean we don't want this engagement?	The risks of having Lunch Co as an audit client would also have been considered at the tender stage (no tender would have been submitted otherwise). However, new information may still come to light – for example, are there any money laundering issues (especially related to client due diligence) that still exist? Question such as, 'Will they pay their fees?' and 'Are there any issues with the company or its directors that we don't yet know about?' would have been considered at the tender stage (especially as it is a newly incorporated business, so there will be very little data to go on).
Have we spoken to the outgoing auditors to see if they can tell us anything about this engagement?	Careful! The question says they have never been audited so there are no previous auditors to contact.

For part (b) we can take the three issues identified from the scenario and consider them in more detail, asking ourselves what impact these points will really have and what else we could say about them. An introductory paragraph will help to set the scene as well.

STEP 5 Write your answer.

(a) The following procedures should be carried out.

   (i) Ensure that my audit team and I are professionally qualified to act and consider whether there are ethical barriers to my accepting nomination.

   (ii) Review the firm's overall work programme to ensure that there are sufficient resources to enable my firm to carry out the audit.

   (iii) Obtain references about the directors, as they are not known personally by me or anyone else in my firm – any integrity or efficiency issues may affect audit quality.

(b) The auditor must use their professional judgement when considering the responses they get to references concerning new clients. The guidance cannot legislate for all situations, so it does not attempt to do so. In the circumstance given above, there is no correct answer, so in practice an auditor would have to make a justifiable decision which they would then document.

Matters to be considered

The reference raises three issues for the auditor considering accepting nomination:

(a) The issue that the director has been difficult to maintain a relationship with in the past

(b) The issue that the director was slow to provide information in the past

(c) The suspicion of a lack of integrity in relation to his tax affairs

The auditor must **consider** these **in the light of several factors**:

(a) The length of time that has passed since the events

(b) What references which refer to the interim time say

(c) The difference between accepting a role of auditing a company and personal tax work

(d) The director's role in the company and therefore the audit

(e) The amount of control exercised by the director:

   (i) Relationships with other directors

   (ii) Influence

At this stage, they **should not be considering** how highly they **value** the **opinion** of the referee. That should have been considered before they sent the reference. At this stage, they should only be considering the implications of the reference for their current decision.

Auditing a company is different from auditing personal affairs in terms of obtaining information and contacting personnel. In this case, the **key issue** is the question over the **integrity** of the director.

As we do not have information about interim references and details of the business arrangements, it is difficult to give a definite answer to this issue. However, Mr Loud is likely to only have **limited control over decisions** of the entity being one of five directors, which might lead to the auditor deciding that the reference was insufficient to prevent him accepting nomination. If Mr Loud were the **finance director**, the auditor would be more inclined not to take the nomination.

Exam success skills diagnostic

Every time you complete a question, use the diagnostic below to assess how effectively you demonstrated the exam success skills in answering the question. The table has been completed below for Hamlyn, Jones and Co to give you an idea of how to complete the diagnostic.

Exam success skills	Your reflections/observations
Good time management	For a 9 mark requirement like this, the total time to answer the question (up to 1.95 minutes per mark) would have been 17½ minutes; the split between reading/thinking/planning time and

Exam success skills	Your reflections/observations
	writing time (something like ¼ to ¾ respectively of the total time) would therefore have been 4½ minutes reading/planning/thinking and 13 minutes writing.
Managing information	Did you pick up on all the information you needed to satisfactorily answer the question – for example, that there were no previous auditors?
Correct interpretation of requirements	Do you think you were able to 'explain' and 'comment' effectively and do you think your answer was pitched at the right intellectual level in each case?
Answer planning	Do you think you got all the points you should have done about acceptance? What would a general list of such matters include and do you think you'd be able to remember it (for reference purposes only!) in the exam?
Effective writing and presentation	Did you manage to carry all the points from your plan through into your final answer? Did you justify the marks for each of parts (a) and (b) in your answers?
Efficient numerical analysis	Not applicable for this question
Most important action points to apply to your next question	

Summary

Practice management includes a number of elements that we haven't touched upon here – for example: quality control; the contents of a tender; determinants of fee-setting; reasons why auditors change their auditors – and in most cases, they lend themselves to using lists to help generate ideas. With the exception of quality control, which is driven by ISA 220, most of these lists contain very practical issues that attempting past exam questions will help you to generate so you have a framework to run with.

Planning and risk assessment

Learning objectives

On completion of this chapter, you should be able to:

	Syllabus reference no.
Define materiality and performance materiality and demonstrate how it should be applied in financial reporting and auditing.	D1(a)
Discuss and demonstrate the use of analytical procedures in the planning of an assignment.	D1(b)
Evaluate and prioritise business risks, audit risks and risks of material misstatement for a given assignment.	D1(c)
Interpret the results of analytical procedures, in an unbiased manner and apply professional scepticism to support the identification of contradictory information and assessment of risks of material misstatement.	D1(d)
Evaluate the results of planning and risk assessment procedures to determine the relevant audit strategy including the auditor's responses.	D1(e)
Recommend additional information which may be required to effectively carry out a planned engagement or a specific aspect of an engagement.	D2(d)
Discuss the importance of the auditor gaining an understanding of the entity including the applicable financial reporting framework, its accounting policies, its significant classes of transactions, balances and disclosures and the entity's system of internal control and recommend additional information which may be required in gaining that understanding.	D1(g)
Recognise matters that are not relevant to the planning of an assignment.	D1(i)

Business and exam context

The issue of audit planning should not be new to you. You learnt how to plan an audit in your previous auditing studies. Why is this chapter here? There are three key reasons:

- To provide you with a technical update
- To **revise** the details that should be included in an **audit plan** and the general considerations included in planning

- To **consider** some of the **finer points of planning** from the point of view of the engagement partner, specifically to consider the issue of the **risk associated with the assignment** (which is a personal risk to the partner in the event of litigation arising)

Risk is an important factor in the audit. It falls into two categories:

- Specific **assignment risk** (which could be either **audit risk** or the **risk of material misstatement**), both of which you have studied previously
- **Business risk** associated with the client, which may form a part of inherent risk and therefore impacts on the audit

Risk is a key issue in an audit, and most auditors take a risk-based approach to auditing.

Section A of the exam will feature a case study set in the context of audit planning, identifying risk areas and planning procedures to audit them. These questions will also draw from other parts of the syllabus (Sections A–D).

Chapter overview

1 ISA 200 – audit objectives

1.1 Overall objectives of the audit

ISA 200 *Overall Objectives of the Independent Auditor and the Conduct of an Audit in Accordance with International Standards on Auditing* states that in conducting an audit of financial statements, the overall objectives of the auditor are:

(a) To obtain **reasonable assurance** about whether the financial statements as a whole are **free from material misstatement**, whether due to fraud or error, thereby enabling the auditor to **express an opinion** on whether the financial statements are prepared, in all material respects, in accordance with an **applicable financial reporting framework**; and

(b) To **report** on the financial statements, and **communicate** as required by the ISAs, in accordance with the auditor's findings (ISA 200: para. 11)

ISA 200 states that the key requirements for the auditor to obtain reasonable assurance and to express an opinion are:

- **Ethics:** Comply with relevant ethical requirements (para. 14)
- **Professional scepticism:** Plan and perform an audit with professional scepticism, recognising that circumstances may exist that cause the financial statements to be materially misstated (para. 15)
- **Professional judgement:** Exercise professional judgement in planning and performing an audit (para. 16)
- **Sufficient appropriate audit evidence and audit risk:** Obtain sufficient appropriate audit evidence to **reduce audit risk to an acceptably low level** thereby enabling reasonable conclusions to be drawn by the auditor for their audit opinion (para. 17)

Managing audit risk allows the auditor to **express an audit opinion** and is therefore central to audit planning and risk assessment.

Essential reading

See Chapter 6 of the Essential reading for more detail on professional scepticism.

The Essential reading is available as an Appendix of the digital edition of the Workbook.

1.2 Audit risk and risk of material misstatement

You will remember this formula from your earlier studies:

Formula to learn

Audit Risk = (Inherent Risk × Control Risk) × Detection Risk

Let's remind you of what each part of the formula relates to, so you know what to look for: you won't be rewarded for stating these definitions in the exam – you only get marks for evaluating specific risks that are relevant to the scenario (source is ISA 200: para. 13):

Audit risk: The risk that the **auditor** expresses an **inappropriate opinion** when the financial statements are materially misstated. Audit risk is a function of the **risk of material misstatement** and **detection risk**.

Risk of material misstatement: The risk that the **financial statements are materially misstated prior to audit**. This consists of **inherent risk** and **control risk**. For the purposes of the ISAs, a risk of material misstatement exists when there is a reasonable possibility of a misstatement occurring (ie its **likelihood**) and being material if it were to occur (ie its **magnitude**).

Inherent risk: The **susceptibility of an assertion** about a **class of transaction, account balance or disclosure** to a **misstatement** that could be **material**, either individually or when aggregated with other misstatements, before consideration of any related controls.

Control risk: The risk that a **misstatement that could occur in an assertion** about a **class of transactions, account balance or disclosure** and that could be **material**, either individually or when aggregated with other misstatements, **will not be prevented, or detected and corrected**, on a timely basis by the entity's controls.

Detection risk: The risk that **the procedures performed by the auditor to reduce audit risk to an acceptably low level will not detect a misstatement** that exists and that could be material, either individually or when aggregated with other misstatements.

These are concepts that you will have already met in your earlier studies. However, for AAA, you will need to consider in greater detail the approach that auditors use when meeting their overall objectives regarding audit risk. This requires you to consider the following ISAs:

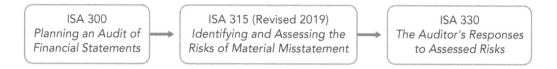

| ISA 300 *Planning an Audit of Financial Statements* | → | ISA 315 (Revised 2019) *Identifying and Assessing the Risks of Material Misstatement* | → | ISA 330 *The Auditor's Responses to Assessed Risks* |

2 ISA 300 – audit planning

The **objective** of ISA 300 is to help the auditor **plan the audit** so it will be performed in an **effective manner** (ISA 300: para. 4). This is done by the adoption of two complementary items:

| An **audit strategy** (characteristics of the engagement that define its scope, for example, as well as those factors that might be felt to be significant in carrying out the engagement) which then leads to... | An **audit plan** (more specific risk assessment procedures via ISA 315, responses to such risks via ISA 330 and any other work required to comply with all other relevant ISAs). |

The specific reasons for planning are to:

- Ensure that appropriate attention is devoted to **important areas** of the audit
- Ensure that **potential problems** are identified and resolved on a timely basis
- Ensure that the engagement is **properly organised** and **managed** in order to be performed in an effective and efficient manner
- Assist in the **proper assignment of work** to engagement team members
- Facilitate the **direction, supervision and review** of engagement team members
- Assist in **co-ordination** of work done by auditors of components and experts

The **nature of the audit** might change during the term of the engagement for a variety of reasons so all such changes and reasons shall be **documented**. The auditor shall also address as part of planning those **ethical issues** under ISA 220 *Quality Control for an Audit of Financial Statements* for **initial audit engagements** such as acceptance and communication with previous auditors.

Planning shall not be a one-off process only carried out at the start of the engagement – it is **iterative** and so the need for any **additional procedures** should be **constantly reviewed**.

PER alert

One of the competencies you require to fulfil **Performance Objective 18** of the PER is the ability to determine the level of audit risk and risk areas, including considering any internal or external information that may have implications for the audit, and to use this to document the audit plan, designing audit programmes and planning audit tests for an internal or external audit. You can apply the knowledge you gain from this chapter of the Workbook to help demonstrate this competency.

Activity 1: Johnson

You are the audit manager planning the audit of Johnson, a listed multinational food and drinks manufacturer. Johnson has plants all over the world and its head office is based in London.

Required

What general matters would you consider when planning the engagement?

Solution

Essential reading

See Chapter 6 of the Essential reading for more detail on planning documentation and planning an initial audit engagement.

The Essential reading is available as an Appendix of the digital edition of the Workbook.

3 ISA 315 (Revised 2019) – risk assessment

3.1 Objectives of ISA 315 (Revised 2019)

The **objective** of the auditor from ISA 315 (Revised 2019) *Identifying and Assessing the Risks of Material Misstatement* is to **identify** and **assess** the **risks of material misstatement**, whether due to **fraud** or **error**, at the **financial statement** and **assertion levels**, thereby providing a basis for designing and implementing **responses** to the assessed risks of material misstatement (ISA 315 (Revised 2019): para. 11).

3.1.1 Risks of material misstatement at the financial statement level

These risks relate to the **entire financial statements** and could affect **many assertions**. The auditor therefore determines the impact of such risks and designs suitable responses.

Examples of these risks and their impact on the financial statements could include the following:

Financial statement level risk	Impact on the financial statements
Operating losses and cash flow problems	Doubt over the appropriateness of continuing to adopt the **going concern** basis of accounting, which could lead to restatement of the financial statements affecting all assertions.
The client's information systems are assessed as poor	Poor internal controls may lead the auditor to conclude that there are misstatements within the **accounting records** that could affect all assertions.
Concerns are raised about the integrity of management at the client	Evidence of a weak control environment may lead the auditor to be sceptical about the quality of **representations** and other judgemental evidence from management, which could affect all assertions.
Increased risk of fraud at the financial statement level (for example, if the client is attempting to secure additional finance)	Fraud of this nature can lead to **manipulation** of the financial statements which could affect all assertions.

Clearly, any of these financial statement level risks could also be considered in more specific terms when assessing risks of material misstatement at the assertion level.

(ISA 315 (Revised 2019): paras. 28(a), 30, A195–198)

3.1.2 Risks of material misstatement at the assertion level

When assessing risks of material misstatement at the **assertion level**, the auditor focuses on assertions about a **class of transactions**, an **account balance** or a **disclosure** and considers these assertions **separately** in the context of the two key components of the risk of material misstatement:

Inherent risk assessment	Control risk assessment
The **susceptibility** of an assertion to any form of misstatement (both fraud and error) varies and will therefore sit on what is known as a **spectrum of inherent risk** which the auditor assesses in terms of **likelihood** and **magnitude** (supplemented by any financial statement level risks of material misstatement as appropriate).	This is the risk that a misstatement is not prevented, detected or corrected by internal controls.
Assessed risks of material misstatement that sit towards the **higher end of the spectrum of inherent risk** are considered to be **significant risks** and will therefore demand **more** of the auditor's attention and will therefore be **prioritised**. Unless specifically required by a separate ISA, the determination of significant risks will be a matter of the auditor's **professional judgement**.	The assessment of control risk is supported by the auditor **testing the operating effectiveness of controls**. However, if such testing is not undertaken, the overall risk of material misstatement is considered to be the same as the auditor's assessment of inherent risk.
Should assertion-level risks be considered to have a **pervasive** effect on the financial statements, they may be classed as financial statement level risks.	When considering controls, the auditor will need to differentiate between: • **Direct controls** (those that are precise enough to address risks of material misstatement at the assertion level); and • **Indirect controls** (those that support direct controls)

(ISA 315 (Revised 2019): paras. 4–6, 12, A5, A218–220)

Spectrum of inherent risk

The assessment of inherent risk requires **professional judgement** by the auditor when determining both **likelihood** (how likely a misstatement is to occur) and **magnitude** (the misstatement itself, which could be expressed in either qualitative or quantitative terms) by reference to the **nature, size and complexity** of an audited entity. The resulting combination of likelihood and magnitude is then evaluated and the higher it gets, the higher the assessment of inherent risk. The ISA points out that for an assessment to be considered high, it does not necessarily require **both** likelihood and magnitude to be assessed as high (ISA 315 (Revised 2019): paras. A208–216).

Significant risks

Clearly, significant risks will require **more of the auditor's attention** and demand that responses are performed with **greater urgency**. Evidence to satisfy significant risks may need to be **more persuasive** than otherwise required. There may also need to be **greater involvement with TCWG**. As a result, such significant risks may be considered **key audit matters (KAMs)**. Some ISAs may automatically direct the auditor to consider certain inherent risks to be significant (such as frauds and ISA 240) but otherwise, it is a matter of **professional judgement** taking issues such as **subjectivity** and **complexity** into account (ISA 315 (Revised 2019): paras. A219–221).

Exam focus point

ACCA has confirmed that question requirements will ask for **significant risks** to ensure that candidates are **focusing** and **prioritising risks** which are at the **upper end of the spectrum** – these will therefore be those that are of greatest **likelihood** and **magnitude**.

Essential reading

See Chapter 6 of the Essential reading for examples of the various components of the risk of material misstatement.

The Essential reading is available as an Appendix of the digital edition of the Workbook.

3.2 The auditor's approach under ISA 315 (Revised 2019)

The auditor will use a variety of procedures as part of their risk assessment:

- **Enquiries** of appropriate individuals (including **internal audit**)
- **Analytical procedures** (including automated tools and techniques such as **data analytics**)
- **Observation** of events and activities
- **Inspection** of documents and other relevant items
- **Sharing information from other sources** (such as **acceptance and continuance** procedures and the **discussions** among audit team members)

Real life example: Automated tools and techniques

ISA 315 (Revised 2019) describes many different applications for the use of automated tools and techniques within the risk assessment process. For example:

- Remote observation tools such as **drones** could be used when inspecting certain assets
- Auditors can obtain digital downloads of accounting records and use **data analytics** techniques (ranging from spreadsheets to more complex systems) to perform analysis that assists in the **prioritisation** of significant risks of material misstatement
- The analysis of accounting records could include **journals** to identify those posted outside of normal working hours or by staff who do not normally post such items
- Entire **populations** of transactions could be **analysed** to identify situations that could indicate a **higher position on the spectrum of inherent risk** (eg account balances that are zero at the reporting date but which have seen significant transactions and journal entries during the period, suggesting possible manipulation)

- To assist the auditor, key messages from data analytics procedures are often presented using a **dashboard** (sometimes referred to as **data visualisation**) which highlights significant matters for the auditor's attention

(ISA 315 (Revised 2019): paras. A31, A35, A137, A161 and A203)

3.2.1 The applicable financial reporting framework

The auditor needs to obtain an understanding of the **applicable financial reporting framework** (including an assessment of the suitability of the client's chosen **accounting policies**) to ensure their assessment of risk of material misstatement within the financial statements addresses all appropriate **classes of transactions, account balances** and **disclosures**.

The auditor may also need to consider the accounting implications for certain higher-risk areas, for example:

- **Revenue recognition** (eg for online retailers and resellers)
- **Industry-specific accounting principles and practices** (eg loans held by for banks or research and development in the pharmaceutical industry)
- Accounting for assets, liabilities and transactions in a **foreign currency**
- Accounting for **unusual** or **emerging issues** (eg cryptocurrency)

(ISA 315 (Revised 2019): para. A82)

3.2.2 The entity and its environment

The auditor also needs to understand **the entity and its environment,** which can comprise the following:

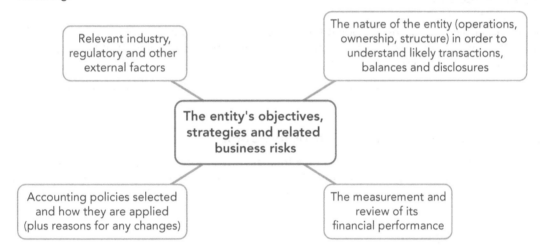

(ISA 315 (Revised 2019): para. 19)

3.2.3 The system of internal control

This understanding also includes the entity's **system of internal control** (illustrated by the diagram below, showing the various components of internal control):

The control environment

The entity's risk assessment process

Control activities

The information system, including the related business processes, relevant to financial reporting, and communication

Monitoring of controls

(ISA 315 (Revised 2019): paras. 21–26)

ISA 315 (Revised 2019) describes the work that the auditor should perform in obtaining an understanding of the various IT applications in use within an entity as well as those risks that arise from the use of IT and from general IT controls.

Essential reading

See Chapter 6 of the Essential reading for examples of the components of internal control (found within the components of the risk of material misstatement) and the work that the auditor should undertake in relation to IT at the client.

The Essential reading is available as an Appendix of the digital edition of the Workbook.

3.3 Scepticism, scalability and standing back

As ISAs adapt over time, they introduce **new themes** that support the overall achievement of the auditor's key objectives. ISA 315 (Revised 2019) uses the **following concepts** to ensure the auditor's identification and assessment of the risks of material misstatement is both thorough and proportionate.

3.3.1 Professional scepticism

You have met professional scepticism many times throughout your studies, but it is mentioned again here to reinforce the importance of challenging management and keeping an open mind to the rapidly changing environment as part of the process of identifying and assessing risks of material misstatement.

Within ISA 315 (Revised 2019) the use of professional scepticism is discussed in terms of the auditor displaying **professional judgement** when determining whether or not a **critical assessment** of risk has been undertaken. It also widens the scope of any risk assessment by referring to the need to be **alert** to **conditions that might indicate possible misstatements** due to fraud or error. Such scepticism could include the following activities:

- Questioning evidence that appears to be contradictory
- Considering responses provided by management and TCWG
- Remaining alert to conditions that could lead to misstatements due to either fraud or error
- Evaluating evidence in the context of the risk assessment big picture (ISA 315 (Revised 2019): paras. A12–13)

Example: Analytical procedures and professional scepticism

Data visualisation techniques may present the findings of analytical procedures, but the auditor still needs to interpret these findings using professional scepticism and identify the **core messages** that support their assessment of the risk of material misstatement.

Assume you work as the auditor for a clothing manufacturer. The company operates its own retail stores and supplies contract customers with a range of bespoke products. It also has a website that sells all product ranges.

You are inspecting the results of your firm's data analytics procedures as part of the audit of revenue and you access the following chart from the dashboard:

The chart suggests that the company's business model is gradually shifting from retail to online sales, which would then direct your attention towards any indications of risk from this change. You might also be inclined to consider the risks presented by IT to rise as the company's reliance on the website increases. However, you also need to conclude that the company's total revenue is falling and direct your assessment of the risk of material misstatement in this direction as well – could actual results be even worse?

3.3.2 Scalability

This is a term that is used frequently within ISA 315 (Revised 2019) and is becoming more prevalent as the ISAs are gradually revised. Concern has been raised by IAASB that audit failure could stem from auditors performing **fewer** and **less thorough procedures** for **smaller audit clients regardless** of the **complexity** they present to the auditor. The concept of scalability attempts to remind auditors that they should actively consider **both** the **size and complexity** of an audit client when determining the nature and extent of required audit procedures.

For example, although the perceived size and complexity of a larger entity would typically increase audit risk, the entity might also have rigorous controls and present far less risk to the auditor than a smaller entity with more ad hoc systems which might seem less risky, simply because of its size.

Similarly, a smaller organisation that does not have access to sophisticated control systems may still present a complex challenge to the auditor when assessing the risk of material misstatement in its financial statements.

The auditor therefore needs to use their professional judgement when assessing risk. The guidance on scalability within ISA 315 (Revised 2019) explains that the standard is flexible enough to be applied to audits of all entities (ie scalable) regardless of size or complexity, and states the following:

'While the size of an entity may be an indicator of its complexity, some smaller entities may be complex and some larger entities may be less complex.' (ISA 315 (Revised 2019): para. 9)

Overall, the message appears to be that auditors should approach an audit engagement without any preconceived ideas about the risks they are expecting to find and should apply ISA 315 (Revised 2019) with an open mind and respond to the results of their risk assessment.

3.3.3 Standing back

Throughout ISA 315 (Revised 2019) you will also find the terms **iterative** and **responsive**. These are used deliberately to reinforce the need for the auditor's identification and assessment of risks of material misstatement to be **actively considered at all stages of the process** and for any **changes** or **developments** to be accommodated to make sure the process can **react** if new information demands it.

This is sometimes referred to as **standing back** and implies that the auditor should **pause, reflect** and **respond accordingly** if new or contradictory information emerges at any point in the process.

3.4 Additional information required?

The auditor will often need to obtain additional information in order to gain the required understanding of the entity, and in order to perform planned procedures. Much of the time, the auditor only has incomplete information about the entity being audited, and it is important to be able to recognise when more is needed. Such is the nature of real-life auditing!

AAA exams often contain a requirement to identify additional information needed in order to either understand the entity or perform a specific part of an engagement. These are often fairly easy marks, and to get them, you need to:

- **Be specific** about what information you need
- State **why** you need the information

It is not necessary at this stage to speculate in too much detail about what might go wrong in each area. Questions will usually contain a little bit of information – eg that a company runs a bonus scheme for managers – but with clear gaps in it – eg how the bonuses are determined will not be stated. All you need to do is to point out this gap and say what information is needed to fill it.

Additional information does not have to be a document, but can be the reason why management has done something in the scenario, for example.

Essential reading

See Chapter 6 of the Essential reading for more detail on additional information required.

The Essential reading is available as an Appendix of the digital edition of the Workbook.

4 ISA 330 – risk response

Given that the auditor has reached ISA 330 *The Auditor's Responses to Assessed Risks*, they must now obtain sufficient appropriate audit evidence regarding the assessed risks of material misstatements through designing and implementing appropriate responses to those risks in order to form an opinion (ISA 330: para. 3). This is where audit testing starts to appear and the auditor will focus on managing detection risk.

ISA 330 asks for the auditor to determine whether controls testing is appropriate or not. The auditor always carries out some substantive testing but, where controls are ineffective, these will not be tested and substantive testing will be relied upon instead.

All conclusions reached using ISAs 300, 315 and 330 must be fully documented to support the audit opinion.

Activity 2: Bauer

You are an audit partner attending the planning meeting for the audit of Bauer, a large technology company with two main divisions. The year end is 31 December. The first division manufactures computer hardware for use by intelligence and security agencies, and the second produces and distributes bespoke and off-the-shelf software for use on the hardware.

As part of your audit planning, you attend a meeting with Bauer's finance director, Jackie. She informs you that there have been no major changes in the business's operations during the year, but the following significant events had occurred:

(1) Owing to an unexplained improvement in the security situation in the Los Angeles area, a significant contract with the US Government for new hardware has not been renewed. This was a surprise and as a result, 100 (out of 1,000) US staff were made redundant during December.

(2) During the year, development commenced on new software for use in satellite tracking of vehicles. This has been capitalised as an intangible asset. In order to commence development, significant staff training costs were incurred.

Required

Evaluate the risks of material misstatement from items (1) and (2). **(5 marks)**

Solution

5 The business risk approach

> **Business risks:** '...result from significant conditions, events, circumstances, actions or inactions that could adversely affect an entity's ability to achieve its objectives and execute its strategies, or from the setting of inappropriate objectives and strategies.' (ISA 315, para. 12)

The business risk model is not a replacement for the traditional audit risk model but rather a vehicle, or mechanism, for the identification of audit risk, recognising that most business risks will eventually have financial consequences and, therefore, an effect on the financial statements.

In adopting a business risk approach, the auditor identifies the risks that the business itself faces, which could threaten the business from meeting its goals, aims and objectives. Once identified, the auditor is then able to identify any corresponding audit risk.

The approach allows the auditor to gain a **greater understanding of the business** and the overall risks it faces and therefore increases the likelihood of identifying the **risks of material misstatement** of the financial statements as well as being able to provide constructive business advice to aid the mitigation (through relevant controls) of such risks.

PER alert

One of the competencies you require to fulfil **Performance Objective 4** of the PER is the ability to evaluate activities in your area and identify potential risks of fraud, error or other hazards assessing their probability and impact. You can apply the knowledge you have obtained from this chapter of the Workbook to help demonstrate this competency.

Activity 3: Business risks vs audit risks

From the following scenario, identify the business risk and any corresponding audit risk:

Solution

Scenario	Business risk	Audit risk
(1) CD Planet operates a chain of retail outlets selling chart CDs.		
(2) Mucha Pasta operates several Italian restaurants and is subject to comprehensive and stringent health and safety food hygiene legislation.		

Scenario	Business risk	Audit risk
(3) XYZ, based in the Eurozone, trades extensively in the US and invoices sales in US$.		

Business risks can be split into **three categories** to enable better identification.

5.1 Financial risk

These are the risks arising from the company's **financial activities** or the **financial consequences** of operations. Examples include the following:

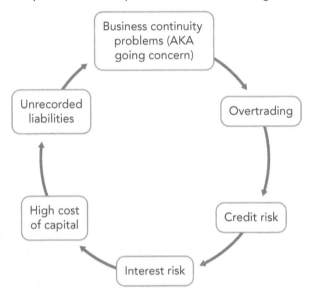

5.2 Operational risk

These are the risks arising from the operations of the business, such as stock-outs, physical disasters, loss of key staff, poor brand management and loss of orders.

Essential reading

See Chapter 6 of the Essential reading for an overview of operational business risks from current and emerging trends in information technology (IT) and e-commerce.

The Essential reading is available as an Appendix of the digital edition of the Workbook.

5.3 Compliance risk

These are the risks arising from non-compliance with laws, regulations, policies, procedures and contracts (as covered in Chapter 1). Examples include the following:

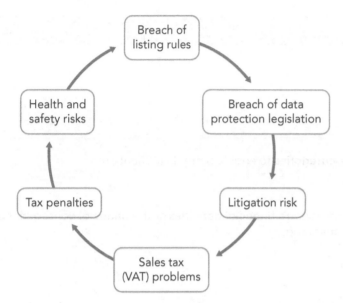

Once risks are identified, management must decide whether they **accept** the risk or what their **control strategy** will be to manage the risk.

Management need to be satisfied that systems of risk management and internal controls are working properly. Internal Audit can make a valuable contribution to the monitoring of risk management.

Activity 4: Melon

Your firm has just been appointed auditor to the Melon Group, which operates a chain of fashion clothing shops for young women. The head office is based in Madrid. There are 280 shops spread across the Iberian peninsula and a further 65 shops across the European Union. The clothing is manufactured mainly in Spain and India by third-party manufacturers and fixed quantities are pre-ordered six months in advance of the season. Most of the shop buildings are held on long leases, although a small number are owned by the Group.

Approximately 40% of the shops outside the Iberian market are run on a franchise basis whereby shop fittings are supplied and installed by the Melon Group and paid for by the franchisee over five years, after which time they are replaced; the clothes are sold at a 40% discount on local retail price to the franchisees on a sale or return basis. Franchisees choose which lines of the full season's range of clothes they wish to hold, based on samples.

Required

Evaluate **FOUR** business risks and **FOUR** audit risks from the Melon Group scenario.

Solution

6 ISA 320 *Materiality in Planning and Performing an Audit*

Materiality: Misstatements, including omissions, are considered to be **material** if they, individually or in the aggregate, could reasonably be expected to influence the economic decisions of users taken on the basis of the financial statements. (ISA 320: para. 2)

An item might be deemed material due to its:

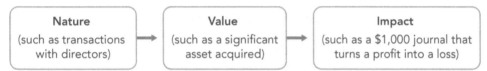

| **Nature** | **Value** | **Impact** |
| (such as transactions with directors) | (such as a significant asset acquired) | (such as a $1,000 journal that turns a profit into a loss) |

The level of materiality set at **planning** will always be a matter of **professional judgement**. Most audit firms set criteria for which benchmark figure to use depending on what is most appropriate. For example:

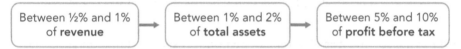

| Between ½% and 1% of **revenue** | Between 1% and 2% of **total assets** | Between 5% and 10% of **profit before tax** |

Example

If profit before tax is given in the question as $350,000, the lowest amount that would indicate a material misstatement in a transaction would be 5% = $17,500. Similarly, if total assets are $2 million, a misstatement in a balance of $20,000 would become material. In some cases, such as inventory, a misstatement might be directly relevant to both transactions and balances, so the auditor would use judgement to decide which of the two amounts indicated a material misstatement (clearly though, the lower amount should be used to adopt the spirit of ISA 320).

The percentage guidelines of assets, revenues and profits that are commonly used for materiality must be handled **with care**. The auditor must bear in mind the **focus** of the company being audited: for example, profit before tax might be more appropriate for a **manufacturer** judged on its performance, but revenues may be a more appropriate for a not for profit entity (ISA 320: para. A8).

The materiality level adopted will have an **impact** on three key areas:

(a) **How many and what items to examine**

(b) **Whether to use sampling techniques**

(c) **What level of error is likely to lead to a modified audit opinion**

ISA 320 also requires the calculation of **performance materiality**.

Performance materiality: The amount or amounts set by the auditor at less than materiality for the financial statements as a whole to reduce to an appropriately low level the probability that the aggregate of uncorrected and undetected misstatements exceeds materiality for the financial statements as a whole. If applicable, performance materiality also refers to the amount or amounts set by the auditor at less than the materiality level or levels for particular classes of transactions, account balances or disclosures. (ISA 320: para. 9)

Materiality levels will be determined when **planning the audit** and may need to be **revised** if new information becomes available during the audit that affects the materiality for the financial statements as a whole.

Essential reading

See Chapter 6 of the Essential reading for more detail on performance materiality.

The Essential reading is available as an Appendix of the digital edition of the Workbook.

7 ISA 520 Analytical Procedures

The auditor should apply analytical procedures as **risk assessment procedures** (ISA 315: para. 6) to obtain an understanding of the entity and its environment and in the overall review at the end of the audit (covered further in Chapter 10).

They can also be used as a source of **substantive audit evidence** when their use is more effective or efficient than tests of details in reducing detection risk for specific financial statement assertions (covered further in Chapters 7 and 8).

Essential reading

See Chapter 6 of the Essential reading for more detail on analytical procedures.

The Essential reading is available as an Appendix of the digital edition of the Workbook.

Analytical procedures include the following type of **comparisons**, using trend analysis and reasonableness tests:

- Prior periods
- Budgets and forecasts
- Industry information
- Predictive estimates
- Relationships between elements of financial information ie ratio analysis
- Relationships between financial and non-financial information eg payroll costs to the number of employees

The following **ratios** should be considered (although you may not be able to calculate all of them – the key thing to remember is that if financial data is presented in an exam question, you must do something with it!)

Ratios mean very little when used in isolation. They should be calculated for **previous periods** and for **comparable companies**. A ratio on its own says nothing – it should **always** be **accompanied** by a **commentary** on that ratio. **For example:**

Stating that revenue has increased by 12% will not score many, if any, marks at all, as it does not assist the auditor in planning the audit: why does it matter?

Commenting that in the context of the scenario, such a growth in revenue seems unusual as the company is in an industry that is experiencing a decline in demand, therefore should be explored further, would score most, if not all, available marks.

The permanent file should contain a section with summarised accounts and the chosen ratios for prior years.

In addition to looking at the more usual ratios, the auditors should consider examining **other ratios** that may be **relevant** to the particular **client's business**, such as revenue per passenger mile for an airline operator client, or fees per partner for a professional office.

Chapter summary

Planning and risk assessment

ISA 200 - audit objectives

Overall objectives of the audit
- Reasonable assurance that F/S are free from material misstatement
- Ethics, professional scepticism, professional judgement
- Sufficient appropriate audit evidence to reduce audit risk to acceptable level

Audit risk and risk of material misstatement
- AR = (IR x CR) x DR
- Risk of Material Misstatement = IR x CR
- Inherent Risk = susceptibility
- Control Risk = not prevented, detected or corrected

ISA 300 - audit planning

- Audit strategy (high level) vs audit plan (more detailed)
- Focus on important areas
- Identify and resolve potential problems
- Engagement is properly organised and managed
- Proper assignment of work
- Facilitates direction, supervision and review
- Assists in co-ordination of others (eg Internal Audit, component auditors or experts)

ISA 315 (Revised 2019) - risk assessment

Objectives of ISA 315 (Revised 2019)
- Identify and assess risk of material misstatement at F/S level (all assertions)
- Identify and assess risk of material misstatement at assertion level (class of transactions, account balance or disclosure)
- Inherent risks assessed along a spectrum determined by likelihood and magnitude
- Inherent risks at higher end of spectrum considered to be significant risks and prioritised
- Control risk assessment considers operating effectiveness

The auditor's approach under ISA 315 (Revised 2019)
- Typical procedures include enquiry, analytical procedures, observation and inspection
- Acceptance and continuance information and discussions among audit team members
- Use of automated tools and techniques (including data analytics)
- Understand requirements of applicable financial reporting framework
- Consider the entity and its environment (eg industry, ownership, strategies, accounting policies etc)
- Consider internal controls (control environment, information systems, risk assessment process, monitoring and control activities)

Scepticism, scalability and standing back
- Professional scepticism - critical assessment of evidence in rapidly changing environment
- Professional judgement required (eg interpreting data analytics)
- Scalability - ISA 315 (Revised 2019) applicable regardless of size or complexity
- Understand requirements of applicable financial reporting framework
- Risk identification and assessment is iterative and responsive, allowing opportunity to stand back and reflect

Additional information required?
Look for the gaps in the scenario and say what you need and why you need it

ISA 330 – risk response

- Design and implement appropriate responses to risk assessment from ISA 315 (Revised 2019)
- Controls vs substantive testing

The business risk approach

- Significant conditions that could adversely affect the entity's ability to achieve its objectives
- Complements the audit risk approach by helping to identify areas at risk of material misstatement

Financial risk

- Risks arising from the company's financial activities or the financial consequences of operations
- Examples: going concern; overtrading; credit risk; interest risk; high cost of capital; unrecorded liabilities

Operational risk

- Examples: stock-outs; physical disasters; loss of key staff; poor brand management; loss of orders

Compliance risk

- Examples: breach of data protection legislation; litigation; tax penalties; health and safety breaches

ISA 320 *Materiality in Planning and Performing an Audit*

- Materiality determines the relative significance or importance of a matter, depending on its nature, value or impact
- Based on the auditor's professional judgement
- Performance materiality < planning materiality levels
- Determines what to examine, how much to sample and what will affect the audit opinion

ISA 520 *Analytical Procedures*

- Used as risk identification and assessment procedures (PLANNING)
- Used as substantive procedures (EVIDENCE)
- Carried out as part of the overall review of the audit (COMPLETION)

BPP
LEARNING
MEDIA

Knowledge diagnostic

1. ISA 200

Overall objectives of the audit are to obtain reasonable assurance that the financial statements are free from material misstatement, via audit procedures designed to reduce **audit risk** to an acceptably low level (ISA 200).

2. Audit risk

Audit risk is the risk that an auditor expresses an **inappropriate opinion** on a set of financial statements. Audit risk is made up of **inherent risk, control risk (risk of material misstatement)** and **detection risk**.

- Perform risk assessment procedures
- Assess the risks of material misstatement
- Respond to assessed risks
- Perform further audit procedures
- Evaluate audit evidence obtained

3. ISA 300

Audit planning aims to focus the audit on key areas, direct the auditor towards priority areas, resolve problems and allocate work efficiently (ISA 300).

4. Risk of material misstatement

Risk of material misstatement is identified and assessed at both F/S and assertion levels, split between **inherent risk** (significant risks sit at higher end of spectrum) and **control risk** (operating effectiveness).

5. Audit approach

Auditor's approach considers specific procedures, plus understanding the applicable financial reporting framework, the entity and its environment and internal controls.

6. Scepticism, scalability and standing back

ISA 315 (Revised 2019) includes iterative guidance on **professional scepticism**, **scalability** and the use of **standing back** to gauge progress and conclusions.

7. Additional information

Additional information may be required to understand the entity or perform an engagement – look for the **gaps** in the scenario and explain **what** you need and **why**.

8. ISA 330

The auditor will design and implement **appropriate responses to risk assessment** (ISA 330).

9. Business risk

Business risks – in order to assess audit risks more effectively, auditors are now required under ISA 315 to understand the risks that a **business** faces in three areas: financial, operational and compliance.

10. Materiality

Materiality is an expression of the relative **significance** or **importance** of a particular matter in the context of financial statements as a whole – items can be material due to their nature, value or impact and the materiality chosen helps the auditor to determine what to examine, whether or not to use sampling techniques and what level of error might lead to a qualified opinion.

11. Analytical procedures

Auditors can use analytical procedures, ratios and other techniques to derive evidence at various stages of the audit:

- At the risk assessment stage (as per ISA 315)
- As part of substantive procedures
- During the overall review at the end of the audit

Further study guidance

Question practice

Now try the following from the Further question practice bank (available in the digital edition of the Workbook):

- Question 9 'Marsden Manufacturing' is excellent practice for evaluating significant audit risks and testing your understanding of materiality in an integrated scenario question.
- Question 11 'Trendy Group' requires a comparison of business risks and audit risks for a consolidated group – make sure you can distinguish between these two types of risk as they are often confused for each other by candidates!

Further reading

There are a number of technical articles on the ACCA website written by members of the AAA examining team which are relevant to some of the topics covered in this chapter that you should read:

- *Exam technique for Advanced Audit and Assurance part 2 – risk*
- *The control environment of a company*
- *Auditing in specialised industries*
- *Professional scepticism* (covered in Chapter 2 but still relevant here)
- *Analytical procedures*
- *Audit risk*

Own research

- In the UK, the FRC has conducted research into various developments in the auditing profession – as an example, you could review the briefing paper on professional scepticism and see what it has to say about risk assessment:

  www.frc.org.uk/auditors/audit-assurance/audit-and-assurance-research-activities

Activity answers

Activity 1: Johnson

Approach

This is really an idea-generation activity, therefore, in addition to using the limited information in the scenario, try and consider the information you have not been given but that you will need to plan this audit engagement.

Suggested solution

- **Logistics** – Assignment of staff to the audit: consider the client's locations and arrange visits where appropriate or consider using staff from other offices/countries if possible; also Johnson is listed, so it is important to consider what reporting deadlines the client is working towards.

- **Time budgets** – The audit of a large multinational will generate a significant fee but is at risk of going over budget; it is therefore important at the planning stage to prepare and communicate a time budget to the audit team and monitor this throughout the engagement.

- **Reporting** – The audit manager should consider what other reports the client may require over and above the statutory auditor's report. A large manufacturer such as Johnson is likely to produce a social and environmental report as part of the annual report; the audit manager should ascertain whether they require assurance on these issues on this report.

- **Client interface** – Consideration should be given to the method and timing of communication with the client management and/or audit committee at certain stages of the audit.

- **Preliminary materiality** – Materiality should be assessed and calculated at the planning stage (although it is likely to be based on draft figures).

- **Risk assessment** – The key aspect of the planning stage of an audit is the performance of a risk assessment. This will ensure that the work performed is focused on the important areas of the accounts.

Activity 2: Bauer

Approach

This activity is getting closer to exam standard – notice that the details are vague, meaning you have to consider what you don't yet know, and why any of the factors presented might lead to each risk of material misstatement. In each case, start with a possible risk and then establish why it might be misstated using your knowledge of IAS/IFRS. Although the question does not explicitly ask for them, you should be focusing on the **significant** risks of material misstatement (ie those of **greatest magnitude and likelihood**).

Suggested solution

(1) As the timing of the redundancies is towards the year end, it is important that the timing of the announcement is ascertained; if it is made before the year end, then a **provision** should be made for any redundancy costs not paid as at 31 December (IAS 37 *Provisions, Contingent Liabilities and Contingent Assets*). If the announcement is made post year end, then the costs would not be recognised until next year.

The **disclosure** of the costs should be considered, as it may be possible to treat them as an exceptional item if they meet the definition in the accounting standards (IAS 1 *Presentation of Financial Statements*).

The unexpected loss of this major contract gives rise to a potential **going concern** problem. Since only 10% of the US staff have been lost as a result, it is unlikely that this in itself would be enough to affect the going concern status of the entire business. However, this should form part of the overall assessment of going concern under ISA 570 *Going Concern*. Consideration should be given as to the reasons for the improvement in the security situation and whether similar improvements may occur in other markets.

(2) Close attention will need to be paid to the **software development costs** to ensure that they meet the criteria laid out in IAS 38 *Intangible Assets* and have been correctly capitalised and disclosed (see the Essential reading for Chapter 8 (available in the digital edition of the Workbook) for more details on the criteria for appropriate research and development costs).

It will be important to ensure that the **training costs** for the new software have not been included in the amounts capitalised. These do not represent a part of the software (which is an intangible asset) and so these training costs should be recognised as an expense when incurred.

Activity 3: Business risks vs audit risks

Approach

Candidates frequently get mixed up with these, so this activity is designed to test how you can distinguish between the things that could get in the way of an organisation achieving each of its objectives (business risks) and the areas of the financial statements that could be misstated (audit risks) from the same issue.

Scenario	Business risk	Audit risk
(1) CD Planet operates a chain of retail outlets selling chart CDs.	• Overstocking of CDs resulting in inventories of ex-chart CDs • Excessive mark down and reductions in order to sell ex-chart inventories • Impact on revenues, profits and cash flows	• Identification of obsolete inventories • Valuation of inventories (possibility of NRV < cost)
(2) Mucha Pasta operates several Italian restaurants and is subject to comprehensive and stringent health and safety food hygiene legislation.	• Breach of legislation could lead to fines, closure, bad press and costly improvement expenses • Potential impact on revenues due to impact on reputation/closure • Financial impact due to fines, legal actions and required improvements	• Provisions/contingent liability disclosure for legal action • Impact on going concern • Appropriateness of the capitalisation of improvements
(3) XYZ, based in the Eurozone, trades extensively in the US and invoices sales in US$.	• Company is exposed to exchange rate risk • Potential impact on profits and cash flows	• Correct retranslation of year-end receivables • Correct treatment of initial sale and receivable • Correct calculation, treatment and disclosure

Scenario	Business risk	Audit risk
		of exchange differences • Compliance with IAS 21

Activity 4: Melon

Approach

You can now start to put together what you have learned in this chapter by analysing the scenario and identifying those areas that could adversely affect the company's ability to meet its objectives (business risks) and those that could lead to material misstatement in the financial statements (audit risks). Note that there are marks now – in the exam it could be up to three marks for successfully evaluating an audit risk: here, you should aim for scoring up to one mark for identifying each risk and a further mark for explaining why it is a risk.

Suggested solution

Business risks – any four from the following:

- *Foreign currency risk:* Many of Melon's supplies are from India and hence cost would depend on exchange rate with the Indian rupee. Also franchisees pay 60% of local retail price to Melon, which passes currency risk to Melon where the franchisees are located outside the Eurozone (eg in the UK).

- *Cash flow/financing risk:* The Group bears an ongoing cash flow risk with respect to the shop fittings provided to franchisees which are not paid for until later. Given that most shop fittings will be for new franchisees, this is coupled with the business risk that those franchisees may fail.

- *Leased vs owned properties:* Leased properties allows the Group the flexibility to open, close or move shops, but also subjects the Group to the risks of the rental market and the potential loss of prime retail sites when the rental agreements are up for renewal. Owned properties are more secure, but are less flexible when the retail centre of a town shifts location over time.

- *Fashion:* The market in which Melon operates is a fast-moving one. Success depends on being at the cutting edge of latest fashions. Given that the clothes are ordered six months in advance, it is essential that Melon's research and buying department calculations are based on accurate information. Miscalculations of the market could result in large amounts of unsaleable inventories to customers or indeed to franchisees. Further, goods unsold by the franchisees can be returned to Melon, increasing its risk.

- *Quality:* All clothing is manufactured by third parties. Controls are necessary to ensure that the quality of goods is adequate across suppliers and consistent between suppliers and over time.

- *Competitors:* There are many players in the fashion market which is becoming more globalised. What in the past may have been a stable national position could quickly turn sour if a new, but established, foreign player enters the market. This needs to be regularly monitored.

- *Supply issues:* Unexpected supply problems could occur for Melon, a foreign investor in India, as a result of local activists criticising the use of cheaper developing world workers.

- *Compliance risk:* Operations in various different markets pose risks due to different regulatory and reporting requirements which must be researched and complied with.

Audit risks – any four from the following:

- *New audit client*: The firm has no previous experience with this client, so the audit risk is high. This lack of familiarity could lead to potential misstatements being overlooked.

- *Overseas transactions:* The activities between Melon and its overseas suppliers and customers present possible risks of misstatement due to foreign currency fluctuations under IAS 21 in terms of statement of profit or loss items (such as revenues and purchases) and assets (such as inventory).

- *Shop fittings and franchises:* Depending on the recoverability of sums due from franchisees, there may be issues with the recognition and valuation of items in shops where a franchise may have ceased operating.

- *Owned vs leased PPE:* There may be a risk of misstatement in shop premises which are recorded as owned but are leased (and vice versa) meaning IAS 16 and/or IFRS 16 may not be adhered to.

- *Inventory:* This will be hard to value due to the volatile nature of fashion goods in general (establishing net realisable value under IAS 2, for example, may be difficult). Also, in cases where goods are returned, there may be a risk of misstatement where ownership of inventory is unclear and it is either carried incorrectly or omitted from Melon's financial statements (this could also affect revenue recognition under IFRS 15 if control of inventory is hard to establish).

Evidence

Learning objectives

On completion of this chapter, you should be able to:

	Syllabus reference no.
Identify and describe audit procedures (including substantive and tests of controls (for both direct and indirect controls)) to obtain sufficient, appropriate evidence from identified sources to support the relevant assertions and disclosures.	D2(a)
Assess and describe how IT can be used to assist the auditor and recommend the use of automated tools and techniques, such as audit software, test data and other data analytics tools where appropriate.	D2(b)
Evaluate and interpret the results of data analytics tools when used during planning or evidence collection.	D2(c)
Explain the planning procedures specific to an initial audit engagement.	D1(f)
Apply the further considerations and audit procedures relevant to initial engagements.	D2(e)
Apply analytical procedures to financial and non-financial data.	D2(f)
Explain the specific audit problems and procedures concerning related parties and related party transactions.	D2(g)
Recognise circumstances that may indicate the existence of unidentified related parties and recommend appropriate audit procedures.	D2(h)
Recognise when it is justifiable to place reliance on the work of an expert (eg a surveyor employed by the audit client).	D4(a)
Evaluate the potential impact of an internal audit department on the planning and performance of the external audit.	D4(b)
Assess the appropriateness and sufficiency of the work of internal auditors and the extent to which reliance can be placed on it.	D4(c)
Recognise and evaluate the impact of outsourced functions, such as payroll, on the conduct of an audit.	D4(d)

Business and exam context

Audit evidence is a vital part of any audit. The basic issues relating to evidence are that:

- Auditors must obtain evidence to support financial statement assertions
- This evidence must be sufficient and appropriate
- Audit evidence must be documented sufficiently

Related parties are a difficult area to obtain audit evidence on. The auditor must bear in mind who the evidence is from and how extensive it is.

In special circumstances, notably the first audit, different considerations and procedures must be followed regarding opening balances.

Sometimes, the evidence the auditor requires is beyond the expertise of the auditor, and they will need to rely on the work of an expert. We also revise internal audit which you studied in some detail in your earlier auditing studies. Internal auditors provide services to the management of a company. Certain considerations arise if the external auditor intends to rely on the work of internal audit. We also consider the impact on the auditor of a client who has outsourced functions such as payroll or accounting services.

Specific audit issues examined in this subject are likely to be at a higher level than in your previous auditing exams. Therefore, the more complex evidence issues of related parties, opening balances and using the work of others are important. You should consider how they link in with specific accounting issues in Chapter 8.

These areas can be tested anywhere in the exam, in either Section A or Section B.

Chapter overview

1 ISA 500 *Audit Evidence*

Audit evidence should be:

Sufficient — **Quantity** of evidence is sufficient to support the audit opinion.

and

Appropriate
- **Relevant** in supporting the financial statement assertions; and
- **Reliable**

Although the use of **assertions** helps to guide the auditor in obtaining sufficient appropriate audit evidence under ISA 500 *Audit evidence*, the assertions themselves are defined within ISA 315 (Revised 2019) *Identifying and Assessing the Risks of Material Misstatement* – this is to reiterate the approach that risks are assessed at both the financial statement and assertion level (ISA 315 (Revised): para. 11).

We need evidence on the validity of the financial statement assertions (essential **characteristics** for items to display in order to be included within the financial statements):

Accuracy – An accurate record of the event or transaction

Completeness – Not understated for both events/transactions and assets/liabilities

Cut off – Items have been placed in the appropriate accounting period

Accuracy, valuation and allocation – Assets and liabilities have been valued correctly

Classification – Events/transactions and assets/liabilities recorded in the proper accounts

Occurrence – Not overstated in respect of events and transactions

Presentation – All events/transactions and assets/liabilities are appropriately aggregated or disaggregated, clearly described and all related disclosures are relevant and understandable

Existence – Not overstated in respect of assets and liabilities

Rights and obligations – There is either a right or an obligation in respect of this item

This can be remembered as **ACCA COPER**.

Completeness, rights and obligations, existence, classification, accuracy, valuation and allocation and presentation relate to **assets and liabilities, and related disclosures**.

Completeness, cut off, occurrence, accuracy, classification and presentation relate **to transactions and events, and related disclosures** (ISA 315 (Revised): para. A190).

Audit evidence is obtained by performing audit tests.

- **Tests of control** – Tests to obtain audit evidence about the suitability of design and effective operation of the accounting and internal control systems
- **Substantive tests** –Tests of detail of transactions and balances, and analytical procedures, performed to obtain audit evidence to detect material misstatements in the financial statements

1.1 Procedures for obtaining evidence

The **objective** of the auditor is to design and perform audit procedures in such a way as to enable the auditor to obtain **sufficient appropriate audit evidence** to be able to draw **reasonable conclusions** on which to base the auditor's opinion (ISA 500: para. 4).

Procedures (ISA 500: paras. A10–A25)	
Inspection of assets	Inspection of assets that are recorded in the accounting records confirms **existence**, gives evidence of **valuation**, but does not confirm **rights and obligations**.
	Confirmation that assets seen are recorded in the accounting records gives evidence of **completeness**.

Procedures (ISA 500: paras. A10–A25)	
Inspection of documentation	Confirmation to documentation of items recorded in accounting records confirms that an asset exists or a transaction occurred. Confirmation that items identified in supporting documentation are recorded in accounting records tests **completeness**. Cut-off can be verified by inspecting a reverse population, that is, checking transactions recorded after the end of the reporting period to supporting documentation to confirm that they occurred **after** the end of the reporting period. Inspection also provides evidence of **valuation/measurement, rights and obligations** and the nature of items (**presentation and disclosure**). It can also be used to compare documents (and therefore test **consistency** of audit evidence) and confirm **authorisation**.
Observation	Observation involves watching a procedure being performed (for example, post opening). It is of **limited use**, as it only confirms the procedure took place when the auditor is watching.
Enquiries	Seeking information from **client staff** or **external sources**. Strength of evidence depends on knowledge and integrity of source of information.
Confirmation	Seeking **confirmation from another source** of details in the client's accounting records, for example confirmation from the bank of bank balances.
Recalculations	**Checking arithmetic** of client's records, for example adding up ledger account.
Re-performance	Re-performance is the auditor's **independent** execution of procedures or controls originally performed as part of the entity's internal control, either manually or using computer-assisted auditing techniques (CAATs). **Data analytics** is a more thorough technique where entire populations can now be audited instead of samples because of the power and capability of technology (see below for examples of how data analytics could be used by the auditor).
Analytical procedures	Analytical procedures consist of **evaluations** of financial information made by a study of plausible relationships among both financial and non-financial data. These can be used as **substantive analytical procedures** (see below for examples).

When assessing the sufficiency and appropriateness of audit evidence, auditors must consider whether the evidence is consistent. Where **contradictory evidence** is discovered, for example, where one piece of evidence suggests that a specific liability has been settled prior to the year end while another piece of evidence throws doubt on this, the auditors must perform any other procedures necessary to resolve the inconsistency (ISA 500: para. 11).

BPP LEARNING MEDIA

1.1.1 Examples of data analytics routines that can be used for gathering evidence

Analysis of sales trends by product, store, month, sales operative, supplier (including margin, frequency etc) ie more detailed than traditional CAATs	Reviewing all purchases to ensure they can be traced back to a matching order, goods received note and invoice	Reviewing journals for any that have been posted outside of office hours and cross-referencing them by originator (useful for fraud or error checks)

You should stay alert to developments in this area as the use of **audit data analytics** is **evolving** at a rapid pace. Not only can larger amounts of more complex data be analysed, the introduction of **data visualisation techniques** (such as dashboards) and **artificial intelligence (AI)** mean that the auditor can now summarise data more easily and interpret the messages locked away in the data for more effectively than ever before.

Essential reading

See Chapter 16 of the Essential reading for more detail on how data analytics is changing the auditor's approach to gathering evidence. Note that there is a technical article produced by the examining team on this as well which you should read.

The Essential reading is available as an Appendix of the digital edition of the Workbook.

1.1.2 Examples of substantive analytical procedures

Simple comparisons

A simple year on year comparison could provide very persuasive evidence that an expense such as rent is correctly stated, providing that the auditor has sufficient knowledge of the business, for example knowing that the same premises have been leased year on year and that there has been no rent review.

Comparisons with estimates prepared by the auditors

A common example of this is where a business may have a large number of items of plant and machinery that are depreciated at different rates. The auditor could perform a quick calculation:

$$\boxed{\text{Closing balance of plant and machinery (cost)}} \times \boxed{\text{Average depreciation rate}}$$

If this estimate was similar to the actual depreciation charge, it would go some way to allowing the auditor to conclude that the charge was materially correct.

Relationship between financial and non-financial information

In making an estimate of employee costs, probably for one specific department, such as manufacturing, the auditor might use information about the number of employees in the department, as well as rates of pay increases. The estimate might be:

$$\boxed{\text{Prior year wages expense}} \times \boxed{\frac{\text{Average no. of employees current year}}{\text{Average no. of employees prior year}} \times \% \text{ pay increase}}$$

If the actual expense does not make sense when compared with the estimate, explanations would need to be sought and corroborated. For example, management might explain that for several months of the year, the factory ran double shifts, so a higher proportion of hours worked were paid at higher overtime rates.

Further examination of production records for those months would be required.

If no explanation is available, then more detailed substantive testing will be required, directed towards possible misstatements, such as mis-postings, or frauds, such as payments to dummy employees. Auditors are essentially looking for enough reliable audit evidence. Audit **evidence usually indicates what is probable** rather than what is definite (it is usually persuasive rather than conclusive) so different sources are examined by the auditors. However, auditors can only give **reasonable assurance** that the financial statements are free from misstatement, so **not all sources of evidence will be examined**.

2 ISA 530 *Audit Sampling*

ISA 530 *Audit Sampling* is based on the premise that auditors do not normally examine all the information available to them, as it would be impractical to do so and using audit sampling will produce valid conclusions.

> **Audit sampling:** Involves the application of audit procedures to less than 100% of the items within a population of audit relevance such that all sampling units have an equal chance of selection in order to provide the auditor with a reasonable basis on which to draw conclusions about the entire population.
>
> **Statistical sampling:** Any approach to sampling that involves random selection of a sample, and use of probability theory to evaluate sample results, including measurement of sampling risk.
>
> **Population:** The entire set of data from which a sample is selected and about which an auditor wishes to draw conclusions.
>
> **Sampling units:** The individual items constituting a population.
>
> **Stratification:** The process of dividing a population into sub-populations, each of which is a group of sampling units, which have similar characteristics (often monetary value).
>
> **Tolerable misstatement:** A monetary amount set by the auditor in respect of which the auditor seeks to obtain an appropriate level of assurance that the monetary amount set by the auditor is not exceeded by the actual misstatement in the population.
>
> **Tolerable rate of deviation:** A rate of deviation from prescribed internal control procedures set by the auditor in respect of which the auditor seeks to obtain an appropriate level of assurance that the rate of deviation set by the auditor is not exceeded by the actual rate of deviation in the population.
>
> **Anomaly:** A misstatement or deviation that is demonstrably not representative of misstatements or deviations in a population.
>
> **Sampling risk:** Arises from the possibility that the auditor's conclusion, based on a sample, may be different from the conclusion if the entire population were subjected to the same audit procedure.
>
> **Non-sampling risk:** Arises from factors that cause the auditor to reach an erroneous conclusion for any reason not related to the sampling risk. For example, most audit evidence is persuasive rather than conclusive, the auditor might use inappropriate procedures, or the auditor might misinterpret evidence and fail to recognise an error.
>
> (ISA 530: para. 5)

Some testing procedures do **not** involve sampling, such as:

- Testing 100% of items in a population
- Testing all items with a certain characteristic (for example, over a certain value) as the selection is not representative of the population

The ISA distinguishes between **statistically-based sampling**, which involves the use of random selection techniques from which mathematically constructed conclusions about the population can be drawn, and **non-statistical methods**, from which auditors draw a judgemental opinion about the population (ISA 530: para. A4). However, the principles of the ISA apply to both methods. You should be aware of the major methods of statistical and non-statistical sampling.

The auditor's judgement as to what is sufficient appropriate audit evidence is influenced by a number of factors.

- Risk assessment
- The **nature** of the **accounting and internal control systems**
- The **materiality** of the item being examined
- The **experience gained during previous audits**
- The auditor's **knowledge of the business** and **industry**
- The **results of audit procedures**
- The **source** and **reliability of information** available

If they are unable to obtain sufficient, appropriate audit evidence, the auditors should **consider the implications for their report.**

3 ISA 510 *Initial Audit Engagements – Opening Balances*

Auditors must make special considerations at the planning stage when they are auditing an entity for the first time, whether because the entity has never required an audit before, or because the entity has simply changed auditor.

New audits generally require a little **more work** than recurring engagements. But it is important to note that this is not because the auditor needs to do a first-time audit more thoroughly than other audits. Rather, it is because there are **specific risks** in relation to an auditor's relative **lack of knowledge** of new audit clients.

The auditor shall obtain **sufficient appropriate audit evidence** about whether the opening balances contain **misstatements** that **materially** affect the current period's financial statements by:

(a) Determining whether the prior period's closing balances have been **correctly brought forward** to the current period or, when appropriate, have been **restated;**

(b) Determining whether the opening balances reflect **the application of appropriate accounting policies;** and

(c) Performing one or more of the following:

   (i) Where the prior year financial statements were audited, reviewing the predecessor auditor's **working papers** to obtain **evidence** regarding the opening balances;

   (ii) Evaluating whether audit procedures performed in the current period provide **evidence** relevant to the opening balances; or

   (iii) Performing **specific audit procedures** to obtain evidence regarding the opening balances

(ISA 510: para. 6)

Essential reading

See Chapter 7 of the Essential reading for more detail on the approach to auditing opening balances.

The Essential reading is available as an Appendix of the digital edition of the Workbook.

3.1 Prior period audited by another auditor

Audit procedures:

Review predecessor's **working papers**, considering the **professional competence** and **independence** of the predecessor auditor	**Read** the most recent set of financial statements and predecessor's auditor's report for information relevant to opening balances	If the prior period auditor's report was **modified**, pay particular attention in the current period to the matter which resulted in the modification

3.2 Prior period not audited (ie first time being audited)

Other audit procedures need to be performed, for example:

Collection or payment of opening **accounts receivable** or **payable** in the current period	Observation of current physical **inventory count** and **reconciliation** back to opening quantities ('roll back')	Examination of records underlying opening **non-current assets and liabilities**, including confirmation from third parties where possible

3.3 Auditor's report

In all cases where there is a new auditor, the auditor's report **must contain an Other Matter paragraph**. This applies whether or not the audit opinion being expressed is modified. ISA 510 gives the following example of an Other Matter paragraph in this case (the example is also found in ISA 710).

Other matter

The financial statements of the Company for the year ended December 31, 20X0 were audited by another auditor who expressed an unmodified opinion on those statements on March 31, 20X1.

(ISA 510: Appendix – Illustration 1)

If there was a **modification** to the opinion and this is **still relevant** in the current period, the auditor expresses a modified opinion in this year's auditor's report in line with ISA 705 and ISA 710 (ISA 510: para. 13). Otherwise, the **opinion** would be modified under the following circumstances:

Unable to obtain **sufficient appropriate evidence** about the opening balances	Qualified 'except for' or disclaimer of opinion
Opening balances contain **material misstatements** affecting current period (either not corrected or not adequately disclosed) This includes the possibility that **accounting policies** may not be consistently applied or accounted for/disclosed properly in the new year.	Qualified 'except for' or adverse opinion
Listed auditor has **difficulty confirming opening balances**	Disclose as a Key Audit Matter in line with ISA 701

4 ISA 230 Audit Documentation

> **PER alert**
>
> One of the competencies you require to fulfil **Performance Objective 19** of the PER is the ability to carry out and document compliance and substantive tests and other audit work in accordance with the audit programme. You can apply the knowledge you obtain in this chapter of the Workbook to help demonstrate this competency.

In general terms, the auditor's documentation should be:

| Repeat | Sufficiently **complete** and **detailed** to enable an experienced auditor with no previous connection with the audit subsequently to ascertain from them what work was performed and to support the conclusions reached. |

| Record | An accurate record of:
(a) The nature, timing and extent of the audit procedures performed to comply with the ISAs and applicable legal and regulatory requirements;
(b) The results of the audit procedures performed, and the audit evidence obtained; and
(c) Significant matters arising during the audit, the conclusions reached thereon, and significant professional judgments made in reaching those conclusions.

This includes the preparation of **working papers reviewed** by an appropriately senior and independent personnel. |

| Reasonings | The auditor's **reasoning** and **conclusions** on all significant matters requiring exercise of judgment. This helps to support the auditor's report conclusions should they require any subsequent justification (eg in response to a negligence claim). |

(ISA 230: para. 8)

5 ISA 620 *Using the Work of an Auditor's Expert*

> **Auditor's expert:** An individual or organisation possessing expertise in a field other than accounting or auditing, whose work in that field is used by the auditor to assist the auditor in obtaining sufficient appropriate audit evidence. An auditor's expert may be either an auditor's internal expert (who is a partner or staff, including temporary staff, of the auditor's firm or a network firm), or an auditor's external expert.
>
> **Management's expert:** An individual or organisation possessing expertise in a field other than accounting or auditing, whose work in that field is used by the entity to assist the entity in preparing the financial statements.
>
> (ISA 620: para. 6)

Relying on the work of a management's expert is covered in ISA 500 *Audit Evidence*. When relying on the work of a management expert's work, the auditor must; evaluate the management's expert's competence, capabilities and objectivity; obtain an understanding of the expert's work, and; evaluate the appropriateness of the work as audit evidence (ISA 500: para. 8).

Reliance on an auditor's expert might be **necessary** in the following situations:

- **Valuation** of certain types of asset, eg land and buildings, precious stones
- Determination of **quantities** or **physical condition** of assets
- Actuarial **valuations** on pensions or insurance liabilities
- **Measurement** of work completed and to be completed on contracts where performance obligations are satisfied over time
- **Legal opinions** re: interpretations of agreements and regulations, or the outcome of litigation

When considering whether to use the work of an expert, the auditors should review:

- The **importance** of the matter being considered in the context of the accounts
- The **risk of misstatement** based on the nature and complexity of the matter
- The **quantity** and **quality** of other available **relevant audit evidence**

The auditor may decide to use an auditor's expert even if the entity has already used a management's expert. This could be the case if:

- The nature, scope or objectives of the management expert's work meant that it was **inadequate** for audit purposes
- The expert was **not independent enough** of management, eg management could control the expert
- The expert's **competence** and **capabilities** were not sufficient

(ISA 620: para. A9)

Essential reading

See Chapter 7 of the Essential reading for more detail on the auditor's use of experts within the audit.

The Essential reading is available as an Appendix of the digital edition of the Workbook.

6 ISA 610 *Using the Work of Internal Auditors*

As part of their role, the external auditors will need to seek **sufficient appropriate audit evidence** in order to reach an opinion. Given the governance-related work on **internal controls** that a company's internal audit function might perform in the 21st century, there is some **logic** in the external auditor relying on this work and reducing time spent on the audit.

Considerations that the external auditor might take into account when reviewing internal audit work include:

- Internal audit's **organisational status** and relevant policies and procedures. Are the internal auditors **objective**?
- The **level of competence** of the internal audit function
- Whether the internal audit function applies a **systematic and disciplined approach**, including **quality control**

(ISA 610: para. 15)

If any of this is found to be unacceptable, the external auditor is unlikely to rely on internal audit evidence and will carry out its **own testing** instead. It may also form part of the external auditor's overall assessment of risk and the company's control environment.

Essential reading

See Chapter 7 of the Essential reading for further content on how to assess the internal audit function.

The Essential reading is available as an Appendix of the digital edition of the Workbook.

7 ISA 550 *Related Parties*

Central to a number of government investigations in various countries have been companies trading with organisations or individuals **other than at arm's length**. Such transactions were made possible by a degree of control or influence exercised by directors over both parties to the transactions. ISA 550 *Related Parties* covers this area.

Related party: A party that is either:

(a) A related party as defined in the applicable financial reporting framework; or

(b) Where the applicable financial reporting framework establishes minimal or no related party requirements:

    (i) A person or other entity that has control or significant influence, directly or indirectly, through one or more intermediaries, over the reporting entity;

    (ii) Another entity over which the reporting entity has control or significant influence, directly or indirectly, through one or more intermediaries; or

    (iii) Another entity that is under common control with the reporting entity through having:

        (1) Common controlling ownership;

        (2) Owners who are close family members; or

(3) Common key management.

(ISA 550: para. 10)

Management is responsible for the identification of related party transactions. Such transactions should be properly approved as they are frequently not at arm's length. Management is also responsible for the **disclosure** of related party transactions.

The **objectives** of the **auditor** are:

(a) Irrespective of whether the applicable financial reporting framework establishes related party requirements, to obtain an understanding of related party relationships and transactions sufficient to be able:

    (i) To recognise fraud risk factors, if any, arising from related party relationships and transactions that are relevant to the identification and assessment of the risks of material misstatement due to fraud; and

    (ii) To conclude, based on the audit evidence obtained, whether the financial statements, insofar as they are affected by those relationships and transactions:

        (1) Achieve fair presentation (for fair presentation frameworks); or

        (2) Are not misleading (for compliance frameworks); and

(b) In addition, where the applicable financial reporting framework establishes related party requirements, to obtain sufficient appropriate audit evidence about whether related party relationships and transactions have been appropriately identified, accounted for and disclosed in the financial statements in accordance with the framework.

(ISA 550: para. 9)

Activity 1: Related parties

What audit procedures should be performed to identify related parties?

Solution

During the audit, **all members** of the **audit team** should be **equally alert** for transactions which may indicate the existence of unidentified related parties. Examples include the following:

- Transactions which have **abnormal terms of trade** such as unusual prices, interest rates, guarantees and repayment terms
- Transactions which **lack a logical business reason** for their occurrence

- Transactions in which **substance differs from form**
- Transactions **processed** in an **unusual** manner
- High volume or significant transactions with **certain customers** or suppliers as compared with others
- **Unrecorded transactions** such as the receipt or provision of services at no charge

The auditor should obtain a **written representation** from management concerning the completeness of information provided concerning related parties and the adequacy of disclosures in the financial statements (ISA 550: para. 26).

Essential reading

See Chapter 7 of the Essential reading for further content on how to respond to the risks of material misstatement due to related parties.

The Essential reading is available as an Appendix of the digital edition of the Workbook.

7.1 Audit conclusions and reporting

If the auditor is unable to obtain sufficient appropriate evidence regarding related parties and transactions with such parties, this gives rise to a qualified opinion due to **insufficient or inappropriate audit evidence**.

If the auditor concludes that the disclosure of related party transactions is not adequate, this gives rise to a modified auditor's report based on **material misstatement**.

8 Outsourcing and ISA 402 Audit Considerations Relating to an Entity Using a Service Organisation

Outsourcing is the use of external suppliers as a source of finished products, components or services. It is also known as 'sub-contracting'.

An audit client using an external supplier in this way does not diminish the ultimate responsibility of the directors for conducting the business of the company.

Business functions that are commonly outsourced include, but are not limited to: payroll, information technology, accounting, recruitment and internal audit.

ISA 402 uses the following terms:

KEY TERM

Service organisation: A third-party organisation (or segment of a third-party organisation) that provides services to user entities that are part of those entities' information systems relevant to financial reporting.

User entity: An entity that uses a service organisation and whose financial statements are being audited.

User auditor: An auditor who audits and reports on the financial statements of a user entity.

Service auditor: An auditor who, at the request of the service organisation, provides an assurance report on the controls of a service organisation.

Type 1 report: A report on the description and design of controls at a service organisation. It comprises:

(a) A description, prepared by management of the service organisation, of the service organisation's system, control objectives and related controls that have been designed and implemented as at a specified date; and

(b) A report by the service auditor with the objective of conveying reasonable assurance that includes the service auditor's opinion on the description of the service organisation's system, control objectives and related controls and the suitability of the design of the controls to achieve the specified control objectives.

Type 2 report: A report on the description, design and operating effectiveness of controls at a service organisation. It comprises:

(a) A description, prepared by management of the service organisation, of the service organisation's system, control objectives and related controls, their design and implementation as at a specified date or throughout a specified period and, in some cases, their operating effectiveness throughout a specified period; and

(b) A report by the service auditor with the objective of conveying reasonable assurance that includes:

(i) The service auditor's opinion on the description of the service organisation's system, control objectives and related controls, the suitability of the design of the controls to achieve the specified control objectives, and the operating effectiveness of the controls; and

(ii) A description of the service auditor's tests of the controls and the results thereof.

(ISA 402: para. 8)

A **user entity** may use a service organisation that **executes transactions** and **maintains related accountability** for them or **records transactions and processes related data** (eg a computer systems service organisation). Such an organisation may also carry out **facilities management** work or even **asset management** on behalf of a user.

Service organisations may undertake activities on a dedicated basis for one company, or on a shared basis, either for members of a single group of entities or for unrelated customers.

User auditors need to obtain sufficient, appropriate audit evidence to express an opinion on financial statements. They therefore need to consider an approach towards the parts of the audit affected by the service organisation.

8.1 Impact on audit planning

One factor that has an impact on the audit of a **user entity** is that the **user auditor** has **no direct contractual relationship** with the **service organisation** (or indeed the **service auditor**) and this may cause problems with **access** and **confidentiality**. In practical terms, however, it is in the interest of the user entity for its **service organisation** to co-operate with the user auditor, but this must still be taken into consideration when planning the audit.

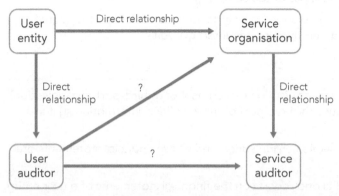

ISA 402 requires the **user auditor** to obtain an **understanding** of the nature and significance of the services provided by the service organisation, starting with the extent of the relationship between user entity and service organisation:

(a) When the services provided by the service organisation are **limited to recording and processing user entity transactions and the user entity retains authorisation and maintenance of accountability,** the user entity may be able to implement effective policies and procedures within its organisation.

(b) When the service organisation **executes the user entity's transactions and maintains accountability,** the user entity may deem it necessary to **rely on policies andprocedures at the service organisation**. In such cases, the auditor needs to design procedures that allow it to manage audit risk effectively.

The auditor needs to understand **how** a user entity uses the services of the service organisation, including:

- The nature and significance of the service provided, including the effect on the controls at the user entity
- The nature and materiality of the transactions processed or accounts/financial reporting processes affected
- The degree of interaction between the user entity and the service organisation
- The nature of the relationship between the two, including the contractual terms
- If the service organisation maintains accounting records for the user entity, whether the arrangements affect the auditors' responsibility to report concerning accounting records

Sources of information include:

- User manuals
- System overviews
- Technical manuals
- The contract/service level agreement
- Reports by the service organisations, internal auditors or regulatory authorities
- Reports by the service organisation auditor

(ISA 402: paras. 9 and A1)

8.2 Obtaining evidence on the quality of a service organisations' controls

The user auditor must evaluate the controls at the user entity that relate to the service organisation and determine whether this gives the auditor sufficient understanding to provide a basis for assessing risks of material misstatement in the user entity financial statements.

If the auditor concludes that this is insufficient, they must carry out one of the following four activities.

- Obtain Type 1 or Type 2 report from the service organisation, if available
- Contact the service organisation to get specific information (with permission)
- Visit the service organisation and perform procedures to obtain the information (with permission)
- Use another auditor to perform procedures at the service organisation (with permission)

It is likely that the auditor will be able to obtain a Type 1 or 2 report, and this will be the most straightforward option. If this action is taken, the auditor needs to be sure that:

- The service organisation's auditor is competent and objective
- The standards under which the report was issued are adequate for the user entity's auditor's purposes
- The report is for an appropriate date (that is, it covers the period the user entity is reporting on)
- The evidence it is based on is sufficient and appropriate for the user entity's auditor's understanding of the internal controls
- If complementary user entity controls are relevant to the user entity, the auditor has obtained an understanding of these

8.3 Responding to assessed risks

The auditor needs to assess whether sufficient appropriate audit evidence is available from records at the user entity. If so, they should carry out **appropriate procedures** at the user entity. If not, they should carry out further audit procedures.

When the user auditor expects controls at the service organisation to be operating effectively, they must obtain evidence that this is the case, by one of the following three methods.

- Obtaining a Type 2 report, if available
- Performing test of controls at the service organisation
- Using another auditor to perform tests of controls at the service organisation

BPP
LEARNING
MEDIA

Again, obtaining a Type 2 report is the most likely option, in which case the entity auditor has to:

- Check that the report is made up to an appropriate date
- Ensure that they have tested complimentary controls at the user entity if necessary
- Check the adequacy of the time period covered by the tests of controls and the time elapsed since those tests of controls were performed
- Ensure the tests of controls performed for the purposes of the report are relevant and provide sufficient appropriate audit evidence for the user entity auditors' purposes

The auditor must also make **enquiries of management** if they are aware or suspect any fraud, non-compliance with law and regulations or uncorrected misstatements at the service organisation that could affect the financial statements of the user entity and evaluate the impact of any matters on their procedures and report.

8.4 Reporting

The key issue to remember is that if the user auditor cannot obtain sufficient appropriate evidence about the impact of the service organisation on the user entity, the auditor must **modify** the auditor's report, as the scope of the audit has been **limited**.

Chapter summary

```
                              ┌──────────────┐
                              │   Evidence   │
                              └──────────────┘
```

ISA 500 *Audit Evidence*

- Evidence should be **sufficient** (enough) and **appropriate** (reliable and relevant)
- Need evidence relevant to the assertions: **ACCA COPER**
- Evidence from **tests of controls** and **substantive testing**
- Procedures: inspection; observation; enquiries, confirmation; recalculations; re-performance and substantive analytical procedures

ISA 530 *Audit Sampling*

- Sample selection methods:
  - Statistical
  - Non-statistical
- Evaluation of results takes cause and impact into account

ISA 510 *Initial Audit Engagements – Opening Balances*

- Ensure that all b/fwd balances are not misstated, are b/fwd correctly and that accounting policies are consistent
- Prior period audited by another auditor:
  - Review predecessor's working papers, read report – modified?
- Prior period not audited (ie first year of audit):
  - Additional procedures re: current assets and liabilities
- **Auditor's report** implications (insufficient and/or inappropriate audit evidence or material misstatement) plus OM paragraph if audited by a previous auditor)

ISA 230 *Audit Documentation*

- Repeat
- Record
- Reasoning

ISA 620 *Using the Work of an Auditor's Expert*

- May be **required** for:
  - Asset valuations
  - Actuarial valuations
  - Inventory counts
  - Stage of completion on contracts where performance obligations are satisfied over time
  - Legal opinions
- Auditor should verify the **credentials** of the expert to ensure they can be trusted as an **objective** source of audit evidence

ISA 610 *Using the Work of Internal Auditors*

- Criteria for assessment:
  - Organisational status (including objectivity)
  - Level of competence
  - Systematic and disciplined approach including quality control

BPP
LEARNING
MEDIA

```
                    ┌─────────────┐        ┌──────────────────────────────┐
                    │  ISA 550    │        │  Outsourcing and ISA 402 Audit │
                    │  Related    │        │  Considerations Relating to an │
                    │  Parties    │        │  Entity Using a Service        │
                    └─────────────┘        │  Organisation                  │
                                           └──────────────────────────────┘
```

- IAS 24 requires entities to disclose who they are related to (**related parties**) and how they have interacted (**related party transactions**).
- The auditor therefore has an obligation to obtain evidence on all related parties and associated transactions and ensure they are all disclosed in the F/S (they are **material by their nature not their size**).

- **Planning** becomes difficult due to lack of direct relationship, so need to assess significance of service organisation and their relevance to the audit
- **Audit procedures** include evidence from site visits and/or service organisation's auditor (plus Type 1 and Type 2 reports using **ISAE 3402** in Chapter 12)

Knowledge diagnostic

1. ISA 500

The auditor must obtain **sufficient appropriate** evidence to support the audit opinion via the assertions (ACCACOPER). Procedures for obtaining evidence need to be appropriate to the client.

2. ISA 530

Auditors can use **sampling** when testing large populations – this approach requires knowing which is the best selection method (random, systematic or haphazard) and then how to **evaluate** results.

3. ISA 510

In most situations, the auditor's work in respect of **opening balances** is quite restricted. More work is required if it is a **new engagement** or if the **prior period was not audited**.

4. ISA 230

Evidence should be adequately **documented** and this is usually achieved if they satisfy the three criteria: **repeat**; **record**; and **reasoning**.

5. ISA 620

The use of an **expert** may be required in certain instances (eg valuations, opinions, measurements). The **competence** of such an expert will need to be assessed just like any other form of evidence.

6. ISA 610

The external auditor will evaluate how much it can **rely** on the work of the **internal auditor** by considering things such as **professionalism, supervision, review, judgement** and **ethical behaviour (all part of sound quality control)**.

7. ISA 550

In line with IAS 24, auditors need to perform a number of tests to ensure that all **related parties and associated transactions** have been **identified** and **adequately disclosed**.

8. ISA 402

Outsourcing is a common practice with many companies engaging service providers to perform non-core functions, for example **internal audit, payroll, recruitment** or **IT**. Clients use these **service organisations** for transactions, maintaining records, processing data, facilities management, training and the maintenance or safe custody of assets. At the planning stage, the external auditor should assess the impact outsourced activities may have on the audit and consider performing **additional procedures** to obtain sufficient appropriate evidence.

Further study guidance

Question practice

Now try the following from the Further question practice bank (available in the digital edition of the Workbook):

- Question 10 'Herzog' tests risks of material misstatement and analytical procedures alongside some procedures for obtaining audit evidence.

Further reading

There are a number of technical articles on the ACCA website written by members of the AAA examining team which are relevant to some of the topics covered in this chapter that you should read:

- *Exam technique for Advanced Audit and Assurance part 4 – audit procedures*
- *Using the work of internal auditors*
- *Data analytics and the auditor*
- *Auditing in a computer-based environment*
- *Specific aspects of auditing in a computer-based environment*
- *Examining evidence*
- *Audit working papers*

Own research

- In the UK, the FRC has conducted research into how audit processes are changing – as an example, you can see how issues you have studied so far interact in the real world by accessing their reports:

  www.frc.org.uk/auditors/report-on-developments-in-audit

Activity answers

Activity 1: Related parties

Approach

As this is an 'idea generation' exercise, you are unlikely to come up with anything as comprehensive as the suggested solution below – however, try and think about where you would look to understand the auditor's objectives: understanding who the related parties could be and how they could be entering into transactions with the entity.

Suggested solution

As part of the risk assessment procedures required by ISA 315 (Revised), the auditor must carry out the following procedures to obtain information relevant to identifying risks associated with related parties.

- Audit team discussion of risk shall include specific consideration of susceptibility of financial statements to material misstatement (ISA 315 (Revised): para. 17) which will need to consider related parties

- Auditor shall inquire of management:
    - The identity of related parties including changes from prior period
    - The nature of the relationships between the entity and its related parties
    - Whether any transactions occurred between the parties, and if so, what
    - What controls the entity has to identify, account for and disclose related party relationships and transactions
    - What controls the entity has to authorise and approve significant transactions and arrangements with related parties
    - What controls the entity has to authorise and approve significant transactions and arrangements outside the normal course of business

        (The auditor may have to perform risk assessment procedures in addition in respect of the latter three points.)

- Stay alert for evidence of related party transactions when obtaining other audit evidence, in particular when scrutinising bank and legal confirmations and minutes of meetings

- If significant transactions outside the normal course of business are discovered, inquire of management the nature of the transactions and whether related parties could be involved

- Share information obtained about related parties with the audit team

(ISA 550: paras. 13–17)

The following procedures may be helpful.

- **Enquire of management** and the directors as to whether transactions have taken place with related parties that are required to be disclosed by the disclosure requirements that are applicable to the entity.

- **Review prior year working papers** for names of known related parties.

- **Review minutes** of meetings of shareholders and directors and other relevant statutory records, such as the register of directors' interests.

- **Review accounting records** for large or unusual transactions or balances, in particular transactions recognised at or near the end of the financial period.

- **Review confirmations of loans receivable** and payable and confirmations from banks. Such a review may indicate the relationship, if any, of guarantors to the entity.

- **Review investment transactions**, for example purchase or sale of an interest in a joint venture or other entity.

- **Enquire** as to the **names** of all pension and other trusts established for the benefit of employees and the names of their management and trustees.
- **Enquire** as to the **affiliation** of directors and officers with other entities.
- **Review the register of interests in shares** to determine the names of principal shareholders.
- **Enquire of other auditors** currently involved in the audit, or predecessor auditors, as to their knowledge of additional related parties.
- **Review the entity's tax returns**, returns made under statute and other information supplied to regulatory agencies for evidence of the existence of related parties.
- **Review invoices and correspondence** from lawyers for indications of the existence of related parties or related party transactions.

If risks relating to related parties and their transactions are identified, they should be treated as **significant risks** in accordance with ISA 315 (Revised). Also, due to the close connection between related parties and possible fraud, the auditor must consider the overlap with ISA 240 here as well.

8

Evaluation and review – matters relating to specific accounting issues

Learning objectives

On completion of this chapter, you should be able to:

	Syllabus reference no.
Design appropriate audit procedures relating to:	D3(a)

- Inventory (including standard costing systems)
- Non-current assets
- Intangible assets
- Biological assets
- Investment properties
- Assets held for sale and discontinued operations
- Financial instruments
- Accounting estimates including fair values
- Government grants
- Leases
- Impairment
- Provisions, contingent liabilities and contingent assets
- Borrowing costs
- Employee benefits
- Share-based payment transactions
- Taxation (including deferred tax)
- Related parties
- Revenue from contracts with customers
- Statement of cash flows
- Business combinations
- The effects of foreign exchange rates
- Segmental reporting
- Financial statement notes and related disclosures
- Earnings per share
- Changes in accounting policy
- Payroll and other expenses

Business and exam context

You must be able to consider four key matters in relation to items appearing in financial statements: risk, materiality, relevant accounting standards and audit evidence. In this chapter, we shall focus primarily on the last two of these, as the first two will depend more on the scenario presented in any given question.

You have previously studied the audit of a basic set of financial statements. At this level, the issues you are presented with will be more complex, but remember that key basic points apply. Bear in mind the relevant **assertions** for the financial statement items.

You need a strong knowledge of all the accounting standards you learnt up to SBR *Strategic Business Reporting* to apply in this exam.

These syllabus areas can be tested in any part of the exam: in Section A, requirements would relate to audit planning and would ask for example procedures or additional information; in Section B, requirements would relate to audit evidence and could be linked in with audit completion or current issues.

Chapter overview

Evaluation and review – matters relating to specific accounting issues

- The importance of financial reporting standards to the auditor
- The audit of deferred tax
- Payroll and other expenses
- Financial instruments
- The audit of revenue
- The audit of leases
- The audit of retirement benefits
- ISA 540 (Revised) *Auditing Accounting Estimates and Related Disclosures*

1 The importance of financial reporting standards to the auditor

This topic deals with the matters that the auditor should consider when testing specific accounting and financial reporting issues. Remember, when faced with a complex accounting issue, the auditor should **consider** a number of different **matters** which will ensure that all relevant areas are covered. These matters could be summarised by the following process:

- **M** • The **materiality** of the issue covered
- **R** • The possible **risk(s)** of misstatement
- **S** • What the relevant **accounting standards** require
- **A** • The **audit evidence** required to address the risk
  • The **audit procedures** used to generate this evidence

Important note

It will not be possible to cover all of the accounting issues mentioned in the syllabus within this topic. Some items are assumed knowledge from previous studies (such as SBR) and others will be covered during the revision phase of your studies. The skills developed in this topic can be used interchangeably between accounting issues.

Essential reading

See Chapter 8 of the Essential reading for an overview of all the relevant accounting issues and audit procedures. **It is essential that you are comfortable with this material in advance of the AAA exam.**

The Essential reading is available as an Appendix of the digital edition of the Workbook.

Let's start by looking at a straightforward illustration of how to put this approach into practice before we go into something more complex!

2 The audit of deferred tax

The auditor should obtain sufficient appropriate audit evidence that the deferred tax liability is correctly calculated.

IAS 12 *Income taxes* requires deferred tax to be calculated on the full provision basis.

Activity 1: Armstrong

You are the manager responsible for the audit of Armstrong, a start-up company producing sporting equipment for the retail market. The draft financial statements for the year ended December 20X6 show profit before taxation of $3 million and total assets of $11.6 million.

The following matters relating to deferred tax have been left for your attention.

At the year end, Armstrong had plant and equipment with a carrying amount of $3.6 million. The tax written down value of the plant and equipment was $2.1 million. (There was no deferred tax provision in the prior year as this is the first year of trade.)

The financial statements have disclosed a deferred tax provision of $450,000 based on a tax rate of 30%.

Required

In respect of the amounts relating to deferred tax in the financial statements of Armstrong, comment on:

(1)   The matters that you should consider

(2)   The evidence you should expect to find

(6 marks)

Solution

3 Payroll and other expenses

You will have already studied the audit of payroll and other expenses for your Audit and Assurance (AA) exam, so for AAA you need to remember the kinds of **procedures** that the auditor might use when assessing the risks associated with these kinds of material costs.

Taking **payroll** as an example, there are a number of **issues** to consider:

*   Processing **starters** and **leavers** (and any other **changes** in people's circumstances)
*   Recording the **amount of work done** (including wages, salaries and overtime)
*   Calculating the **amounts to be paid** to staff and others (such as the tax authorities)
*   Prompt and complete **payment** to appropriate individuals and organisations
*   Accurate **records** of payments and disclosures in the financial statements

The **size, structure** and **complexity** of an audit client could make a big difference to the audit approach when considering payroll (and indeed any other expenses): for example, the degree of **technology** used in processing the payroll, the **ease** of being able to collect evidence and even the relative **expertise** of the staff working for the client.

As payroll could also be an **outsourced function**, the requirements of ISA 402 from Chapter 7 could come into play here as well.

Activity 2: Payroll

Considering the issues discussed above, suggest examples of typical audit procedures that could be used in the audit of payroll. Your answer should include a number of different approaches for collecting audit evidence.

Solution

4 Financial instruments

The accounting requirements for financial instruments are found in **IFRS 9 Financial Instruments, IFRS 7 Financial Instruments: Disclosures** and **IAS 32 Financial Instruments: Presentation**. You need to be familiar with the examinable parts of these standards from your earlier FR/SBR studies.

Activity 3: Buddy Co

You are the manager on the audit of Holly Co; the audit team have left the following information for your attention.

In November 20X7, Holly Co purchased 500,000 shares in Buddy Co; this purchase gave Holly approximately 18% of the issued share capital of Buddy. The shares were purchased for $2 each and transaction costs amounted to 1% of the value of the shares. The Finance Director of Holly has stated that he has no intention of selling the shares in the near future as he doesn't like to speculate and he sees this as a long-term investment that he may add to in the future.

The share price of Buddy at the year end was $2.25.

You should assume that the purchase price of the shares and the transaction costs are both material to the financial statements of Holly Co.

Required

In respect of the audit of this transaction, comment on:

(1)   The matters you would consider; and

(2)   The evidence you would expect to find.

(7 marks)

Solution

---

5 The audit of revenue

The audit of revenue requires an awareness of **IFRS 15** *Revenue from Contracts with Customers* which sets out the process of recognising revenue using the following five steps:

Step 1	**Step 2**	**Step 3**	**Step 4**	**Step 5**
Identify the contract(s) with a customer	Identify the performance obligations in the contract	Determine the transaction price	Allocate the transaction price to the performance obligations in the contract	Recognise revenue when (or as) the entity satisfies a performance obligation

Clearly, with so many steps to consider, including meeting the requirements of performance obligations, IFRS 15 is a very examinable area for AAA.

 Activity 4: Laxman Co

You are an audit senior on the audit of Laxman Co, a wholesale seller of stationery and office products.

Recognised within revenue are a series of credit sales of inventory totalling $200,000 that took place close to the year end. Laxman Co continues to hold the legal title to this inventory.

Laxman Co holds a bank loan whose covenants impose on it a number of conditions, one of which is that its financial statements show an acid test ratio of more than one.

The following amounts are shown in Laxman Co's draft financial statements.

	$
Revenue	1,200,000
Current assets	1,000,000
Inventory	100,000

	$
Current liabilities	800,000

Required

Identify and explain the principal matters to consider when auditing the revenue of Laxman Co.

Solution

6 The audit of leases

IFRS 16 *Leases* defines a lease as a contract that 'conveys the right to control the use of an identified asset for a period of time in exchange for consideration' (para. 9). For **lessees**, this includes an assessment of whether the contract allows both of the following:

- The right to obtain substantially all the economic benefits from use of the identified asset
- The right to direct the use of the identified asset (known as a '**right-of-use asset**')

For a right-of-use asset (and hence lease) to be recognised, the asset should:

- Not be easily substituted by lessors; and
- Not be an exempt item, such as some intellectual property, assets related to mineral extraction, agricultural items or service contracts.

Revenue and liabilities from maintenance elements for assets must be shown separately from the lease liability within the lessee's financial statements.

A **right-of-use asset is recognised at cost**, including any fees and dismantling costs at the end of the lease term.

Depreciation is on a **straight-line basis**. Leases can be revalued if market conditions (including impairment reviews) support this.

A **lease liability** is created for all right-of-use assets – this includes all relevant financial commitments, eg the present value of lease payments not yet paid and any purchase options.

Some leased assets can be **exempt** from this accounting treatment: short-term leases (less than 12 months) and low-value assets (likely to be <$5,000) can be expensed instead.

IFRS 16 requires right-of-use assets and lease liabilities to be shown separately, either on the face of the statement of financial position (SoFP) or within the notes.

Disclosure includes:

- Depreciation charges and carrying amounts for any right-of-use assets held at the reporting date
- Interest expenses on lease liabilities
- Gains and losses from sale and leaseback transactions
- Expenses incurred on short-term and low-value leases
- Total cash outflow for leases

Disclosure is not required for leases where the information is deemed to be non-material.

Lessors follow a different approach under IFRS 16 *Leases* must be differentiated between 'finance leases' (where substantially all the risks and rewards of ownership are passed to the lessee, and the asset is derecognised in the lessor's financial statements once the lease terminates) and 'operating leases' (basically any other lease where the asset is held on the lessor's SoFP while income is received from the lessee) in their financial statements.

Activity 5: Leases

What would you consider to be the most significant audit risks for leases?

How would the auditor respond to some of these risks?

Solution

7 The audit of retirement benefits

IAS 19 *Employee Benefits* provides guidance on how companies should account for retirement benefit schemes. There are two types – **defined contribution** and **defined benefit** – and it is the latter type that tends to be inherently more risky as such schemes are set up to maintain funds for current and future payments to former employees and their dependants.

Consider the variables that exist in respect of such schemes:

(a) The **fundassets** are **valued** by following the market, which we know is inherently volatile.

(b) The **liabilities** of the fund can be affected by the **number** and **turnover** of qualifying employees, their **life expectancy**, the **terms** of their benefits and even future rates of pay.

In both cases, there is a risk that, from one year to the next, changes in these variables will result in a fall in assets or a rise in liabilities, or worse, both of these, which could lead to an overall deficit in the fund if not adequately managed under the terms of the standards. The auditor should obtain sufficient appropriate audit evidence that all liabilities and assets are reasonably valued, correctly accounted for and properly disclosed.

Activity 6: Jake's Pegs

You are planning the audit of Jake's Pegs, a global producer of clothes pegs and other domestic items. The company has been in existence for 35 years and is profitable. This is the first year your firm has performed the statutory audit.

The audit planning was virtually complete when the Finance Director informed you that the company operates a defined benefit pension scheme for all 750 of its employees. When challenged over the delay, the Finance Director apologised and said the scheme had 'slipped her mind'; she said she was confident that the scheme was in surplus but she was still waiting for the actuarial report which might not be available until the week before the reporting deadline.

Required

1   What **additional** audit risks arise due to this new information regarding the pension scheme?

2   Assuming the scheme is accounted for in accordance with IAS 19, what audit procedures would you expect to carry out in respect of the pension scheme for Jake's Pegs?

Solution

8 ISA 540 (Revised) *Auditing Accounting Estimates and Related Disclosures*

The objective of the auditor is to obtain **sufficient appropriate audit evidence** about whether accounting estimates and related disclosures in the financial statements are reasonable in the context of the applicable financial reporting framework.

(ISA 540: para. 11)

8.1 The nature of estimates

Right from the start of your accounting studies, you will have been aware of some of the main types of accounting estimates. **Examples** include:

•   Allowances for **receivables** or to **reduce inventories** to net realisable value

- The assessment of useful lives for the **depreciation** of non-current assets
- Amounts set aside for **warranty provisions** or for **losses on lawsuits**

The risk of misstatement in these areas is obvious, not least because they tend to concern areas where the auditor may not possess sufficient expertise to assess them adequately themselves. If management intended to **overstate profits**, for example, they are much more likely to reduce the amount of the allowance for receivables than, say, to omit the last week's worth of supplier invoices received in the financial year.

In recent years, developments that were required to consider the accounting treatment for more complex or volatile amounts, such as **financial instruments**, have led to the need for greater scrutiny over the approach used by auditors when assessing accounting estimates.

8.2 The audit approach

ISA 540 (Revised) *Auditing Accounting Estimates and Related Disclosures* was issued in December 2018 and still emphasises the basic requirement to obtain sufficient appropriate audit evidence. However, the standard **also** requires the auditor to obtain an **understanding** of the following in relation to accounting estimates and their disclosure:

(a) **Complexity** (although in cases of simple estimates such as a publicly quoted share price, the audit approach can be scaled down accordingly)

(b) **Subjectivity** (or the reasonableness of any judgement used in arriving at an estimate)

(c) **Estimation uncertainty** (any inherent lack of precision in the measurements used)

(d) Other **inherent risk factors** that may specifically affect the generation of an estimate that goes into the financial statements (such as reliance on a standard which may be open to interpretation) – in essence, this means that a separate assessment of inherent risk is required when the auditor is considering accounting estimates

(e) An understanding of the **controls relating to accounting estimates in operation at the client**, focusing on their design, implementation and operating effectiveness

(ISA 540: paras. 4, 5, 16–17)

The auditor's consideration of the **internal controls** relevant to assessing accounting estimates at a client could cover a significant amount of activities, such as the systems of **oversight and governance** in place, the use of **specialist expertise** and the role of **data** and **information systems** (ISA 540: paras. A28–44).

Once the auditor has understood these factors at the audited entity, they should respond to each of them by considering where and how they will obtain **sufficient appropriate audit evidence**. The auditor should consider the following sources of evidence in descending order:

- **Evidence from subsequent events** (such as using sales prices in the new year to assess the valuation of inventory at the reporting date)
- **Test management's own estimate** (known as 'management's point estimate') by considering the suitability of the process used by management, as well as the controls in place at the entity and the underlying data and any assumptions applied by the entity in addressing complexity, subjectivity and estimation uncertainty
- Should there be evidence that **management has failed to take account of estimation uncertainty** or that **management's point estimate cannot be relied upon**, the **auditor should consider developing their own estimate** (known as the 'auditor's point estimate', which may be either one figure or a specified range) using a process, data and assumptions that the auditor can trust (they may even consider the use of an auditor's expert in such cases)

(ISA 540: paras. 18, 27–19)

8.3 Evaluation of results

The auditor must **assess** any **variances** between the estimates derived from subsequent events and management's point estimate (as well as any auditor's point estimate or range developed). They must then determine whether a **misstatement** exists in the accounting estimate and whether it could be **material** (this could relate to qualitative **disclosures** as well as the estimates themselves). Finally, the auditor considers the implications for the **auditor's report**. (ISA 540: paras. 33–36)

Essential reading

As a priority, you should note that Chapter 8 of the Essential reading really is **essential reading** for the AAA exam and covers all examinable accounting issues and audit procedures, up to and including, the knowledge that you should have learned for SBR.

The Essential reading is available as an Appendix of the digital edition of the Workbook.

Chapter summary

Evaluation and review – matters relating to specific accounting issues

The importance of financial reporting standards to the auditor

- <u>M</u>ateriality
- <u>R</u>isk of misstatement presented
- Relevant accounting <u>S</u>tandards
- <u>A</u>udit evidence and procedures

The audit of deferred tax

- IAS 12 *Income taxes*
- Full provision basis
- Amounts due to temporary differences
- Recalculation as audit evidence

Payroll and other expenses

- Consider the audit approach required in each case
- Agree work done, numbers of employees, rates of pay due and payments made

Financial instruments

- IAS 32, IFRS 7 and IFRS 9
- Valuation of instruments
- Treatment of changes in value

The audit of revenue

- IFRS 15 *Revenue from Contracts with Customers*
- 5 step process:
  - Step 1 – Identify contracts
  - Step 2 – Identify performance obligations
  - Step 3 – Determine transaction prices
  - Step 4 – Allocate prices to performance obligations
  - Step 5 – Recognise revenue on satisfaction of a performance

The audit of leases

- IFRS 16 Leases
- Valid right-of-use asset?
- Authorised lease?
- Any excluded assets (including low value or short term leases?)
- Verify existence of asset
- Recalculate depreciation, lease liability and interest values
- Ensure that disclosure is satisfactory

The audit of retirement benefits

- IAS 19 *Employee Benefits*
- Defined contribution and defined benefit schemes
- Fund assets are valued by the market (FV)
- Fund liabilities depend on a number of variables – assessment by actuary
- Assessment of any gains or losses on fund – amounts posted to other comprehensive income
- Fund in surplus or deficit – balance on statement of financial position

ISA 540 (Revised) *Auditing Accounting Estimates and Related Disclosures*

- Auditor needs to assess **inherent risks** associated with accounting estimates
- Specific consideration of **complexity, subjectivity** and **estimation uncertainty** as well as any evidence of **management bias**
- Audit approach:
  - Looking at events after the end of the reporting period
  - Testing how management made their own point estimate
  - Looking at relevant controls
  - Developing an auditor's point estimate to compare against

Knowledge diagnostic

1. MRSA

For AAA you need to consider the following:

- The **materiality** of the issue(s) presented
- **Risk(s)** presented by each accounting issue
- What the accounting **standard** requires
- The **audit evidence/procedures** required

2. IAS 12

Remember that **IAS 12** requires deferred tax to be calculated on a **full provision basis** – remember how to apply the 'materiality, risk(s), standards and evidence' approach.

3. IAS 2

Auditors need to be able to consider the issues surrounding inventory in line with **IAS 2** (such as **impairment, value** and **quantity**) especially given the material nature of such balances.

4. Financial instruments

Auditors must use their knowledge of **IAS 32, IFRS 7** and **IFRS 9** to ensure that this **complex area** is accounted for accurately.

5. IFRS 15

The audit of revenue requires the application of the 5 steps from **IFRS 15**:

- Step 1 – Identify contracts in place with customers
- Step 2 – Identify performance obligations in the contract
- Step 3 – Determine transaction prices
- Step 4 – Allocate transaction prices to performance obligations in the contract
- Step 5 – Recognise revenue on satisfaction of a performance obligation

6. IFRS 16

You should be familiar with **IFRS 16** and be able to consider the audit risks posed:

- Is it a **right-of-use asset** that is not excluded?
- Is this a **low-value asset** or a **short-term** lease?
- Are **right of use assets and lease liability** values accurate?
- Is the accounting **disclosure** correct?

7. IAS 19

Defined contribution schemes are usually straightforward but **defined benefit schemes** present more risk to auditors and companies due to the possibility of **fund assets** being outweighed by **fund liabilities,** as well as the inherently risky issue of scheme liabilities in the first place. The treatment of **actuarial gains and losses** needs to be fully understood as well – **IAS 19** is key here.

8. Estimates

There are many **estimates** used in the production of a set of financial statements so the auditor needs to be comfortable with the method of their calculation. Auditors should consider **complexity, subjectivity** and **estimation uncertainty** associated with estimates which could lead to material misstatement (especially from **management bias**).

9. IAS 37

Provisions (under **IAS 37**) require a constructive obligation, probable occurrence and a realistic estimate to be recognised – otherwise a contingent liability should be disclosed. Contingent assets should not be recognised unless virtually certain.

10. Intangible assets

Intangible assets include research and development, brands and goodwill and require professional scepticism to ensure they have not been impaired.

11. IAS 41

Biological assets (IAS 41) is a complex area that requires an understanding of the differences between agricultural produce and inventory for the financial statements.

12. IAS 40

Investment properties (IAS 40) need to be distinguished from non-current assets such as **PPE (IAS 16)**, leased assets (IFRS 16) and even **assets held for sale (IFRS 5)**.

13. IAS 20

Government grants (IAS 20) requires an understanding of the grant conditions and an awareness of whether the grant is capital or income based.

14. IAS 23

Borrowing costs (IAS 23) should be capitalised but only in relation to qualifying activities.

15. IFRS 2

Share based payment transactions (IFRS 2) can be equity and/or cash-settled but should be traced back to the contracts to ensure they do not present an audit risk.

16. IAS 7

The **statement of cash flows (IAS 7)** is an important indicator of going concern but must also be audited as part of the financial statements in an audit.

17. IAS 21

The effect of **foreign exchange rates** under **IAS 21** requires monetary items to be translated at the closing rate, but non-monetary items to be translated at the date of the transaction.

18. IFRS 8

Segmental reporting is covered by **IFRS 8 *Operating Segments*** and is all about disclosure of reportable segments – you need to know the criteria that identify part of a business as a reportable segment.

19. IAS 33

Earnings per share (EPS) is required under **IAS 33** and requires disclosure of basic and diluted EPS.

20. Changes in accounting policy

Changes in accounting policy must be disclosed and applied retrospectively (but changes in accounting estimates are only applied prospectively).

21. Payroll and other expenses

Payroll and other expenses can often be a material cost, requiring an understanding of the amounts payable, the various parties involved and compliance with a number of systems, so should be prioritised for testing using a variety of techniques, including substantive, controls-based and even data analytics testing.

Further study guidance

Question practice

Now try the following from the Further question practice bank (available in the digital edition of the Workbook):

- Question 13 'Locksley' tests the audit of development expenditure and non-current assets
- Question 14 'Bainbridge' tests inventories, PPE and a convertible debenture using the MRSA approach from the chapter.
- Question 16 'Henshelwood' tests share based payment, pension costs and provisions.
- Question 17 'Keffler' tests intangibles, PPE and provisions using the MRSA approach from the chapter.
- Question 18 'Griffin' tests group accounting, going concern and laws and regulations using the MRSA approach from the chapter – however, as some of these issues relate to subsequent chapters, you may wish to leave this until you have studied them.

Further reading

There are a number of technical articles on the ACCA website written by members of the AAA examining team which are relevant to some of the topics covered in this chapter that you should read:

- *Exam technique for Advanced Audit and Assurance part 3 – accounting issues*
- *IAASB exposure draft – Proposed International Standard on Auditing 540 (Revised) Auditing Accounting Estimates and Related Disclosures*
- *Massaging the figures*

Own research

- In the UK, the FRC has conducted research into how audit processes are changing – as an example, you can see how issues you have studied so far interact in the real world by accessing their reports

  www.frc.org.uk/auditors/report-on-developments-in-audit

Activity answers

Activity 1: Armstrong

> **Approach**
>
> Questions such as these have their roots in quality control – imagine you are reviewing the work of your team and you want to make sure they have considered everything relevant to the matters described in the scenario. How will you do this?
>
> Use the template in the solution space to apply the four stages discussed at the start of this chapter: materiality, risks and auditing standards for the matters you should consider; audit evidence and the procedures to generate them for evidence you should expect to find.

Suggested solution

(1) The matters that you should consider

Materiality:

At 15% of profit before tax and 3.8% of total assets, the deferred tax provision is material to both the statement of profit or loss and the statement of financial position.

Risk(s) presented:

- Whether the deferred tax provision and charge are complete
- Whether the deferred tax provision and statement of profit or loss charge have been properly presented and are supported by the appropriate disclosures
- Whether the correct tax rate has been used
- Whether the deferred tax provision has been calculated correctly

Standards:

- IAS 12 *Income Taxes* requires that deferred tax is calculated at a rate that is 'substantively enacted' and expected to apply when the deferred tax is to be settled.
- IAS 12 also requires that the amount is based on accurate temporary/timing differences relating to the plant and equipment.
- Disclosure needs to be made for the items forming the deferred tax provision, the movement on the liability and the major components of income tax expense.

(2) The evidence you should expect to find

Evidence/procedures

- Schedule of temporary/timing differences relating to the plant and equipment agreed to plant and equipment schedules and tax computations
- Agreement of tax rate used (30%) to 'substantially enacted' rate of tax (note the rate used should be the rate substantively enacted, not merely 'announced')
- Enquire of directors and review plant and equipment schedules and tax computation for evidence of temporary/timing differences not provided for
- Recalculation of provision: Carrying amount $3.6m — written down value $2.1m = $1.5m @ 30% = $450,000

- Review of disclosure in the notes to the financial statements to ensure the appropriate disclosures are made in accordance with IAS 12

Activity 2: Payroll

> ### Approach
>
> This is an idea generation activity, so first try and think about the various approaches that could be used by the auditor and then suggest suitable examples in each case. You may find your answers here are quite theoretical, but in a real exam question, you will obviously have a scenario to work from, so remember that application is still important when considering any audit procedures.

Suggested solution

Audit approach	Suggested audit procedures
Substantive analytical procedures (to test the population as a whole)	Compare actual payroll costs with budget and prior year amounts and investigate any variances Combine non-financial information to derive a proof-in-total (eg multiply rates of pay by the number of staff employed and investigate any variances)
Tests of detail (to test certain assertions or areas of the financial statements)	Trace a sample of new starters in the payroll back to their human resources (HR) records (occurrence) and reconcile the amounts paid to their terms and conditions (accuracy) Select a sample of leavers from HR and test subsequent payrolls to confirm they have not been included in error (occurrence) For a sample of months throughout the year, reconcile the payroll expense in the nominal ledger to the payroll expense created by the payroll system Confirm the amounts paid in payroll each month are consistent with the amounts leaving the client's bank account
Tests of control (to ensure that the payroll system can be relied upon to create reliable figures)	For a sample of months throughout the year, confirm that the payroll processed was authorised by the chief accountant For a sample of overtime payments, trace each one back to a valid authorisation, such as a signature on a timesheet For each month's statutory deductions from pay, confirm that the amounts were reviewed by a senior employee
Audit data analytics (to leverage efficient audit procedures in all of the above) **Note.** This would only be possible for clients with payroll systems that are compatible with this type of data analysis	Recalculate the entire payroll by reference to source documents such as timesheets and establishment headcounts and amounts due Recalculate the amounts due for tax and other statutory deductions throughout the year by reference to employee details and current legislative requirements Analyse the bank details used in each payroll run to search for duplicates that may indicate the existence of fraud

Audit approach	Suggested audit procedures
	Interrogate the payroll system for patterns to identify cases where segregation of duties is missing when processing the payroll

Activity 3: Buddy Co

Approach

This is very similar to Activity 1 ('Armstrong') but is testing your knowledge of financial instruments. Don't worry if you cannot remember everything there is to know about the accounting treatment – there are always marks available for calculating materiality and obtaining routine pieces of evidence to support assertions in the financial statements. If you need a reminder of the accounting treatment, refer to the Essential reading in the digital edition of this Workbook.

Suggested solution

(1) Matters to consider

Materiality has already been assessed here, but in the exam you will probably need to calculate this.

Risks presented and **standards** can be discussed at the same time. For example, the number of shares owned in Buddy is 18% – if Holly's stake was 20% (or there was evidence of significant influence) according to **IAS 28 Investment in Associates**, this would cease to be an investment and would need to be accounted for under the equity method (assuming consolidated financial statements are already being produced, which is happening here as there is a subsidiary).

If this was just an investment in shares, however, ownership of 18% of the shares in Buddy would need to be confirmed to ensure Holly has the right to carry these on the statement of financial position and be entitled to any dividends distributed.

Has Holly made the irrevocable election to hold these shares at fair value with any changes going through other comprehensive income (OCI)? If so, the **fair value of consideration plus transaction costs** would be recognised initially and any gains at year end would be recognised in OCI. If this election is **not made**, initial recognition would be at the **fair value of acquisition only** and the transaction costs would be **expensed** through profit or loss (P/L) with any fair value gains at the end of the year also being recognised in P/L.

IFRS 7 Financial Instruments: Disclosures specifies that the financial statements should disclose both the significance and the nature/extent of any risks associated with financial instruments, including an estimate of the level of market risk the shares represent to Holly.

(2) Evidence you expect to find

Copies of the Buddy Co share certificates in Holly's name which verify Holly's ownership of 500,000 shares in Buddy as at November 20X7.

Inspection of Buddy's statutory share records to verify Holly owns 18% of all issued shares and a review of board minutes to ascertain whether Holly holds any significant influence over Buddy.

Inspection of Holly's bank statements and cash book to confirm the transaction occurred in November 20X7.

Request a representation from the Finance Director of Holly regarding any election to treat fair value gains through OCI not P/L.

Recalculation of the payment of the purchase price ($2 × 500,000 = $1,000,000) and the transaction costs (1% × $1,000,000 = $10,000) and confirmation that the fair value initially recognised on Holly's statement of financial position matches the appropriate treatment ($1,010,000 if going through OCI; $1,000,000 if going through P/L).

Trace amounts for transaction costs through to correct locations (either as part of fair value on recognition or P/L depending on whether any election was made by Holly).

Copies of invoices or brokers' notes to corroborate the value paid (including transaction costs) plus third-party confirmation of Buddy's share price on the date of purchase (eg agree $2 per share to the quoted price in the Financial Times on the purchase date).

Recalculation of the $115,000 increase in the fair value of the shares in Buddy ($2.25 × 500,000 = $1,125,000 minus $1,010,000) and a copy of any relevant working papers completed by Holly.

Reconciliation that the gain has been allocated to the correct place (OCI or P/L depending on any election made by Holly).

A copy of the journal showing the increase in value of the Buddy investment at the reporting date (eg debit financial asset, credit profit or loss) and confirmation from a third party (eg Financial Times again) of the share price ($2.25) at the reporting date.

A copy of the draft financial statements of Holly to ensure that the shares have been recorded as owned by Holly together with an indication of the levels of risk presented (eg market risk).

Activity 4: Laxman Co

> ### Approach
> The two principal matters to consider here are interrelated: whether IFRS 15 has been properly applied to Laxman Co's inventory, and whether Laxman Co is in breach of the conditions of its bank loan. However, remember to think outside the box a little and consider whether anything else is relevant here.

Suggested solution

(1) Inventory

IFRS 15 states that revenue is recognised when the entity has transferred the goods to the buyer, meeting the performance obligations of the contract (para. 9).

In this case, the legal transfer of title has not yet occurred and so it would therefore appear that these items should not be recognised within revenue.

However, as auditors, it will be necessary to obtain further information regarding the sale, as in accordance with IFRS 15, the transfer of legal title is not sufficient evidence that control has been transferred (and performance obligations met). It is possible, for instance, that legal title has been retained in order to protect Laxman Co against the possibility of non-payment by the receivable, even though, in substance, a sale has in fact occurred.

Further audit evidence must be obtained in order to form a judgement over whether IFRS 15 has been breached.

(2) Loan condition

Laxman Co appears to be within the criteria laid down by the bank: it has an acid test ratio of 1.125 (= ($1,000,000 − $100,000) ÷ $800,000).

However, if the revenue recognised in respect of the inventory above has not been recognised in accordance with IFRS 15, the financial statements may need to be amended. The amendment could be by as much as $200,000 (decreasing receivables and increasing inventory) which would not affect current assets as the switch from receivables to inventory would balance itself out, but would change the acid test ratio to 0.875 (= ($1,000,000 − $300,000) ÷ $800,000).

If the conditions set by the bank have been broken, then it is likely that some negative consequence would result from this. This could range from a fine or penalty that would need to be recognised in the financial statements, to the possibility of Laxman Co having to repay the loan. If this were the case, it would be necessary to consider very carefully whether significant doubts exist over Laxman Co's ability to continue as a going concern.

(3) Possibility of fraud

The auditor needs to consider the possibility that management has engaged in fraudulent financial reporting in respect of revenue recognition in order not to breach the conditions set by the trade organisation. If this were the case, the auditor will need to re-examine any representations it has already received from management.

Activity 5: Leases

Approach

This is simply designed to get you up to speed with IFRS 16. There is far more detail included here than required by the question, but it shows the depth of knowledge that you will need for the exam. Remember that you should always apply your IFRS knowledge to the scenario and respond accordingly.

Suggested solution

Audit risks

Audit risks for lessors

Whether a lease is an operating or finance lease – the treatment of lease repayments will vary (either receivables or income) and the asset will need to be derecognised at the end of the lease term if it is a finance lease.

Audit risks for lessees

Leases may be inappropriately recognised as leases (or not recognised when they should be) because one or more of the necessary conditions under **IFRS 16 Leases** has not been observed:

- The lessor does not have the right to substantially all the economic benefits of an identified asset.
- The asset may be easily substituted by the lessor so cannot be part of a lease agreement.
- The lessor does not have the right to direct or control the asset included in the lease.
- The conditions for recognising a 'right-of-use asset' may apply but have been ignored.

A combined contract to provide both a leased asset and servicing of the asset may not have been split into its constituent parts which could lead to incorrect recognition of the service element.

Initial recognition of the lease liability may be either incomplete or inaccurate due to some/all of the constituent elements being missed/misstated:

- The PV of the lease payments not yet paid and the discount factor used
- Any penalties for relevant early termination
- Uncertainty over any options to purchase the asset at the end of the lease term
- The agreed or implied lease term

Similarly, lease assets may be misstated due to failure to correctly account for any of the following:

- Initial fees and other charges which may have been ignored.
- Failure to account for any impairments or revaluations that have occurred during the lease term.
- Failure to account for dismantling and restoration provisions that might be required at the end of the lease term.

Assets may be treated as either short-term leases or low-value assets when they are neither (so would need to have assets and liabilities recognised on the statement of financial position).

Disclosures may be inadequate or incomplete for either lessees or lessors based on what IFRS 16 requires in each case.

Sale and leaseback agreements

Companies sometimes agree to sell assets such as land and buildings which they intend to keep on using in return for paying the new owners a fee – the sale creates either a gain or loss in the seller's financial statements when compared with the cost value of the asset on disposal. This also means that the continued use of the asset needs to be reflected in the company's accounts as a lease, so IFRS 16 needs to be followed here to create a right-of-use asset for the lessee, along with an associated lease liability.

However, this situation can be exploited by companies attempting to conceal the true purpose of an asset's disposal: sometimes, there may be an agreement for the company to repurchase the asset after a set period of time, usually for a higher price than it was sold for. When the substance of such a transaction is considered, it may appear that the initial disposal amount was, in fact, a loan and the repurchase amount is actually a repayment and the company has simply attempted to conceal this form of financing from its financial statements.

The requirement for IFRS 16 to show all material leases as both assets and liabilities is likely to reduce the risk of this as all such leases would need to reflect IFRS 16.

Auditors need to consider whether the sale part of the agreement satisfies the requirements of **IFRS 15** *Revenue from Contracts with Customers* – if not, the seller (who has now become lessee) needs to continue to recognise the asset they are leasing and recognise a financial liability under **IFRS 9** *Financial Instruments* for the consideration received from the new lessor/buyer. IFRS 16 requires the IFRS 15 criteria for a sale to be met in order for the transaction to be accounted for as a sale and leaseback.

The auditor's response

Typical audit procedures

In an exam question, it is likely that there will also be a requirement to consider suitable audit procedures as the auditor's response to any of these risks, and you should therefore consider how you would obtain sufficient and appropriate audit evidence in such cases – for example:

- Obtaining copies of lease contracts to confirm the details of any agreements (including the right-of-use asset specified in the contract, evidence of exclusivity of right-of-use and the possibility of any substitute assets being introduced)

- Recalculating the amounts included at both initial recognition and subsequent measurement for right-of-use assets and associated liabilities (including lease repayments, interest rates used, initial fees paid and incentives granted)

- Verifying any conditions related to either extensions or early termination based on evidence collected from the lessee and/or elsewhere (for example, sale contracts in the case of a sale and leaseback to establish if it really is a sale)

- Verifying that a right-of-use asset cannot be either substituted or controlled by any party other than the lessee (such as from site visits, documentary evidence or enquiries)

- Obtaining copies of draft financial statements to review the level of disclosure for adequacy

Activity 6: Jake's Pegs

Approach

There is no mark allocation here, so you do not know the detail your answer should go into. However, in any question, carefully reading the requirement will help you: in part 1 it's just the **additional** risks that the emergence of the pension scheme creates, not the risks already present. For part 2 you should consider breaking your answer down into the main areas of the financial statements where such a pension arrangement will be reflected and the considering the work you would do to audit each part.

1   Suggested solution

Additional risks

The delay in informing the firm of the existence of the scheme will increase the inherent risk of the audit. This may imply that the information regarding the scheme is not fully prepared yet.

The client has withheld information regarding the scheme and claimed that it was an oversight. The pension scheme is a major part of the company's financial structure and it is unlikely the Finance Director would forget about it. The auditor should respond to this with elevated levels of professional scepticism and consider the impact on other areas of the audit. Care should be taken before reliance is placed on representations provided by management.

The fact that the actuarial report may not be ready until late in the audit will increase the risk as the auditor may be under time pressure to complete the work inside the reporting deadline.

The impact of the scheme on the statement of profit and loss and other comprehensive income and statement of financial position will be dependent on the actuarial valuation of the scheme assets and liabilities. These are judgemental and complex areas and the auditor may not have the expertise to audit these effectively. The audit plan should include an expectation of the need to apply ISA 620 *Using the Work of an Auditor's Expert*.

The pension scheme could have a significant detrimental impact on the statement of financial position of Jake's Pegs. The Finance Director appears confident that the scheme is in surplus but this may be unrealistic. It is likely the scheme's assets will be held, to a large extent, in the form of shares and property, both of which might have fallen in value. This may create a significant deficit on the scheme, which is likely to be highly material to the statement of financial position. This could call into question the going concern status of the company.

2   Suggested solution

Audit procedures

The finance department at Jake's Pegs would have needed to account for the scheme in line with the standards, and this would have led to some specific steps that the auditor would need to review (covered below in the table).

General procedures

We should enquire of the directors as to the accounting policy regarding the treatment of actuarial gains and losses. The actuarial gain or loss should be recalculated by the auditor.

Specific procedures

Work undertaken by Jake's Pegs	Specific audit procedures in respect of these
Actuarial assumptions should be used to make reliable estimates of the amounts of future benefits that the scheme will have to pay out currently and in the future (eg employee turnover, sign-up rates for the scheme, mortality rates, future salary increases) in order to have an estimate of the present value of future benefit obligations.	As mentioned above, there may be some need for an expert under the terms of ISA 620 to question the specific assumptions and calculations made by the actuary. The auditor can review the logic used and the consistency of the assumptions with prior years and general market conditions. Written representations from management may be helpful here although, given the heightened level of scepticism we are deploying, this may only serve as protection in the event of unwelcome (and unspecified) audit liability claims in the future.

Work undertaken by Jake's Pegs	Specific audit procedures in respect of these
The **fair value** of any **scheme assets** should be established.	Review the market data used to agree the value of the fund and verify to an independent source.
Any **actuarial gains or losses** in the value of the liabilities and any difference between the return on the plan assets and the interest income calculated for the plan assets must be determined in order to agree on the amount to be recognised in the financial statements.	Such gains or losses must be recalculated and confirmation obtained from accounting records of their appropriate recognition in the financial statements.
Any **changes** that need to be made to the **scheme's benefits** should be accounted for appropriately.	Auditors should ensure that any potential shortfalls are adequately identified and disclosed in the financial statements.

9 Group audits and transnational audits

Learning objectives

On completion of this chapter, you should be able to:

	Syllabus reference no.
Recognise the specific matters to be considered before accepting appointment as group auditor to a group in a given situation.	D5(a)
Identify and describe the matters to be considered and the procedures to be performed at the planning stage, when a group auditor considers the use of the work of component auditors.	D5(b)
Identify and explain the matters specific to planning an audit of group financial statements including: • Assessment of group and component materiality, • The impact of non-coterminous year ends within a group, • Changes in group structure or a complex group structure.	D5(c)
Recommend and discuss the communications and content therein to be provided by the group auditor to the component auditor in a given situation.	D5(d)
Recognise the audit problems and describe audit procedures specific to: • A business combination, including the classification of investments, • The determination of goodwill and its impairment, • Group accounting policies, • Intra-group trading, • Equity accounting for associates and joint ventures, • Changes in group structure, including acquisitions and disposals, and • Accounting for a foreign subsidiary.	D5(e)
In respect of the consolidation process, identify and explain the relevant audit risks and audit procedures necessary to obtain sufficient appropriate evidence.	D5(f)
Consider how the group auditor should evaluate the audit work performed by a component auditor.	D5(g)
Explain the responsibilities of the component auditor before accepting an appointment, and the procedures to be performed in a group situation.	D5(h)

	Syllabus reference no.
Justify the situations where a joint audit would be appropriate.	D5(i)
Explain the implications for the auditor's report on the group financial statements of an entity where the opinion on a component is modified in a given situation.	E3(f)
Discuss how transnational audits may differ from other audits of historical financial information (eg in terms of applicable financial reporting and auditing standards, listing requirements and corporate governance requirements).	D1(h)

Business and exam context

This is a new auditing topic for you, one which is concerned with practical difficulties of communication between auditors and the issues of geography.

When auditing group accounts, as in so many other areas, the auditors require detailed accounting knowledge in order to fulfil their responsibilities.

Group audits fall into two categories:

(a) Where the same firm of auditors audits the whole group

(b) Where one firm of auditors has responsibility for the opinion on the consolidated accounts and a different firm audits part of the group

Even where the audit of each individual company in the group is carried out by the same firm, there may be administrative complications where some audits are carried out by different branches, perhaps overseas, with different practices and procedures.

Group audits can be tested in Section A or Section B of the exam. Questions may focus on any aspect of the group audit, although auditor reporting will not be examined in Section A. Groups tend to offer plenty of suitable audit risks for AAA – consequently, it is possible that the scenario in Section A will be a group audit.

Chapter overview

1 ISA 600 *Special Considerations – Audits of Group Financial Statements (Including the Work of Component Auditors)*

Essential reading

See Chapter 9 of the Essential reading for an overview of group accounting issues that you should have learned from your previous studies (including SBR).

The Essential reading is available as an Appendix of the digital edition of the Workbook.

As you know from your financial reporting studies, in a group situation the parent company will have to prepare its own audited financial statements, together with the audited **consolidated financial statements** incorporating **all component companies**.

> **Component:** An entity or business activity for which the group or component management prepares financial information that should be included in the group financial statements.
>
> **Component auditor:** An auditor who, at the request of the group engagement team, performs work on financial information related to a component for the group audit.
>
> **Component materiality:** The materiality level for a component determined by the group engagement team.
>
> **Group:** All the components whose financial information is included in the group financial statements. A group always has more than one component.
>
> **Group audit:** The audit of the group financial statements.
>
> (ISA 600: para. 9)

2 Responsibilities

The **group auditor** has sole responsibility for the opinion on the group financial statements. In most countries, this responsibility is not diminished by reliance on the work of any **component auditors,** who are a source of evidence only and are not referred to within the group auditor's report. There will be a **group engagement team** led by the **group engagement partner** who will be responsible for the performance of the group audit and providing an auditor's report on the group financial statements.

The group auditor must decide how much **reliance** they will place on the work performed by the **component auditor**. In order to do this, they will consider the qualifications, experience, competence, ethical standpoint and resources of the component auditors.

ISA 600 states that if a component company is audited by a component auditor and is deemed by the group auditor either to be so **significant in size or to pose a significant risk of material misstatement**, they can stipulate:

- That **further audit procedures** must be carried out; and
- The **extent** that the component auditor is involved (if at all).

The group auditor may not be able to access all the information it needs about components or component auditors, because of laws relating to confidentiality or data privacy, for example. The effect on the group audit opinion depends on the **significance of the component**.

If the **component is not significant,** then it may be sufficient just to have a complete set of financial statements, the component auditor's report, and information kept by group management.

If the **component is significant,** then it is possible that there will be an **inability to obtain sufficient appropriate audit evidence** about the component, in which case the audit opinion is either **qualified** or a **disclaimer of opinion** is issued. In this instance, it would also be impossible to comply with ISA 600's requirement to be involved with the work of the component auditor (for significant components), which would also lead to an inability to obtain sufficient appropriate audit evidence.

2.1 Significant components

> **Significant component:** A component identified by the group engagement team: (a) that is of individual significance to the group, or (b) that, due to its specific nature or circumstances, is likely to include significant risks of material misstatement of the group financial statements. (ISA 600: para. 9(m))

ISA 600 states that a significant component can be identified by using a **benchmark** (para. A5). If component assets, liabilities, cash flows, profit or turnover (whichever is the most appropriate benchmark) **exceed 15% of the related group figure**, then the auditor may judge that the component is a **significant component.**

If a component is financially significant to the group financial statements, then the group engagement team or a component auditor will perform a full audit based on the component materiality level.

The group auditor should be involved in the assessment of risk in relation to significant components. If the component is otherwise significant due to its nature or circumstances, the group auditors will require **one** of the following.

Specified audit procedures relating to identified significant risks

An audit of specified account balances related to identified significant risks

A full audit using component materiality

Components that are not 'significant components' will be subject to analytical procedures at a group level – a full audit is not required for the purpose of the group audit/consolidated financial statements.

2.2 The component auditor

2.2.1 Understanding the component auditor

ISA 600 requires the group engagement team to obtain an **understanding** of the component auditor. This involves an assessment of the following.

(a) Whether the component auditor is **independent** and understands and will comply with the ethical requirements that are relevant to the group audit

(b) The component auditor's **professional competence**

(c) Whether the group engagement team will be **involved in the work of the component auditor** to the extent that it is necessary to obtain sufficient appropriate audit evidence

(d) Whether the component auditor operates in a **regulatory environment** that actively oversees auditors

2.2.2 Involvement with the component auditor

The extent of **involvement** by the group auditor at the planning stage will depend on the:

- Significance of the component
- Risks of material misstatement of the group financial statements
- Extent of the group auditor's understanding of the component auditor

The basic rule is that **where the component is significant, the group auditor must be involved in the component auditor's work.**

The **component auditor** should consider whether there might be any **restrictions** on them providing the group auditor with access to information, such as laws relating to **confidentiality** or data privacy. It should be borne in mind that in general, the component auditor is **not normally**

obliged to co-operate with the group auditor (unless they are operating in a jurisdiction which requires them to do so). In practice, this means that the same audit firm will often be appointed as auditor of the group and its significant components.

2.2.3 Assessing the component auditor

For all companies in the group, the group auditor is required to perform a **review of the work done by the component auditor**. This is normally achieved by reviewing a report or questionnaire completed by the component auditor which highlights the key issues which have been identified during the course of the audit. The effect of any uncorrected misstatements and any instances where there has been an inability to obtain sufficient appropriate audit evidence should also be evaluated. On the basis of this review, the group auditor then needs to determine whether any additional procedures are necessary. These may include:

- Designing and performing further audit procedures. These may be designed and performed with the component auditors, or by the group auditor.
- Participating in the closing and other key meetings between the component auditors and component management
- Reviewing other relevant parts of the component auditors' documentation

2.2.4 Communicating with the component auditor

The group engagement team shall **communicate its requirements to the component auditor** on a timely basis. This communication shall set out the work to be performed, the use to be made of that work and the form and content of the component auditor's communication with the group engagement team (ISA 600: para. 40).

The group engagement team shall **request the component auditor to communicate matters** relevant to the group engagement team's conclusion with regard to the group audit (ISA 600: para. 41).

Essential reading

See Chapter 9 of the Essential reading for more detail on the communication between group and component auditors (specifically ISA 600: paras. 40–41).

The Essential reading is available as an Appendix of the digital edition of the Workbook.

2.2.5 Communicating with group management and those charged with governance

ISA 600 identifies the following as matters which should be communicated to group management.

- Material deficiencies in the design or operating effectiveness of group-wide controls
- Material deficiencies that the group engagement team has identified in internal controls at components that are judged to be significant to the group
- Material deficiencies that component auditors have identified in internal controls at components that are judged to be significant to the group
- Fraud identified by the group engagement team or component auditors or information indicating that a fraud may exist

Where a component auditor is required to express an audit opinion on the financial statements of a component, the group engagement team will request group management to inform component management of any matters that they, the group engagement team, have become aware of that may be significant to the financial statements of the component. If group management refuses to pass on the communication, the group engagement team will discuss the matter with those charged with governance of the group. If the matter is still unresolved, the group engagement team shall consider whether to advise the component auditor not to issue the auditor's report on the component financial statements until the matter is resolved.

2.2.6 Communication with those charged with governance of the group

The following matters should be communicated to those charged with governance of the group.

- An overview of the type of work to be performed on the financial statements of the component

- An overview of the nature of the group engagement team's planned involvement in the work to be performed by the component auditors on significant components
- Instances where the group engagement team's evaluation of the work of a component auditor gave rise to a concern about the quality of that auditor's work
- Any limitations on the group audit, for example, where the group engagement team's access to information may have been restricted
- Fraud or suspected fraud involving group management, component management, employees who have significant roles in group-wide controls or others where fraud resulted in a material misstatement of the group financial statements

Activity 1: Communication

Communication is a two-way process. This is especially true in the context of the dialogue between the group auditor and the component auditor.

Required

(1) Suggest some of the requirements that the group auditor would communicate to the component auditor.

(2) Suggest some of the matters that the component auditor needs to tell the group auditor.

Solution

2.3 Illustration of a simple group

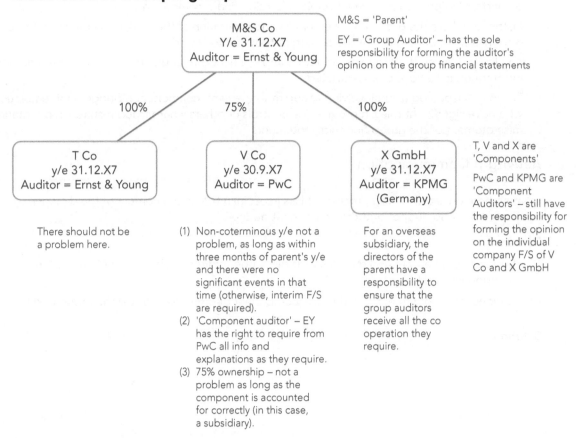

M&S Co
Y/e 31.12.X7
Auditor = Ernst & Young

M&S = 'Parent'

EY = 'Group Auditor' – has the sole responsibility for forming the auditor's opinion on the group financial statements

100%   75%   100%

T Co
y/e 31.12.X7
Auditor = Ernst & Young

V Co
y/e 30.9.X7
Auditor = PwC

X GmbH
y/e 31.12.X7
Auditor = KPMG
(Germany)

T, V and X are 'Components'

PwC and KPMG are 'Component Auditors' – still have the responsibility for forming the opinion on the individual company F/S of V Co and X GmbH

There should not be a problem here.

(1) Non-coterminous y/e not a problem, as long as within three months of parent's y/e and there were no significant events in that time (otherwise, interim F/S are required).

(2) 'Component auditor' – EY has the right to require from PwC all info and explanations as they require.

(3) 75% ownership – not a problem as long as the component is accounted for correctly (in this case, a subsidiary).

For an overseas subsidiary, the directors of the parent have a responsibility to ensure that the group auditors receive all the co operation they require.

Other considerations

Are any of the components immaterial? If so, obtain draft financial statements from them and perform an analytical review only. If this review suggests any errors exist, more detailed work will be needed.

Have there been any **changes** to the group structure? Changes such as acquisitions, disposals (or even part-disposals) are required under ISA 600 para. A12 as part of understanding the group. Is the **going concern** status of any component dependent on the parent's ongoing support? If so, a letter of support or comfort letter should be obtained by the auditor.

Given the nature of most consolidated groups in the 21st century, the group auditor's job is extremely **complex** and likely to be subject to a number of risks not faced during the audit of the parent company alone:

(a) Understanding the **structure of the group**, paying close attention to any **changes** and the risk of 'hidden' or 'shell' companies, as discovered during the Enron scandal

(b) Consideration of **group-wide controls** (controls designed, implemented and maintained by group management over group financial statements) to ensure there are no inherent problems in the audit

(c) The fact that their group opinion is **often based upon the work of others** and as such, this demonstrates significant audit risk

Consequently, **great care** must be taken when deciding whether or not to **accept** such work.

3 Matters to consider before accepting appointment as parent company auditor

Taking factors from Section 2 into account, the group auditor should consider whether or not their participation is sufficient to be able to act as the group auditor. For this purpose, the group engagement partner **must obtain an understanding of the group before acceptance** (ISA 600: para. 12) which should include the following:

- The **materiality** of the portion of the financial statements which the group auditor audits (and therefore, by implication, **the proportion that they do not audit**)
- The group auditor's degree of **knowledge** regarding the business of the components
- The **risk** of material misstatements in the financial statements of the components audited by the component auditor(s)
- The ability, where necessary, to perform **additional procedures** to enable them to act as group auditors
- The nature of the group auditor's **relationship** with the firm acting as component auditor

Under ISA 600, the group auditor will consider the following:

- The **quality of work** from **component auditors**;
- The ability of the group auditor to get involved with component auditors to obtain **sufficient appropriate audit evidence** if necessary; or
- The availability of **information on consolidation from the client**.

If the group auditor has **concerns** about any of these issues and are unlikely to be able to deliver anything other than a disclaimer of opinion, they should not consider either **accepting or continuing** with the engagement (ISA 600: para. 13).

4 Issues arising when a component is located abroad

When a component is located abroad a number of potential difficulties could arise such as the following:

Different accounting policies might be used in the foreign country. The component accounts must be brought into line with the accounting policies used by the parent company in order to consolidate properly. The group auditor will use the checklist mentioned above to determine the accounting policies used.

There may be **cultural problems** unique to the country in which the component operates. The group auditor will need to be sensitive to these during dealings with the component auditors. **Language problems** might also arise.

There may be issues in existence which are **specific to the country** in which the component operates. For example, some countries are subject to hyperinflation; accounts produced in these circumstances will need to be adjusted prior to consolidation with the parent. If the component is located in a developing country, there may be aspects of business infrastructure missing (eg education, technology or even anti-bribery legislation). Factors such as these will need to be identified for each component and tackled as appropriate during the audit.

5 The correct classification of investments

Essential reading

See Chapter 9 of the Essential reading for an overview of Associates and Joint Ventures that you should have learned from your previous studies (including SBR).

The Essential reading is available as an Appendix of the digital edition of the Workbook.

You know from your accounting studies that an investment is treated as a **subsidiary** when the parent company has **control** over that company. Where **significant influence** is held, the investment is treated as an **associate**. It is important that the degree of control exercised by the parent company is tested by the group auditor.

The auditor needs to consider how an investment fits into the activities of the group. They should **review board minutes** for evidence of the degree of influence exercised by the parent. They should also discuss the matter with the parent directors.

The existence of **other significant shareholders** may indicate that the parent company has little **influence**. The auditor should check the register of members to determine the level of shareholding and potential influence held by other shareholders.

The auditor should also consider how easy it is to obtain **information** about another company. This could also be an indicator of significant influence.

6 Consolidation audit procedures

There are a number of procedures that should be performed by the group auditor:

- Confirming the balances extracted from the financial statements of each component prior to their inclusion on the consolidation schedule
- Reviewing the disclosures necessary for the group accounts, such as related parties
- Gathering evidence appropriate to the various consolidation adjustments

Essential reading

See Chapter 9 of the Essential reading for an overview of the problems with consolidations and associated audit procedures that you should have learned from your previous studies (including SBR).

The Essential reading is available as an Appendix of the digital edition of the Workbook.

Activity 2: Consolidation

What are the major types of consolidation adjustment required for group financial statements?

Solution

Goodwill is calculated in accordance with **IFRS 3 _Business Combinations_,** to provide more transparency of the value of **non-controlling interests (NCI)**. The standard allows measurement of NCI, either at share of subsidiary net assets or fair value (FV). The latter results in 100% of goodwill on acquisition analysed between parent and NCI elements for consolidation.

FV is used to determine assets and liabilities for these calculations. Share price on acquisition is used for the FV of the NCI. The overall approach the auditor should follow for determining FV can be summarised as follows:

- Obtain an understanding of the entity's process for determining FV

- Identify and assess the risks of material misstatement at the assertion level
- Perform audit procedures on the data used to develop the FV
- Evaluate whether the FV measurements have been properly determined

Activity 3: Wolf Co

You are the group auditor for Bad Co and are currently reviewing the consolidation adjustments for goodwill in respect of the acquisition of Wolf Co. Bad Co acquired 7.5 million of the 10 million ordinary shares in Wolf Co for $12 million. At the time of acquisition, the FV of Wolf Co's net assets was $10 million and the share price was $1.50 each. Bad Co operates a policy of valuing NCI at fair value.

Required

Calculate goodwill on the acquisition of Wolf Co and explain the principal audit procedures you would perform on the goodwill calculation schedule.

	$'000
Consideration transferred	
Non-controlling interest	_____
Net assets acquired	_____
Goodwill	_____
Non-controlling interest at fair value	
Non-controlling interest at share of net assets	_____
Goodwill attributable to NCI	_____
Goodwill attributable to Bad Co shareholders	_____
Goodwill attributable to NCI shareholders	_____

Solution

7 Implications for the auditor's report where a component's report has been modified

In a group situation, **materiality** and **risk** must be assessed in the context of the group as a whole. The group auditor must consider the materiality of any modifications to a component's auditor's report in relation to the whole of the consolidated financial statements.

This can lead to situations where a **component** may have a **material qualification** that has **no impact on the group opinion** which would then remain unmodified. Similarly, a **pervasive** modification in a component's auditor's report may only have a **material impact** on the group opinion.

Ultimately the decision as to the impact of a modification to a component's auditor's report on the consolidated opinion is a matter of **judgement** for the group auditor. Where the group auditor concludes that **adequate evidence** about the work of the component auditor cannot be obtained and has been unable to perform sufficient additional procedures with respect to that component, they should consider the **implications** for the auditor's report. A subsequent modification in these circumstances would be on the grounds of **insufficient inappropriate audit evidence**.

8 Joint audits

A joint audit means an audit where two or more auditors are responsible for an audit engagement and jointly produce an auditor's report to the client.

Reasons for joint audits

Two or more firms could act as joint auditors for the following reasons:

(a) In a new **acquisition**, the parent may insist that their auditor acts jointly with those of the new subsidiary.

(b) A company operating from widely **dispersed locations** may find it useful to have joint auditors.

(c) **Foreign subsidiaries** may need to employ local audit firms to satisfy the laws of the country in which they operate. These local auditors may act jointly with the group auditors.

(d) Some companies may prefer to use **local accountants**, while at the same time, enjoying the wider range of services offered by a large national firm.

Before accepting appointment as a joint auditor, it will be necessary to consider the **experience** and **standards** of the other firm.

The allocation of work between the firms needs to be agreed and the auditors should agree whether joint or separate engagement letters will be sent.

Both firms must sign the auditor's report and both are responsible for the whole audit. They are **jointly liable** in the event of litigation. Such joint audits can therefore be seen to be complex to manage and potentially expensive.

9 Transnational audits

A transnational audit means an audit of financial statements which are, or may be, relied upon **outside the entity's home jurisdiction** for purposes of significant lending, investment or regulatory decisions. This will include audits of all financial statements of companies with listed equity or debt and other public interest entities which attract particular public attention because of their size, products or services provided.

The growth in such transnational engagements has led to a number of issues that clients are more aware of in the 21st century:

(a) Variations in **audit approaches** and the role of regulators across different jurisdictions has led to variable degrees of engagement quality.

(b) The incomplete nature of ISA adoption worldwide has led to **variations** in audit approach.

(c) **Cultural differences** worldwide have also led to different audit approaches.

In response to this trend towards globalisation and the issues associated with transnational audits, a **Forum of Firms (FOF)** was created, initially by the 'Big Four' firms but now with over 20 member firms.

To support and provide guidance to the FOF the IAASB has set up the **Transnational Auditors Committee**.

Specific responsibilities of the TAC include the following:

- Identifying audit practice issues. When the issues suggest changes in auditing or assurance standards may be required, recommending to the appropriate IFAC standard-setting boards that the issue be reviewed.

- Providing a forum to discuss 'best practices' in areas including quality control, auditing practices, independence, and training and development.

- Proposing members to the IFAC Regulatory Liaison Group and identifying qualified candidates to serve on IFAC standard-setting boards.

- Acting as a formal conduit for interaction among transnational firms and international regulators and financial institutions with regard to audit quality, systems of quality control, and transparency of international networks.

Chapter summary

Group audits and transnational audits

ISA 600 Special Considerations – Audits of Group Financial Statements (Including the Work of Component Auditors)

- **Group auditor:** Sole responsibility for audit opinion on group financial statements
- **Group engagement team** performs the group audit
- **Component auditor:** Used as a source of evidence only - need to be assessed for quality and reliability
- Group auditor can request **further work** on a component if component is of significant size and/or risk (with or without component auditor's involvement)
- Need to consider **issues** such as non-coterminous year-ends (<3 months = adjust for significant events only; >3 months = interim F/S) and part ownership
- Group auditor requires from component auditor(s):
  - Independence requirements
  - Areas of special interest in the component
- Component auditor requires questionnaire of timetables
- Responsibilities from group auditor

Responsibilities

- Parent company produces own financial statements, audited by own auditor
- Components in a group include:
  - Division
  - Branch
  - Subsidiary
  - Joint Venture
  - Associate
- Group accounts audited by parent company auditor
- Subsidiary accounts audited by component auditor

Matters to consider before accepting appointment as parent company auditor

- Materiality of components not audited by group auditor
- Knowledge of business of components not audited
- Risk of components not audited:
  - Ability to perform additional procedures
  - Nature of relationship with component auditors
  - Group auditor may consider that if insufficient and/or inappropriate evidence is available – Disclaimer – continue or decline?

Issues arising when a component is located abroad

- Different accounting policies
- Cultural problems
- Language problems
- Country specific problems

The correct classification of investments

- Control = subsidiary
- Significant influence = associate
- Auditor must look for evidence of who is actually in control (eg board minutes, correspondence etc)

Consolidation audit procedures

- Calculation of goodwill and any impairments
- Cancellation of any inter-company balances
- Provisions for unrealised profits
- Fair Value (FV) adjustments
- Retranslation of F/S from overseas components
- Correct value of components in parent F/S

```
                 ┌──────────────────────────────────────────────────────────────────────────┐
         ┌───────┴───────┐            ┌───────────┐               ┌──────────────┐
```

Implications for the auditor's report where a subsidiary's report has been modified	Joint audits	Transnational audits

- Group auditor must assess materiality for the group as a whole
- The degree of modification (material or pervasive) may be different in the component auditor's report than for the group
- Group auditor uses judgment to decide whether or not there is a material impact or a lack of sufficient/appropriate audit evidence

- Why?
  - New acquisition
  - Dispersed location
  - Foreign subsidiaries
  - Client choice
- Need to consider standards and experience of other firm
- Joint liability
- Impacts on the profession?

- Audits where the F/S may be relied on in a different country to where the entity is based
- Different approaches and regulations have led to varying levels of audit quality
- Forum of Firms (Big Four plus others)
- IAASB – Transnational Auditors Committee (TAC):
  - Identifying audit practice issues
  - Discussing best practice
  - Membership of IFAC committees
  - Formal conduit for promoting interaction between firms

Knowledge diagnostic

1. ISA 600

Group auditors are responsible for the audit of the parent company and group financial statements, while **component auditors** are responsible for the opinion on component financial statements. The group auditor can ask for **more work** to be done by the component auditor or even dispense with their opinion if risk of material misstatement dictates.

2. Group auditors

Auditors must consider whether or not they are happy to **accept or continue** in such engagements such as, for example, when there are concerns over the amount known about this audit or the **risk of misstatement on audits not covered by them**.

3. Overseas components

Issues arising when a component is located abroad are often of a very practical nature and can impact on the auditor's ability to perform the tasks necessary for the audit opinion.

4. Classification of components

The correct classification of investments is key to how group financial statements are presented – Subsidiary vs Associate vs Joint venture vs Investment.

5. Goodwill

Auditors need to be able to calculate the **consolidation adjustments** required for the consolidated accounts, including **goodwill** based on the correct **FV** of the group's assets and liabilities.

6. Impact on the auditor's report

Depending on the **size** and **nature** of any component modification, the impact may range from immaterial to pervasive.

7. Joint audits

In some cases, there may be a need for more than one audit firm to act as group auditor and each has to be aware of the issues before agreeing to act.

8. Transnational audits

As the impact and financing of consolidated groups become **more global**, the auditing profession has set up an **FOF** supported by the IAASB to address the needs of how best to provide consistent quality and approaches.

Further study guidance

Question practice

Now try the following from the Further question practice bank (available in the digital edition of the Workbook):

- Question 19 'Annabella' tests audit planning in a group context, including the audit procedures required to test a consolidation.
- Questions 11 'Trendy Group' and 18 'Griffin' also cover groups, although they have been set for earlier chapters – make sure you revisit these in the context of what you have learned here.

Further reading

There is one technical article on the ACCA website, written by members of the AAA examining team, which is relevant to the contents of this chapter that you should read:

- *Group audits*

Own research

- Find a copy of a set of financial statements for a consolidated group and review them for the various disclosures made by both management and auditors to see what such an engagement actually includes.
- Use the following link to read up on the Transnational Auditors Committee (TAC) and the Forum of Firms (FOF):

  www.ifac.org/who-we-are/committees/transnational-auditors-committee-forum-firms

Activity answers

Activity 1: Communication

> **Approach**
>
> This is an opportunity for you to consider some very practical points about the dialogue between group auditors and component auditors. Pretend that you are the group auditor and you know nothing about the firm on whose work you will be relying: What do you need to know in order to be able to trust them?
>
> Consider:
>
> (a) What you need the component auditor to either know or confirm to the group auditor; and
>
> (b) What you really need to know about the outcome of the audit that the component auditor has conducted on your behalf.

Suggested solution

(1) **These communications include:**

   (i) A request that the component auditor confirms their co-operation with the group engagement team

   (ii) The ethical requirements that are relevant to the group audit and in particular, independence requirements

   (iii) In the case of an audit or review of the financial information of the component, component materiality and the threshold above which misstatements cannot be regarded as clearly trivial to the group financial statements

   (iv) Identified significant risks of material misstatement in the group financial statements, due to fraud or error that are relevant to the work of the component auditor; the group engagement team requests the component auditor to communicate any other identified significant risks of material misstatement and the component auditor's responses to such risks

   (v) A list of related parties prepared by group management and any other related parties of which the group engagement team is aware; component auditors are requested to communicate any other related parties not previously identified

(2) **This communication often takes the form of a memorandum, questionnaire or report of work performed and includes the following:**

   (i) Whether the component auditor has complied with ethical requirements that are relevant to the group audit, including independence and professional acceptance

   (ii) Whether the component auditor has complied with the group engagement team's requirements

   (iii) Identification of the financial information of the component on which the component auditor is reporting

   (iv) Information on instances of non-compliance with laws and regulations that could give rise to material misstatement of the group financial statements

   (v) A list of uncorrected misstatements of the financial information of the component (the list need not include items that are below the threshold for clearly trivial misstatements)

   (vi) Indicators of possible management bias

   (vii) Description of any material deficiencies identified in internal control over financial reporting at the component level

   (viii) Other significant matters that the component auditor communicated or expects to communicate to those charged with governance of the component, including fraud or suspected fraud involving component management, employees who have significant roles in internal control at the component level or others where the fraud resulted in a material misstatement of the financial information of the component

(ix) Any other matters that may be relevant to the group audit or that the component auditor wishes to draw to the attention of the group engagement team, including exceptions noted in the written representations that the component auditor requested from component management

(x) The component auditor's overall findings, conclusions and opinion on the component's financial statements

Activity 2: Consolidation

Approach

This should be idea-generation again – you should get used to the need to recall certain items rapidly as this may happen in the real exam. Consider what you have learned about consolidations from FR and SBR and then consider what adjustments you have completed when attempting questions for these subjects!

Suggested solution

- The calculation of any goodwill, including any impairment reviews as appropriate
- Cancellation of intra-group balances and transactions, such as dividends
- Provisions for unrealised profits resulting from intra-group transactions
- Fair value adjustments on assets and liabilities
- Retranslation of financial statements for overseas components
- The correct value of any components included in the parent company's financial statements

Activity 3: Wolf Co

Approach

Calculations of NCI at the year end will require this acquisition figure plus any share of identifiable net assets. Review the Essential reading in the digital edition of this Workbook for fuller details of ISA 600 and IFRS 3 and how to calculate this schedule. Once you have the numbers, work your way down each line and consider what evidence you could seek to back each one up.

Suggested solution

Calculation of goodwill at acquisition:

	$'000
Consideration transferred	12,000
Non-controlling interest (2.5m shares × $1.50 per share)	3,750
Sub-total	**15,750**
Net assets acquired	(10,000)
Goodwill (difference)	**5,750**
Non-controlling interest at fair value (above)	3,750
Non-controlling interest at share of net assets (25% × $10m FV)	2,500

	S'000
Goodwill attributable to NCI (difference)	**1,250**
Goodwill attributable to Bad Co shareholders (balancing figure)	4,500
Goodwill attributable to NCI shareholders (above)	1,250
Total goodwill (above)	**5,750**

Principal audit procedures:

- Obtain a copy of the goodwill calculation from Bad Co and recalculate to ensure accuracy.
- Confirm the consideration of $12 million to a broker's invoice and Bad Co's bank statements.
- Confirm Bad Co's ownership of the shares, the date of the transaction and the number of shares owned by inspecting copies of the share certificates.
- Confirm the share price paid on the date of transfer using a third-party source (eg Bloomberg).
- Obtain working papers confirming the fair value of $10 million for Wolf Co's net assets.
- Confirm the total number of ordinary shares in existence for Wolf Co.
- Confirm choice of correct accounting treatment by reading board minutes for adoption of IFRS 3.

Skills checkpoint 3

Planning the audit and gathering evidence

Chapter overview

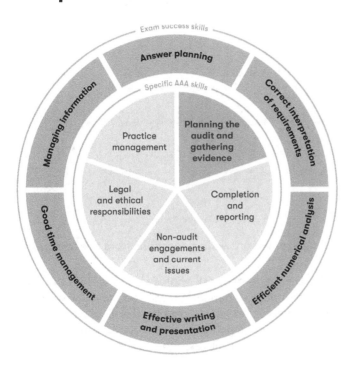

Introduction

Now that you have reached the midway point of the syllabus it makes sense to start thinking about the exam in a bit more detail. Question 1 in the exam will be a 50-mark scenario question with a number of requirements that should test some, if not all, of the following:

- Risks (audit risks, risks of material misstatement or business risks)
- Other planning issues
- Audit procedures and evidence required to verify specific parts of the scenario
- Ethical and professional points related to the scenario

In this skills checkpoint, we will go through an audit risk question, showing you how to use the scenario to draw up a detailed answer. We will also show you all of the exam success skills as they relate to Question 1 so you can start to practise them as part of your home study.

AAA Skill: Planning the audit and gathering evidence

A step by step technique for approaching questions testing this part of the syllabus now follows (you may find that some of these techniques are suitable for other parts of the syllabus as well – why not start practising them now?)

> **STEP 1:**
> Confirm the requirement (evaluating audit risk) by reference to the verb, the marks and the timing.

> **STEP 2:**
> Annotate the scenario with ideas of audit risks.

> **STEP 3:**
> Perform analytical procedures on the data supplied (including conclusions).

> **STEP 4:**
> Create an answer plan that takes Steps 1, 2 and 3 into account.

> **STEP 5:**
> Write your answer.

Exam success skills

There are some key exam skills that will help you when answering questions from this topic which are summarised below:

- **Managing information.** Planning in AAA takes the form of risk analysis coupled with the use of audit procedures to generate sufficient appropriate evidence. You will need to know what could be misstated in a set of financial statements and how to confirm this via suitable audit procedures, usually in the context of a scenario where you will need to apply technical knowledge. Therefore, there are two key areas that you will need to know about in order to score well.

  The first is your **technical knowledge of accounting and financial reporting matters** – the AAA examinable documents are the same as those used on Strategic Business Reporting (SBR) so it is vital that you have studied that subject by the time you attempt AAA. **Chapter 8** of this Workbook covers specific accounting issues; there is also an **Appendix** that covers these standards in more detail if you require a recap of the key issues.

  The second relates to **obtaining evidence** and it is here that you can use **mnemonics** to help you identify evidence and the procedures used to generate it.

  Let's start with a question approach for the following type of requirement, usually set in the context of a quality control review where you need to work out what happened in an engagement and make sure that the audit team performed the right procedures and generated the right evidence:

  'Comment on the matters to be considered and state the evidence that you should expect to see'

  The mnemonic to use here is **MRSA** (covered more in Chapter 8):

  M What is the materiality of the item that is being discussed?

  R What is the risk of misstatement presented here?

  S How does the standard suggest this should be dealt with?

  A What audit evidence should the team have collected and put on file for review?

There are other mnemonics that can help you to generate ideas for suitable audit procedures that are covered in Chapter 7 (**AEIOU** and **ACCACOPER**).

One final piece of advice when generating an audit procedure is to consider the specific elements of a good procedure – ideally it should include as many of the following as possible:

WHAT you are doing; **WHY** and **HOW** you are doing it; **WHERE** you may need to go to do it; to **WHOM** you will need to speak; and what **DOCUMENTATION** you will need to obtain.

- **Efficient numerical analysis.** You will see more of this when the question is attempted later in this skills checkpoint, but overall, if financial statement extracts and other forms of financial or non-financial data is presented in a scenario (especially Question 1 of the AAA exam) you will need to do something with it – it is not there for either decoration or distraction!

  The use of suitable analytical procedures will be required in such cases and you should be using them as a **starting point** for your analysis and planning.

- **Correct interpretation of requirements.** In Question 1 of the AAA exam, the requirement will be presented differently to other questions – it is known as an 'embedded email requirement' and you need to be prepared for it.

  Consider the following example taken from the AAA Specimen Exam Question 1:

  Required

  Respond to the instruction in the email from the audit engagement partner. (46 marks)

  Note. The split of the mark allocation is shown within the partner's email (Exhibit 1).

  Professional marks will be awarded for the presentation and logical flow of the briefing notes and the clarity of the explanations provided. **(4 marks)**

  (50 marks)

  The partner's email has been **embedded** earlier in the scenario for that question:

  "Using this information, I require you to prepare briefing notes for my use, in which you:

  (i)   Evaluate the audit risks to be considered in planning the audit of the Group. Your evaluation should utilise analytical procedures for identifying relevant audit risks. **(20 marks)**

  (ii) Explain the matters to be considered, and the procedures to be performed, in respect of planning to use the work of Clapton & Co. **(8 marks)**

  (iii) Design the principal audit procedures to be performed in respect of the following balances recognised as non-current assets in the Group statement of financial position:

   (1) $12 million recognised as investment in associate, and **(5 marks)**

   (2) $8 million recognised as a brand name. **(5 marks)**

  (iv) Using the information provided in Exhibit 4, identify and evaluate any ethical threats and other professional issues which arise from the requests made by the Group audit committee. **(8 marks)**

  Thank you."

  It is essential that you split up these requirements into discrete tasks and create a plan that delivers the minimum number of points for each requirement in line with the mark scheme. This requires a form of 'scaffolding' that will be discussed in a later skills checkpoint.

- **Effective writing and presentation.** In the example above, taken from the AAA Specimen Exam, there are four professional marks – what are they and how do you earn them?

  Basically, these marks allow you to demonstrate an awareness of the professional nature of how the modern-day accountant should communicate, as well as to present answers in a format that is both professional and appropriate to the circumstances of the scenario.

  How can you earn these professional marks? This is what the examining team recently suggested:

  "*Candidates who presented their answers in a logical and reasoned manner with sub-headings and references scored well. Again candidates are advised to consider their exam technique in this area, for example only one concise paragraph is necessary as an*

introduction, not a whole page. Candidates are advised to space out their work and start a new page for each sub-section."

You should always respond according to what's been requested. The embedded email above requests answers in the format of a **briefing note** (a document that presents key details for someone else to be adequately briefed during a meeting). Other documents might be requested, for example **reports, emails** or **letters** but in most cases, you will probably be briefing the audit partner. You must ensure that **at no point in your answer do you mention your own name** – the examining team suggests the use of the name **'Audit Manager'** in your answer. **Suggested layouts** are shown below:

Report	Briefing note/Emails	Letter
'Title'	**From:** *A. Manager*	Your address
Prepared by: *A. Manager*	**To:** *A. Partner*	Recipient's name
Date: *13/7/20X5*	**Date:** *13/7/20X5*	Recipient's address
Executive summary	**Subject:**	13/7/20X5
Not always required, but can look extremely professional.	**Introduction**	*Dear Recipient,*
Introduction	• Restate requirements	**Subject of letter.....**
Including terms of reference and scope of engagement.	**Detailed sections**	*Details of letter*
Detailed sections	• **Sub-heading 1**	*'If I can be of any more help, please do not hesitate to contact me at the address above...'*
	Content	*'Yours faithfully,'*
Conclusions	• **Sub-heading 2**	(if addressed to 'Sir' or 'Madam')
	Content	or
Recommendations	• **Etc**	*'Yours sincerely,'*
Action plans, including staff responsible for implementing recommendations and timescales.	**Conclusions**	(if addressed to a named party)
	• Summary points	*Your name*
	Appendices (if required)	**Your title**
Appendices	**Signed**	
	Audit Manager	
	Audit Manager	

Professional marks are also awarded for an appreciation of the **tone** of a required answer – again, as nearly qualified professional accountants, candidates should be able to produce something appropriate.

• **Good time management and answer planning.** Although there is **no separate reading and planning time** in this exam, and **no choice of questions either**, you still have a number of **key decisions** to make when it comes to allocating your timings during the exam. Skill 3 will discuss how to allocate enough time to individual requirements, but for now, let's consider the overall balance between (i) reading and planning and (ii) writing your answer during the exam, and how to use time effectively in each case.

Even if you are not a planner by nature, planning can help you cope with your nerves when you start the exam. It can also be a way of giving yourself crucial time to think before you start writing, potentially saving you from wasting time by going down the wrong path. The **examining team** recently commented that candidates should:

"...invest time upfront in analysing what the requirement is asking for rather than spending time detailing points which do not address the requirement... For candidates preparing for this exam, it is especially important to focus on tailoring the number of points written to the marks available and to take note of areas that the requirement flags as not required."

Investing time upfront means making a conscious decision to set aside specific reading and planning time **as well as** writing time for each question. This should be anything from a

quarter to a third of the time required for each question, and should allow you to fully understand what's required before you write it. For example, the exam could look like this:

	Reading/planning time	Writing time	Total time for question
Question 1 = 50 marks	24 minutes	74 minutes	98 minutes
Question 2 = 25 marks	12 minutes	37 minutes	49 minutes
Question 3 = 25 marks	12 minutes	36 minutes	48 minutes
	25%	75%	195 minutes (3¼ hours)

Perhaps you could just use the term 'thinking time' instead of reading and planning to help you remember to do it!

Here's the question that we will be using for this checkpoint:

Your firm has recently been appointed as the auditor of Forsythia, a small limited liability company which offers garden landscaping services. You have been assigned the task of planning the audit for the year ended 31 December 20X9.

Extracts from the draft financial statements are shown below:

	Year ended 31 December 20X9	Year ended 31 December 20X8
	$'000	$'000
	Draft	Actual
Revenue	3,112	2,549
Gross profit	301	277
Operating profit	278	167
Non-current assets	412	412
Trade receivables	621	431
Cash in hand and at bank	0	22
Trade payables	155	178

Forsythia is partly owned by three business associates, Mr Rose, Mr White and Mr Grass, who each hold 10% of the shares. The major shareholder is the parent company, Poppy Co. This company owns shares in 20 different companies, which operate in a variety of industries. One of them is a garden centre, and Forsythia regularly trades with it. Poppy Co is in turn owned by a parent, White Holdings Co.

The management structure at Forsythia is simple. Of the three non-corporate shareholders, only Mr Rose has any involvement in management. He runs the day to day operations of the company (marketing, sales, purchasing etc) although the company employs two landscape gardeners to actually carry out projects. The accounts department employs a purchase clerk and a sales clerk, who each deal with all aspects of that function. The sales clerk is Mr Rose's daughter, Justine. Mr Rose authorises and produces the payroll. The company ledgers are kept on Mr Rose's personal computer. Two weeks after the year end, the sales ledger records were severely damaged by a computer virus. Justine has a single printout of the balances at the year end, which shows the total owed by each customer.

Forsythia owns the equipment used on projects and pays the gardeners a salary and a bonus based on performance. Mr Rose is remunerated entirely on a commission basis relating to sales; plus, as a shareholder, he receives dividends annually, which are substantial.

Forsythia does not carry any inventory. When materials are required for a project, they are purchased on behalf of the client and charged directly to them. Most customers pay within the 60-day credit period, or take up the extended credit period which Forsythia offers. However, there are a number of accounts that appear to have been outstanding for a significant period.

Justine and her father do not appear to have a very good working relationship. She does not live at home and her salary is not significant. However, she appears to have recently purchased a sports car, which is not a company car.

Required

Evaluate the audit risks to be considered in planning the audit of Forsythia. **(14 marks)**

Skill activity

STEP 1 Confirm the requirement by considering the verb, the marks and the timings required.

Evaluate the audit risks to be considered in planning the audit of Forsythia. (14 marks)

Remember that audit risks are the risk of the auditor issuing an incorrect audit opinion – historically at this level, candidates have sometimes mistaken audit risks for business risks (the risk that an organisation will not achieve its objectives). Make sure you know what kind of risks you are looking for!

'Evaluate' is a higher level verb, so will probably score up to 2 marks for each audit risk, but you will need to work hard to score the full marks – traditionally, the examining team would have allowed ½ mark for each issue that was identified and then a further 1 to 1½ marks for the explanation of why this represented an audit risk.

Consequently, this might require 7 issues × 2 marks each = 14 marks. However, the results of analytical procedures might also attract marks as well, up to a ceiling, so you would probably not need any more than 7 audit risks.

Finally, 14 marks would require just over 27 minutes work – allowing around 25% of this time for reading/planning/thinking (7 minutes) that would leave 20 minutes to write the answer in full.

STEP 2 Annotate the scenario with ideas of audit risks areas.

Marking up the scenario will help you identify the areas where you believe the risk of issuing an incorrect opinion will be greatest and allow you to focus on the logic of why.

Your firm has recently been appointed[11] as the auditor of Forsythia[12], a small limited liability company which offers garden landscaping services[13]. You have been assigned the task of planning the audit for the year ended 31 December 20X9.

Extracts[14] from the draft financial statements are shown below:

[11] Detection risk: opening balances and comparatives - audited or not?

[12] Any group audit issues? Who are the group auditors?

[13] Receivables likely to be significant

[14] Analyse variances and ratios – days, margins and changes

	Year ended 31 December 20X9	Year ended 31 December 20X8
	$'000	$'000
	Draft	Actual
Revenue	3,112	2,548
Gross profit	301	277
Operating profit	278	167
Non-current assets	412	412
Trade receivables	621	431
Cash in hand and at bank	0	22
Trade payables	155	178

Forsythia is partly owned by three business associates, Mr Rose, Mr White and Mr Grass, who each hold 10% of the shares. The major shareholder is the parent company, Poppy Co. This company owns shares in 20 different companies, which operate in a variety of industries.[15] One of them is a garden centre, and Forsythia regularly trades with it. Poppy Co is in turn owned by a parent, White Holdings Co.[16]

The management structure at Forsythia is simple. Of the three non-corporate shareholders, only Mr Rose[17] has any involvement in management. He runs the day to day operations of the company (marketing, sales, purchasing etc) although the company employs two landscape gardeners to actually carry out projects[18]. The accounts department employs a purchase clerk and a sales clerk, who each deal with all aspects of that function. The sales clerk is Mr Rose's daughter, Justine. Mr Rose authorises and produces the payroll. The company ledgers are kept on Mr Rose's personal computer[19]. Two weeks after the year end, the sales ledger records were severely damaged by a computer virus[20]. Justine has a single printout[21] of the balances at the year end, which shows the total owed by each customer.

[15] Complicated corporate structure – why?

[16] Controlling party? Any connection to Mr White?

[17] Key man? Over-reliance?

[18] Odd that the business is not owned by landscape gardeners?

[19] No segregation of duties and poor controls

[20] Poor controls

[21] Limitation? And given below, suspicion of fraud? Teeming and lading?

Forsythia owns the equipment used on projects and pays the gardeners a salary and a bonus based on performance. Mr Rose is remunerated entirely on a commission basis relating to sales; plus, as a shareholder, he receives dividends annually, which are substantial.

Forsythia does not carry any inventory. When materials are required for a project, they are purchased on behalf of the client and charged directly[22] to them. Most customers pay within the 60-day credit period, or take up the extended credit period[23] which Forsythia offers. However, there are a number of accounts that appear to have been outstanding[24] for a significant period.

[22] How accounted for? Errors possible?

[23] Any relevant laws and regulations?

[24] Problem with receivables?

Justine and her father do not appear to have a very good working relationship. She does not live at home and her salary is not significant. However, she appears to have recently purchased a sports car, which is not a company car.[25]

[25] Fraud risk - how can she afford this?

STEP 3 Perform analytical review procedures on the data supplied.

There is no set order or checklist of procedures to perform, but the general rule is that if there are financial statement or other data presented, you will need to do something with them!

The data are telling you a story; you need to understand the language they use so the story makes sense.

The broad categories of analytical procedures are as follows, with an overview of the ratios that you can calculate in each category:

Profitability	Gross margin (gross profit/revenue as a %)
	Operating margin (operating profit/revenue as a %)
Efficiency	Receivables days (receivables/revenue × 365 days)
	Inventory days (closing or average inventory/purchases or cost of sales × 365 days)
	Payables days (payables/purchases or cost of sales × 365 days)
	Remember, the reciprocals of these without multiplying by the 365 days will create turnover figures instead – as the amount gets lower, things will be getting worse for the audited entity (beware being given a reporting period of lower than 365 days!)
	Current ratio (current assets/current liabilities as a ratio)
	Quick ratio (as above but excluding inventory, again as a ratio)
Gearing	Debt to equity ratio (can be calculated as debt/debt + equity to be more meaningful)
	Interest cover (usually profit before interest and tax/finance costs)

Forsythia's analytical review shows the following:

	Draft 20X9	Actual 20X8	Variance	Conclusion
	$'000	$'000		
Revenue	3,112	2,549	22%	Significant rise – manipulated?
Gross profit	301	277	9%	Hasn't increased in line with above
Operating profit	278	167	66%	Significant rise – misallocations?
Non-current assets	412	412	0%	Why no movement – error?
Trade receivables	621	431	44%	Double rise in revenue – why?
Cash	0	22	-100%	Where has this gone – O/D now?
Trade payables	155	178	-13%	Why fallen – understated?

Calculations

	Draft 20X9	Actual 20X8		Conclusion
Gross margin	10%	11%		As above – should both move in similar direction – misallocations?
Operating margin	9%	7%		

	Draft 20X9	Actual 20X8		Conclusion
Assumed Cost of Sales (required for calculations)	2,811	2,272		
Receivables days	72.8	61.7		Greater than terms – overstated?
Payables days	20.1	28.6		Fallen for no reason – understated?

Remember that analytical review without a conclusion will not score many (if any) marks, so you need to have built the results into your answer – usually they would lead to further questions, as analytical procedures frequently identify issues that require further investigation.

STEP 4 Draw up an answer plan using the results of Steps 1, 2 and 3.

Not all the points you notice will necessarily be **relevant** and you may also find that you do not have **time** to mention all the points in your answer. You should prioritise your points in a more formal answer plan and then write your answer.

Audit risks

Inherent	Control
Related party transactions/group issues Receivables – increase in amount and days Fraud – possible indicators, professional scepticism Profit driven management – sales and margins Credit extended – accounting/law and regs Trade payables – understated? Non-current assets – why no movement? Cash – really zero and what if now O/D?	Lack of segregation of duties – op vs gross margins? PC/virus Suspicion of fraud? Key man insurance
	Detection First audit Opening bals and comparatives – audited?

Engagement risks

Some questions raised which makes business look odd:

- Group (complex/different auditors/who controls?)
- Nature of business – yet landscape gardeners hired

Indicators of potential fraud

Possible indicators of money laundering (complex structure/cash business)

STEP 5 Write your solution in full.

Note. Audit risks do not necessarily require the split between inherent/control/detection risks, but if it helps you to identify them more easily, you should continue to use them.

Audit risks – inherent

Related parties and group issues

Forsythia is part of a **complicated group structure**. This raises several issues for the audit.

- There is a risk of related party transactions existing and not being properly disclosed in the financial statements in accordance with IAS 24 *Related Party Disclosures*.
- Similarly, there is a risk that it will be difficult to ascertain the controlling party for disclosure.
- There is likely to be some group audit implications. My firm may be required to undertake procedures in line with the group auditors' requirements if Forsythia is to be consolidated.

Receivables

Forsythia is a **service provider**, and it **extends credit** to customers. This is likely to mean that **trade receivables** will be a significant audit balance. The draft financial statements show an increase of 44% in trade receivables for 20X9, with receivables days increasing from 61.7 in 20X8 to 72.8 in 20X9. These both suggest that trade receivables is overstated. However, there is **limited audit evidence** concerning trade receivables due to the effects of a computer virus. There are also indicators of a **possible fraud**.

Fraud

There are various factors that may indicate a sales ledger fraud has taken/is taking place.

- Lack of segregation of duties
- Extensive credit offered (as demonstrated by the increasing receivables days calculations)
- The virus only destroyed sales ledger information – too specific?
- Poorly paid sales ledger clerk – with expensive lifestyle
- Sales ledger clerk is daughter of a well-paid shareholder and they do not have a good relationship

None of these **factors** necessarily point to a fraud individually, but **added together raise significant concerns**.

Profit-driven management

Mr Rose is motivated for the financial statements to show a profit for two reasons:

- He receives a commission (presumably sales driven, which impacts on profit).

- He receives dividends as shareholder, which will depend on profits.

From the draft financial statements, revenue has increased by 22% and operating profit has risen by 66%. Operating margin has also risen from 7% to 9%. Consequently, there is a risk that revenue is overstated in the draft financial statements as a result of **management bias.**

Credit extended

We should ensure that the credit extended to customers is standard business credit. There are unlikely to be any **complications,** for example interest, but if there were, we should be aware of any **laws and regulations** which might become relevant when attempting to chase such overdue debts, and any **accounting issues** which would be raised by allowances should doubts persist.

Trade payables

The absence of inventory due to the arrangements between Forsythia and its customers appears unusual, and may be masking either fraud or error. Trade payables have gone down by 13% and trade payables days have moved from 28.6 days in 20X8 to 20.1 days in 20X9. This indicates possible understatement of the trade payables balance.

Other areas of possible misstatement

From the analytical procedures performed on the extracts from the draft financial statements, two further issues emerge – **non-current assets** have stayed the same and **cash** has dropped to zero. Non-current assets should have reduced as depreciation is charged – additions may balance out this charge, but the firm should investigate this further to ensure there is no misstatement. Similarly, the cash balance may have dropped to zero, especially if the company's credit control is as poor as it appears, but the true cash position could be one of overdraft which may have further consequences (such as bank covenants and going concern issues) that we would need to evaluate as part of the audit.

Audit risk – control

There are three significant control problems at Forsythia.

Segregation of duties

There appears to be a **complete lack of segregation of duties** on the three main ledgers. This may have led to a **fraud** on the sales ledger. The fact that there is no segregation on payroll is also a concern as this is an area where fraud typically occurs.

Lack of segregation of duties can also lead to **significant errors** being made and not being detected by the system. The draft financial statements show that gross margin has fallen from 11% to 10% but operating profit has risen from 7% to 9%. While not significant, they may indicate misclassification in costs that indicate **misstatements** which may be material. This problem also means that **control risk** will have to be assessed as **high** and **significant substantive testing** will need to be undertaken.

Personal computer

A PC is used for the accounting system. This is likely to have **poor built-in controls** and further exacerbate the problems caused by the lack of segregation of duties.

The **security** over PCs is also often poor, as has been the case here, where a **virus** has destroyed evidence about the sales ledger.

Key man

The fact that Mr Rose is dominant in management may also be a control problem, particularly if he were ever to be absent.

Audit risk – detection

The key detection risk is that this is the **first audit**, so we will have no prior understanding of the entity to draw on. We have not audited the **opening balances** and **comparatives**. We should have contacted any previous auditors and therefore be aware of whether these have been audited. If there were no previous auditors, these are unaudited. We must ensure that our auditor's report is clear on this issue.

There is also significant detection risk in relation to **related parties,** as discussed above.

Engagement risk

There are several indicators that Forsythia may be an 'odd' company.

The first indicator is that it is part of a **complex and unexplained group**, and that the group is not audited by the same firm of auditors, although it is unclear how many firms of auditors are involved in the group audit. There may be good reasons for this audit policy, but we should **investigate those reasons**, in case any other issues arise.

Another indicator is that it seems slightly odd that a small company should exist to provide landscape gardening services, when it appears that the owners are not landscape gardeners, or at least, if they are, they do not work in the business. Again, there may be valid reasons for this, but we should **discover and document them**.

It is particularly important that these issues are cleared up. A complex group structure and a company dealing in cash transactions (Forsythia's potentially are) could indicate the possibility that the owners are trying to **launder money**. There are also indicators of **fraud**. If either of these issues exist, the auditor may have **significant responsibility** to report and co-operate with relevant authorities, and the **professional relationship of client and auditor could be compromised.** Therefore, the audit firm must ensure that it has suitable 'know your client' procedures in place and the appropriate systems for making reports should a suspicion arise. The partners must ensure that staff have appropriate training so that they are able to comply fully with legal requirements in relation to money laundering.

Exam success skills diagnostic

Every time you complete a question, use the diagnostic below to assess how effectively you demonstrated the exam success skills in answering the question. The table has been completed below for Forsythia to give you an idea of how to complete the diagnostic.

Exam success skills	Your reflections/observations
Good time management	For a 14 mark requirement like this, the total time to answer the question (up to 1.95 minutes per mark) would have been 27½ minutes; the split between reading/thinking/planning time and writing time (something like ¼ to ¾ respectively of the total time) would therefore have been 7½ minutes reading/planning/thinking and 20 minutes writing.
Managing information	Did you pick up on all the information you needed to satisfactorily answer the question – for example, the complex ownership structure and the numerous instances of fraud that were implied?
Correct interpretation of requirements	Did you evaluate the audit risks by showing sufficient judgement and justification in your answer?
Answer planning	Did you manage to identify all the points in the solution? You didn't need them all to pass, so would you still have passed in the time you had?
Effective writing and presentation	Did you manage to carry all the points from your plan through into your final answer?
Efficient numerical analysis	Did you use the results of your analytical procedures to identify areas of audit risk?
Most important action points to apply to your next question	

Summary

Planning the audit and gathering evidence could represent the majority of the marks you need to pass this exam, so getting used to the skills and techniques described here is essential. Fortunately, there are many questions that test these skills in the Practice and Revision Kit, so you should be adept at this when you come to sit the exam for real.

10

Completion

Learning objectives

On completion of this chapter, you should be able to:

	Syllabus reference no.
Design audit procedures designed to identify subsequent events which may require adjustment to, or disclosure in, the financial statements of a given entity.	E1(a)
Evaluate indicators that the going concern basis may be in doubt and recognise mitigating factors.	E1(b)
Recommend audit procedures, or evaluate the evidence that might be expected to be available and assess the appropriateness of the going concern basis in given situations.	E1(c)
Assess the adequacy of disclosures in financial statements relating to going concern and explain the implications for the auditor's report with regard to the going concern basis.	E1(d)
Apply analytical procedures for the purposes of evaluation and review and evaluate the results in the context of other audit evidence.	E2(a)
Assess whether an engagement has been planned and performed in accordance with professional standards.	E2(b)
Evaluate whether reports issued are appropriate in the relevant circumstances.	E2(c)
Evaluate as part of the final review the matters (eg materiality, risk, relevant accounting standards) and audit evidence to confirm if sufficient and appropriate evidence has been obtained.	E2(d)
Justify the review procedures which should be performed in a given assignment, including the need for an engagement quality control review and recommend additional procedures or actions needed in the circumstances.	E2(e)
Evaluate the use of written representations from management to support other audit evidence.	E2(f)
Describe appropriate audit procedures relating to: (xxi) Events after the end of the reporting period	D3(a)

	Syllabus reference no.
Explain how the auditor's responsibilities for corresponding figures, comparative financial statements and 'other information' are discharged.	D3(b)
Discuss the courses of action available to an auditor if a material inconsistency or material misstatement exists in relation to other information, such as contained in the integrated report.	E3(h)

Business and exam context

Towards the end of an audit, a series of reviews and evaluations are carried out. You should be familiar with them from your previous auditing studies.

We start with the **overall review** which is undertaken on the financial statements as a whole and the review of misstatements and potential misstatements. The section then discusses the details of a **quality control review of an individual audit**.

Often the auditors will have to rely on **written representations** about related parties and other issues. Written representations are subjective evidence, and the auditor must proceed with caution when dealing with them. The auditor conducts reviews of the period between the period end and the signing of the auditor's report **(subsequent events)** and of the **going concern** presumption.

The issue of **comparatives** is also discussed. The auditor has different responsibilities for corresponding figures and for comparative information. Finally, the auditor must review **other information** to establish whether it contradicts the financial statements. The detailed procedures and requirements are discussed in Section 4.

Going concern is a particularly important audit review which could be relevant in risks or evidence questions. Bear in mind the links with planning, knowledge of the business and analytical procedures. **Subsequent events, corresponding figures** and **other information** could also come up in an exam question in the context of auditor's reports.

Questions in syllabus sections E–G can only be examined in Section B of the exam, and will not be part of the audit planning question. It is theoretically possible that events after the reporting period could be examined in Section A of the exam, but this is very unlikely.

Chapter overview

1 Overall review of financial statements

1.1 ISA 220 *Quality Control for an Audit of Financial Statements*

⚠ PER alert

One of the competencies you require to fulfil **Performance Objective 20** of the PER is the ability to review the performance of an audit, ensuring the process has been undertaken effectively and that all work undertaken is accurate and complete and that sufficient evidence has been obtained. You can apply the knowledge you have obtained from this chapter of the Workbook to help demonstrate this competency.

At the completion stage, the auditor performs an **overall review** of all work done to ensure the audit **complies** with **professional standards** and all applicable **legal and regulatory requirements**, and that **evidence** is a **suitable basis for the audit opinion** (ISA 220: para. 6).

The auditors should also consider whether the **accounting policies** applied are in accordance with accounting standards, properly disclosed, consistently applied and appropriate to the entity. When examining the accounting policies, auditors may use a **checklist** and should consider the following.

Policies **commonly adopted** in particular industries	Policies for which there is **substantial authoritative support**	Whether any **departures** from applicable accounting standards are necessary	The financial statements reflect the **substance** of the underlying transactions

Some audits (such as those for listed companies and other public interest entities) require an **independent engagement quality control review**, which evaluates **significant judgements** and conclusions reached by the audit team and ensures this has all been done in full and before the auditor's report is signed by the engagement partner (ISA 220: para. 20).

Essential reading

See Chapter 10 of the Essential reading for more detail on ISA 220.

The Essential reading is available as an Appendix of the digital edition of the Workbook.

1.2 ISA 520 *Analytical Procedures*

Relevant trends and ratios are **recalculated** by the auditor at the completion stage in order to ensure the consistency of the final version of the financial statements with the evidence that has been collected during the audit.

Examples of the areas that the analytical procedures at the final stage must cover:

- Important accounting ratio
- Related items
- Changes in products and/or customers
- Price and mix changes
- Wages changes
- Variances
- Trends in production and sales
- Changes in material and labour content at production
- Other statement of profit or loss expenditure
- Variations caused by industry or economic factors

The analytical procedures performed at the completion stage are no different from those performed elsewhere in the audit process. The only difference is that by this time, the auditor should know enough about the client to be able to point to evidence explaining the issues highlighted by the analytical review.

If the auditor finds a previously unrecognised risk of material misstatement at this stage, then it will have to revise its assessment of audit risk. This may affect materiality, for example, and may mean that further audit evidence is needed in certain areas.

> ### PER alert
>
> One of the competencies you require to fulfil **Performance Objective 19** of the PER is the ability to evaluate evidence collected, demonstrating professional scepticism, investigating areas of concern and ensuring documentation is complete and all significant matters and areas of judgement are highlighted. You can apply the knowledge you gain from this chapter of the Workbook to help demonstrate this competency.

1.3 ISA 450 (revised) *Evaluation of Misstatements Identified During the Audit*

By the end of the audit, there may be a number of misstatements that have been identified as a result of the auditor's procedures (including **disclosures** where details could have been either omitted or misstated and which could indicate **fraud**). Those that are clearly **trivial** will be ignored, while those that the client has already **agreed to amend** will be reviewed to ensure this has occurred. What about any remaining misstatements though?

The auditor must consider the impact on the financial statements of **uncorrected misstatements**, especially those that are not individually material, because in **aggregate**, their cumulative effect may become material (ISA 450: para.11). The auditor needs to evaluate these misstatements and differentiate between those that are **factual misstatements** (those that are clearly misstated), **judgemental misstatements** (those relating to accounting policies or estimates) and **projected misstatements** (which cannot be quantified specifically) (ISA 450: para. A6).

Should the **aggregate** of uncorrected misstatements **start to become material**, then the auditor can either perform **further procedures** or request management to **adjust the financial statements**. Ultimately, this could lead to a **modification of the audit opinion** if corrections are not made, so it is essential to discuss this with those charged with governance.

During this stage of the audit, materiality may **change** due to adjustments made by management, so the auditor should be alert to the risk that some misstatements may now become material.

The **summary of uncorrected misstatements** will not only list misstatements from the current year, but also those from the previous year(s). This will allow misstatements to be highlighted which are reversals of misstatements in the previous year, such as in the valuation of closing/opening inventory. **Cumulative** misstatements may also be shown, which have increased from year to year. It is normal to show both the statement of financial position and the statement of profit or loss and other comprehensive income effect, as in the **example** given here.

Schedule of uncorrected misstatements

	20X2				20X1			
	Statement of profit or loss		Statement of financial position		Statement of profit or loss		Statement of financial position	
	Debit	Credit	Debit	Credit	Debit	Credit	Debit	Credit
	$	$	$	$	$	$	$	$
(a) ABC Co receivable unprovided	10,470			10,470	4,523			4,523
(b) Opening/ closing inventory undervalued*	21,540			21,540		21,540	21,540	
(c) Closing inventory undervalued		34,105	34,105					
(d) Opening unaccrued expenses								
Telephone*		453	453		453			453
Electricity*		905	905		905			905
(e) Closing unaccrued expenses								
Telephone	427				427			
Electricity	1,128				1,128			
(f) Obsolete inventory write off	2,528			2,528	3,211			3,211
Total	36,093	35,463	35,463	36,093	9,092	21,540	21,540	9,092
*Cancelling items	21,540			21,540				
		453	453					
		905	905					
	14,553	34,105	34,105	14,553				

2 ISA 580 Written Representations

The **objectives** of the auditor under ISA 580 are:

(a) To **obtain appropriate representations from management** and, where appropriate, those charged with governance that they believe that they have fulfilled their **responsibility** for the preparation of the financial statements and for the completeness of the information provided to the auditor;

(b) To **support other audit evidence** relevant to the financial statements or specific assertions in the financial statements by means of written representations if determined necessary by the auditor or required by other ISAs; and

(c) To **respond appropriately** to written representations provided by management and, where appropriate, those charged with governance, or if management or, where appropriate, those charged with governance do not provide the written representations requested by the auditor (ISA 580: para. 6).

2.1 If the client refuses to provide representations

If the responsible party refuses to provide requested representations, this constitutes 'insufficient/inappropriate audit evidence' **leading to a disclaimer of opinion** (this would also be the case if there was doubt over management's integrity) (ISA 580: paras. 19–20).

2.2 Contents of a typical letter of representation

- Responsibilities for preparing the financial statements, including significant assumptions
- Related party relationships and transactions
- Events subsequent to the date of the financial statements
- The effects of uncorrected misstatements (and confirmation that they are not material)
- Confirmation that access has been granted to all information
- All transactions have been recorded in the accounting records
- All information in relation to fraud or suspected fraud that management is aware of
- Known instances of non-compliance or suspected non-compliance with laws and regulations

3 ISA 560 *Subsequent Events*

Subsequent events are defined as 'both events occurring between the period end and the date of the auditor's report and facts discovered after the date of the auditor's report' (ISA 560: para. 5). Such events can be either those that have an effect on the financial statements or those that do not (**adjusting** or **non-adjusting events** as per IAS 10 *Events After the Reporting Period*).

Activity 1: Subsequent events

What procedures should the auditor perform just prior to signing the auditor's report to ensure there are no unidentified material subsequent events that require adjustment or disclosure in the financial statements?

Solution

Essential reading

See Chapter 10 of the Essential reading for more detail on subsequent events, especially how audit procedures can vary depending on where you are in the subsequent events timeline.

The Essential reading is available as an Appendix of the digital edition of the Workbook.

4 ISA 570 *Going Concern*

4.1 Management and auditor responsibilities

Management	• Assess entity's ability to continue as a going concern and present the financial statements accordingly.
	• The assessment should cover at least 12 months from the date of the financial statements (the auditor shall request that directors extend their assessment if this period is not covered).
Auditor	• Consider the appropriateness of management's use of the going concern basis of accounting (even if the local GAAP does not require it).
	• Consider if there are material uncertainties threatening the client's going concern status that need to be disclosed (ISA 570: para. 9).

4.2 Indicators of going concern problems

Financial	Operational	Other
• Net liability or net current liability position • Inability to pay payables on due dates • Arrears/discontinuance of dividends • Fixed-term borrowings approaching maturity without realistic prospects of renewal or repayment • Withdrawal of financial support by receivables and other payables • Negative operating cash flows • Adverse key financial ratios • Substantial operating losses or significant fall in value of cash generating assets • Inability to comply with terms of loan agreements • Change from credit to cash on delivery transactions with suppliers • Inability to obtain financing for essential new product development or other essential investments	• Management intentions to liquidate entity or to cease operations • Shortage of supplies • Emergence of highly successful competitor • Loss of key management without replacement • Loss of major market, franchise, licence, or principal supplier • Labour difficulties or shortages of important supplies	• Uninsured or underinsured catastrophes when they occur • Non-compliance with capital or other statutory requirements • Pending legal or regulatory proceedings that may, if successful, result in claims that are unlikely to be satisfied • Changes in legislation or government policy expected to adversely affect the entity

The auditor should **evaluate** the assessment made by management using a variety of techniques:

- **Analysing and discussing cash flow**, profit and other forecasts with management
- **Analysing and discussing** the entity's latest available **interim financial statements**
- **Reading the terms of debentures and loan agreements** and determining whether any have been breached
- **Reading minutes** of the meetings of shareholders, those charged with governance and relevant committees for reference to financing difficulties
- **Enquiring** of the entity's legal counsel regarding **litigation and claims**
- **Confirming the existence, legality and enforceability** of arrangements to provide or maintain financial support with related and third parties and **assessing** the **financial ability** of such parties to **provide additional funds**
- Evaluating the entity's plans to deal with **unfilled customer orders**
- **Performing audit procedures regarding subsequent events** to identify those that either mitigate or otherwise affect the entity's ability to continue as a going concern
- Confirming the existence, terms and adequacy of **borrowing facilities**
- Obtaining and reviewing reports of **regulatory actions**
- Determining the adequacy of **support for any planned disposal of assets** (ISA 570: para. A16)

4.3 Auditor's report implications

> Going concern assumption appropriate, but a material uncertainty exists

If the material uncertainty is **adequately disclosed,** the auditor should express an **unmodified opinion,** but add a separate paragraph called '**Material uncertainty related to going concern**' which also states that the auditor's opinion is not modified in this respect.

If there is **inadequate disclosure,** the auditor expresses a **qualified** or **adverse opinion.**

> Going concern assumption inappropriate

The auditor should express an **adverse opinion** if the financial statements have been prepared on a going concern basis when this is no longer appropriate for the entity. Assuming an **alternative accounting treatment** is applied appropriately (such as on a **break-up basis**) an **Emphasis of Matter paragraph** could be used to draw attention to this.

> Management unwilling to make or extend an assessment

This would represent insufficient or inappropriate audit evidence and would lead either to a **qualified** or **disclaimer of opinion**, depending on the severity of the circumstances.

Going concern and the auditor's report are covered in more detail in Chapter 11 *Reporting*.

5 ISA 710 *Comparative Information – Corresponding Figures and Comparative Financial Statements*

According to ISA 710 para. 6, comparative information can be of two types:

(a) **Corresponding figures**: Where amounts and disclosures for the preceding period are included as part of current period financial statements

(b) **Comparative financial statements**: Where amounts and disclosures for the preceding period are included **separately** as an entire statement for comparison purposes

The auditor's opinion relates to the current period financial statements **as a whole,** so corresponding figures are not separately identified. The auditor should obtain sufficient appropriate evidence that **accounting policies** used are **consistent** with those of the current period and that the **amounts agree** to those presented in the prior period (ISA 710: para. 7).

The extent of any **additional audit procedures** and the **impact on the auditor's report** all depend on whether the prior period financial statements were audited and, if so, by whom.

5.1 Preceding period financial statements were NOT audited by our firm

For **both** corresponding figures and comparative financial statements:

The preceding period F/S were audited by another firm	The preceding period F/S were not audited
If there is no legal prohibition from using one, an 'Other Matter' paragraph states:	This can be stated in an '**Other Matter**' paragraph.
• That the F/S were audited by another auditor • The opinion issued plus any modifications • The date of that report	

In each case, audit procedures from **ISA 510** for agreeing **opening balances** then apply.

5.2 Preceding period financial statements were audited by our firm

For **corresponding figures,** there are two separate scenarios that need to be considered:

There was no modification to the preceding period F/S audit opinion, but a material issue with these figures is identified during the audit of the current period:	There was modification to the preceding period F/S audit opinion in relation to the corresponding figures:
• If the issue is **resolved** in the current year's corresponding figures, the auditor's report remains **unmodified** (an Emphasis of Matter paragraph may be used here). • If the issue remains **unresolved** in the corresponding figures, the auditor's opinion is modified in line with the issue's nature and extent.	• If the issue is now **resolved** in the current year's corresponding figures, the auditor's report remains **unmodified** in this respect. • If the issue remains **unresolved** in the corresponding figures, the auditor's opinion is modified in line with the issue's nature and extent.

For **comparative financial statements**, the auditor should separately identify each period reported on within the auditor's report. If the opinion on that period has changed since the original opinion was issued, an 'Other Matter' paragraph should be used to explain why.

6 ISA 720 *The Auditor's Responsibilities Relating to Other Information*

The auditor is required to give an opinion as to whether the financial statements give a true and fair view.

The annual report containing the audited financial statements will also include **other information** which the auditor may be required to report on as a separate engagement, such as:

(a) The directors' or management's report, including names of directors

(b) Financial summaries, ratios or highlights

(c) Employment data

(d) Selected quarterly data

(e) An integrated report

6.1 Material misstatements

The auditor must **read the other information** and be alert for material inconsistencies:

• Between the other information and the financial statements; and/or

• Between the other information and the auditor's knowledge obtained during the audit.

If any such material inconsistency appears to exist, the auditor shall **discuss this with management** and conclude whether there is a **material misstatement** in either the other information or the financial statements, or if the **auditor's understanding** of the entity and its environment needs to be updated (ISA 720: para. 16).

In any event, inconsistencies between the other information and the financial statements should always be **communicated to those charged with governance**.

Amendment necessary to	Auditor response if uncorrected
Audited financial statements	Consider **further audit procedures** as required by ISAs and the effect (if any) on the **auditor's report**. Evaluate the misstatement(s) in line with **ISA 450**.
The other information	**Understand the issue** (an expert may be required) and **ask management to revise the other** information if it still requires restatement (if they refuse, ask those charged with governance). If still not corrected, consider the **impact on the auditor's report** (see below) or **withdraw** from the engagement.

Amendment necessary to	Auditor response if uncorrected
Auditor's understanding	Respond in line with other ISAs (such as ISA 315).

6.2 Reporting other information in the auditor's report

The auditor's report will always include a separate section on other information, but how it is presented will vary depending on the circumstances (highlighted for key differences).

When the **other information contains no material misstatement:**

Other Information

Management is responsible for the other information. The other information comprises the [information included in the X report, but does not include the financial statements and our auditor's report thereon.]

Our opinion on the financial statements does not cover the other information and we do not express any form of assurance conclusion thereon.

In connection with our audit of the financial statements, our responsibility is to read the other information and, in doing so, consider whether the other information is materially inconsistent with the financial statements or our knowledge obtained in the audit or otherwise appears to be materially misstated. If, based on the work we have performed, we conclude that there is a material misstatement of this other information, we are required to report that fact. We have nothing to report in this regard.

The other information **may not be available to the auditor**, so the following is used instead:

Other information

Management is responsible for the other information. The other information comprises the [information included in the X report, but does not include the financial statements and our auditor's report thereon]. The X report is expected to be made available to us after the date of this auditor's report.

Our opinion on the financial statements does not cover the other information and we do not express any form of assurance conclusion thereon.

In connection with our audit of the financial statements, our responsibility is to read the other information identified above when it becomes available and, in doing so, consider whether the other information is materially inconsistent with the financial statements or our knowledge obtained in the audit or otherwise appears to be materially misstated. If, based on the work we have performed, we conclude that there is a material misstatement of this other information, we are required to report that fact. We have nothing to report in this regard.

There may be cases where the auditor is able to conclude that **there is a material misstatement to the other information** and it has **not been corrected by management**. In such cases, the section on other information is **moved up the auditor's report** to a position **immediately after the 'Basis for opinion' section (above key audit matters):**

Other information

Management is responsible for the other information. The other information comprises the [information included in the X report, but does not include the financial statements and our auditor's report thereon.]

Our opinion on the financial statements does not cover the other information and we do not express any form of assurance conclusion thereon.

In connection with our audit of the financial statements, our responsibility is to read the other information and, in doing so, consider whether the other information is materially inconsistent with the financial statements or our knowledge obtained in the audit or otherwise appears to be materially misstated. If, based on the work we have performed, we conclude that there is a material misstatement of this other information, we are required to report that fact. We have nothing to report in this regard. As described below, we have concluded that such a material misstatement of the other information exists.

[Description of the material misstatement of the other information.]

Chapter summary

```
                          ┌─────────────────┐
                          │   Completion    │
                          └─────────────────┘
```

Overall review of financial statements

- **ISA 220:** Evidence supports the proposed audit opinion, accounting policies are consistent and (if required) an **engagement quality control review (EQCR)** has been performed (dated no earlier than the date of the auditor's report)
- **ISA 520:** Final **analytical procedures** to confirm consistency with audit evidence
- **ISA 450:** Evaluation of misstatements identified during the audit – consider **uncorrected misstatements** (especially their **aggregate** impact on the F/S) and establish which are **factual, judgmental and projected misstatements**

ISA 580
Written Representations

- Objectives of auditor under ISA 580:
  - Obtain **written representations** from management (or those **charged with governance**) that they have fulfilled their **responsibilities** for preparing F/S and supplying all necessary **information**
  - Support audit evidence obtained by written representations if more detail is required (eg related parties, subsequent events, fraud, NOCLAR, uncorrected misstatements etc)
  - **Respond appropriately** when representations are provided (or when they are not but should be!)
- For more guidance on both going concern and completing the audit, please refer to the examining team's technical articles.

ISA 560
Subsequent Events

- Period up to auditor's report
- Period after report is signed

BPP LEARNING MEDIA

ISA 570 Going Concern

- Responsibilities?
  - Management: Assess ability to continue as a going concern.
  - Auditor: Consider appropriateness of use of going concern basis of accounting – if uncertainties exist but are disclosed, the auditor's report should be modified (see overleaf).

Indicators of going concern problems

- Financial
- Operational
- Other

ISA 710 Comparative Information – Corresponding Figures and Comparative Financial Statements

- Corresponding figures
- Comparative financial statements

ISA 720 The Auditor's Responsibilities Relating to Other Information

- Material inconsistencies between (i) items audited within F/S, (ii) items presented outside the F/S and not audited ('Other Information') and/or (iii) the auditor's knowledge obtained during the course of the audit – which one needs correction?
- Discuss with management to establish whether there is material misstatement or if the auditor's understanding of the entity needs to be updated:
  (i) Amendment required to F/S? Consider further audit procedures and possible modified opinion if not amended
  (ii) Amendment required to 'Other Information'? Understand, request revision – if not corrected, either withdraw or modify report (see overleaf)
  (iii) Auditor's understanding inadequate? Respond in line with ISAs (such as ISA 315).

Knowledge diagnostic

1. Overall review of the financial statements

Overall review of financial statements will determine whether or not **appropriate accounting policies** have been used, if information published is **compatible with audit findings**, if disclosure is adequate and if information **complies** with all statutory and regulatory requirements. The stage of the audit just before the opinion is signed is crucial and the auditor must perform a **final quality control review**. This review will also involve an evaluation of any **misstatements identified during the audit** to ensure the correct treatment of any that remain **uncorrected**.

2. Representations

Representations from those responsible for the financial statements are used to **supplement** the opinion where no other evidence exists. There are procedures for obtaining them and auditors must be aware of what to do if these representations are either not provided or lead to further questions.

3. Subsequent events

Auditors need to be aware of any **subsequent events (adjusting or non-adjusting)** that may occur either before or after they issue their auditor's report to ensure they still give the right opinion in light of these events.

4. Going concern

Both **management** and **auditors** have responsibilities regarding **going concern**, but auditors should be mindful of any issues that indicate possible going concern problems in any financial, operational or other areas of the business.

5. Corresponding figures and comparatives

Auditors need to be aware of the implications for their auditor's reports if there are issues with either **corresponding figures** or **comparative financial statements** in the financial statements.

6. Other information

As well as the audited accounts, the auditor has to be aware of any **other information** within the financial statements and ensure that it is both consistent and factually correct. In the event of any **material misstatements** or **cases where the auditor's understanding of the entity and its environment needs to be updated**, the auditor must determine what requires amendment and how best to act.

Further study guidance

Question practice

Now try the following from the Further question practice bank (available in the digital edition of the Workbook):

- Question 20 'Bestwood Electronics' tests theory and application related to subsequent events.
- Question 21 'Bingham Engineering' tests your knowledge of going concern and how you might apply certain procedures when reaching any conclusions about the going concern status of an entity.
- Question 22 'Lambley Properties' tests your ability to apply your knowledge of written representations to a more complex scenario.

Further reading

There are some technical articles on the ACCA website written by members of the AAA examining team which are relevant to some of the topics covered in this chapter that you should read:

- *Evaluation of misstatements*
- *Completing the audit*
- *Going concern*

Own research

Obtain a copy of a recent set of financial statements for an organisation and find as many real-life examples of the following issues discussed in this chapter as you can:

- Going concern
- Other information
- Subsequent events
- Corresponding figures

Activity answers

Activity 1: Subsequent events

> **Approach**
>
> This is revision from AA – what would you do if you wanted to be as sure as you could that there are no issues still outstanding when you sign the auditor's report?

Suggested solution

- Review procedures management has established to ensure that subsequent events are identified.
- Read minutes of board meetings, shareholder meetings and audit committees that have taken place since the year end.
- Obtain and review the latest available interim financial statements and/or management accounts, budgets and other related management reports.
- Enquire of the entity's legal counsel concerning litigation and claims.
- Enquire of management as to whether any subsequent events have occurred which might affect the financial statements.

Reporting

Learning objectives

On completion of this chapter, you should be able to:

	Syllabus reference no.
Determine the form and content of an auditor's report and assess the appropriateness of the contents of an auditor's report containing an unmodified opinion.	E3(a)
Recognise and evaluate the factors to be taken into account when forming an audit opinion in a given situation, including the effect of uncorrected misstatement, and justify audit opinions that are consistent with the results of audit procedures.	E3(b)
Critically appraise the form and content of an auditor's report in a given situation.	E3(c)
Assess whether or not a proposed audit opinion is appropriate.	E3(d)
Advise on the actions which may be taken by the auditor in the event that a modified auditor's opinion is issued.	E3(e)
Recognise when the use of an emphasis of matter paragraph, other matter paragraph and KAM disclosure would be appropriate and recommend and justify the content of each.	E3(g)
Critically assess the quality of a report to those charged with governance and management.	E4(a)
Advise on the content of reports to those charged with governance and management in a given situation.	E4(b)

Business and exam context

At this level, you are not only expected to know what the audit opinion is and how it is presented, but are also required to determine audit opinions and also assess the appropriateness of an audit opinion formed by another person.

In this chapter we shall also consider the form of the auditor's report, the criticism that it receives and whether it enables an auditor to express properly a true and fair view. Recent developments are considered, dwelling in detail on the inclusion of key audit matters in some auditor's reports. We shall also look at the auditor's requirements in relation to reporting to those charged with governance.

Auditor reporting questions at this level tend to be challenging, but 'do-able', particularly if you have practised similar questions and have established a step by step approach to questions on forming an auditor's opinion. You are very likely to encounter a question on auditor's reports in Section B of the exam, and are guaranteed a question on syllabus Section E (covering completion, subsequent events and going concern, and reporting).

Chapter overview

1 ISA 700 – an overview

The **primary objective** of the audit is to express an **opinion** on the **truth** and **fairness** of the financial statements. The format of the basic auditor's report is laid down in **ISA 700** *Forming an Opinion and Reporting on Financial Statements*. This is supported by **ISA 701** *Communicating Key Audit Matters in the Independent Auditor's Report*.

> ### PER alert
>
> One of the competencies you require to fulfil **Performance Objective 20** of the PER is the ability to prepare auditors' reports in accordance with relevant standards on auditing, or equivalent standards, and applicable regulations and legislations. You can apply the knowledge you obtain in this chapter of the Workbook to help demonstrate this competency.

2 Standard unmodified report with unmodified opinion

The standard report as laid down by ISAs 700, 701 and 720 looks like this (in overview):

INDEPENDENT AUDITOR'S REPORT

To the shareholders of the company [or other appropriate addressee.]

Opinion

[Includes the individual statements and the reporting period under review for the company being audited. It can use either 'give a true and fair view' or 'presents fairly, in all material respects' and states the relevant GAAP adopted.]

Basis for opinion

[This is always presented after the opinion and explains how the audit was conducted: the role of ISAs and the IESBA Code of Ethics as well as the audit evidence being sufficient and appropriate to provide a basis for the auditor's opinion.]

Key audit matters

[As per ISA 701, matters of most significance from the audit; required for all listed entities.]

Other information

[As per ISA 720, communicates that there is nothing to report regarding other information.]

Responsibilities of management and those charged with governance for the financial statements

[Preparation and fair presentation of the financial statements, including internal controls, and the assessment of the company's ability to continue as a going concern.]

Auditor's responsibilities for the audit of the financial statements

[A detailed summary of the auditor's objectives, starting with obtaining reasonable assurance about the financial statements being free from material misstatements due to fraud or error. Stresses the role of professional judgement and scepticism over accounting policies and estimates, judgements, internal controls, presentation, disclosure and communicating key audit matters and other issues with those charged with governance.]

Report on other legal and regulatory requirements

[Form and content of this section of the auditor's report will vary depending on the nature of the auditor's other reporting responsibilities.]

Signed

[Auditor's name and/or signature, address and date of the auditor's report.]

Essential reading

See Chapter 11 of the Essential reading for more on the auditor's report, including a full reproduction of the auditor's report.

The Essential reading is available as an Appendix of the digital edition of the Workbook.

2.1 ISA 260 *Communication with those Charged with Governance*

In addition to reporting to shareholders, the external auditor is expected to communicate matters of **audit importance** to those charged with governance (TCWG) – usually the directors, but this could be an **audit committee** as well, so the auditor should establish **to whom they must report**. This should be an ongoing, two-way dialogue and is initiated at the engagement stage to avoid any omissions, as well as **how** (in writing) and **when** (described in the ISA as 'timely').

The **items to be communicated** relate to the **auditor's responsibilities** as part of the audit and information relevant to the audit **from TCWG**, as well as any **issues arising** from the audit. This is sometimes referred to as the **report to management** and includes **significant findings** from the audit, such as views about the chosen **accounting policies**, **difficulties** encountered **during the audit** and any other matters relevant to the **oversight of the financial reporting purpose**.

2.2 ISA 265 *Communicating Deficiencies in Internal Control to those Charged with Governance and Management*

This standard deals with any **specific internal control issues** identified to ensure they are communicated promptly for the right action to be taken. The issues communicated are only those identified **during the course of the audit** as **necessary to the creation of the financial statements under review**: they are not an assessment of the overall adequacy of the accounting and internal control systems currently operated by management.

Deficiencies are classified as **significant** if they warrant the attention of TCWG. Findings are usually presented along with **recommendations** and a **timescale**.

Essential reading

See Chapter 11 of the Essential reading for more on how the auditor reports their findings to those charged with governance and management.

2.3 ISA 701 *Communicating Key Audit Matters in the Independent Auditor's Report*

If the auditor has a responsibility to report **matters of audit significance** under ISAs 260 and 265, why are key audit matters (KAMs) included in the auditor's report? **ISA 701 requires the auditor to determine KAMs** from the matters communicated to TCWG and, having already formed an opinion on the financial statements, **communicate those matters to shareholders and other users of the financial statements** by describing them in the auditor's report before reporting them as KAMs to TCWG.

The auditor should keep appropriate documentation of all KAMs: they are defined as being those matters that, in the auditor's professional judgement, were **of most significance** in the audit of the financial statements of the current period. They are **required for all listed entity auditor's reports** and are part of the standard unmodified report (so they are not the same as Emphasis of Matter or Other Matter paragraphs and do not lead to a modification of the auditor's opinion).

Identifying such matters requires the auditor to use **professional judgement** – for example:

- **Material, complex** or **subjective** items, especially any associated misstatements
- Matters where the auditor encountered **difficulty** or required **extra audit effort**
- Areas where audit procedures were **difficult to apply** or where **several issues converged**

It should be obvious that KAMs are **audit matters**, not just difficult areas of financial reporting. The decision-making framework looks like this:

(Source: IAASB Determining and Communicating Key Audit Matters (IAASB 2016b))

KAMs should be disclosed within the 'Key audit matters' section of the auditor's report stating **why** they were assessed as KAMs, **how** they were addressed during the audit and the **note** from the financial statements where more detail is supplied by the audited entity. If it is felt that disclosure would compromise the need for confidentiality (eg in cases of money laundering) or if the law precludes it, the auditor can choose not to communicate specific KAMs.

It is extremely unlikely that there will be **no KAMs** from an audit but if this is the case, there is still a section headed 'Key audit matters' stating that there are none. **Going concern uncertainty** is not treated as a KAM, as that would have its own section if required within a modified auditor's report (see below).

Essential reading

See Chapter 11 of the Essential reading for further details of how the auditor's report has become more informative over recent years, including the perceived benefits of using KAMs.

The Essential reading is available as an Appendix of the digital edition of the Workbook.

3 Modifications to the auditor's report

Note. The ISAs do not specifically use the terms 'modified report' or 'unmodified report' but you will find they are often used to help clarify certain situations, including those when the auditor's report has some form of additional communication (such as the use of a going concern or emphasis of matter paragraph) but the audit opinion remains unmodified. In addition, remember that the term 'present fairly' can be used instead of 'true and fair view' when expressing an unmodified opinion on the financial statements.

4 Modified report with unmodified opinion

4.1 ISA 706 *Emphasis of Matter Paragraphs and Other Matter Paragraphs in the Independent Auditor's Report*

In the auditor's opinion, it may be **necessary** to **draw users' attention** to matters presented **within the financial statements** or **other information** in the annual report that are of such importance they are **fundamental to users' understanding** of either the financial statements or the rest of the audit including the report.

An **'Emphasis of matter'** paragraph draws users' attention to issues that are **adequately disclosed within the financial statements** that they **need to see** in order to understand them properly, such as:

- Uncertainties relating to future outcomes of exceptional litigation or regulatory action (where there are multiple uncertainties, the auditor may feel it is appropriate to express a disclaimer of opinion instead – however, **'Emphasis of matter' paragraphs are not used to address going concern uncertainties,** as a separate section of the auditor's report is used to communicate such matters – see below)
- Early application of new accounting standards
- A major catastrophe that has had, or continues to have, a significant effect on the entity's financial position
- If a new auditor's report is issued (such as when ISA 560 *Subsequent Events* applies)

It is important to understand the **distinction** between **KAMs** (matters of most significance to the audit) and **emphasis of matter paragraphs** (fundamental to users' understanding of the financial statements). Emphasis of matter paragraphs should not be used as a **substitute** for any required KAMs, while **KAMs that are fundamental to users' understanding** of the financial statements should be **prioritised within the KAMs section** of the auditor's report. Similarly, matters that **did not require significant auditor attention** but which may still be **fundamental to users' understanding** of the financial statements should form part of an emphasis of matter paragraph (ISA 706: paras. A1–3).

The additional paragraph should be added immediately **after the basis for opinion paragraph** in the auditor's report, using the heading **'Emphasis of matter'** including **full details** of the matter and the **location** within the financial statements which explains the issue further. It is up to the auditor's judgement whether to place the Emphasis of Matter paragraph **before or after the 'Key audit matters' section**.

The paragraph states that the auditor's **opinion** is **not modified in respect of this matter** – the use of such a paragraph **must only occur** if the matter in question has been **adequately treated and disclosed** in the financial statements and the auditor is in agreement with this.

An **'Other matter'** paragraph draws users' attention to issues **outside the scope of the financial statements** (so therefore items not addressed by 'Emphasis of matter' paragraphs) and can include anything else that users need to know about the audit, such as:

- Issues related to **ISA 510 *Initial Engagements – Opening Balances***
- Items relating to the conduct of the audit (eg being unable to withdraw as auditor)
- Disclosure or comment required by laws, regulations or local GAAP

Other Matter paragraphs must not refer to KAMs as other matters are by definition beyond the scope of the audited financial statements. Similarly, **ISA 720 *The Auditor's Responsibilities Relating to Other Information*** regarding **other information** does not make use of an 'Other matter' paragraph either, as this is referred to within a separate section of the auditor's report.

The additional paragraph is headed **'Other matter'** and shall be included **after the basis for opinion paragraph, after any 'Emphasis of matter' paragraph** and **after the 'Key audit matters' section**.

4.2 Modification of the auditor's report due to going concern issues

In previous sections of these materials, we learned that if there was a material uncertainty related to going concern but the use of the going concern assumption was still appropriate, as long as the disclosure made by the audited entity was deemed adequate by the auditor, an unmodified opinion could be issued but a **separate disclosure** was required within the auditor's report.

This appears **immediately after the 'Basis for opinion' section**: remember that any uncertainty related to going concern is not a KAM and does not get reported by an Emphasis of matter paragraph.

The following is an illustration of what this section of a modified auditor's report would look like (taken from **ISA 570 *Going Concern***):

Material Uncertainty Related to Going Concern

We draw attention to Note 6 in the financial statements, which indicates that the Company incurred a net loss of ZZZ during the year ended 31 December 20X1 and, as of that date, the Company's current liabilities exceeded its total assets by YYY. As stated in Note 6, these events or conditions, along with other matters as set forth in Note 6, indicate that a material uncertainty exists that may cast significant doubt on the Company's ability to continue as a going concern. Our opinion is not modified in respect of this matter.

Activity 1: Spot the ball

On the proforma, indicate where the following items would appear on a modified auditor's report:

(1) A **misstatement of the other information** presented within the document containing the financial statements

(2)   A **material uncertainty related to going concern** adequately disclosed in the financial statements

(3)   An **Emphasis of matter paragraph** explaining an uncertainty related to ongoing litigation

(4)   An **Other matter paragraph** explaining that the prior year financial statements were audited by another firm

INDEPENDENT AUDITOR'S REPORT

Opinion

Basis for opinion

Key audit matters

Other information

Responsibilities of management and those charged with governance for the financial statements

Auditor's responsibilities for the audit of the financial statements

Report on other legal and regulatory requirements

Signed

---

5   Modified audit opinions

5.1   ISA 705 *Modifications to the Opinion in the Independent Auditor's Report*

There are **three types of modified opinion** that the auditor can issue (depending on the **cause** or **nature of the matter** giving rise to any modification and the **impact** or **pervasiveness** of that matter on the financial statements):

(a)   A qualified opinion;

(b)   An adverse opinion; or

(c)   A disclaimer of opinion.

From ISA 705 para. 5a, the term **'pervasive'** has the following **definitions**:

The matters giving rise to any modifications:

- Are **not confined** to **specific elements**, accounts or items of the financial statements;

- If so confined, represent or could represent a **substantial proportion** of the financial statements; or

- In relation to disclosures, are **fundamental** to users' understanding of the financial statements.

The types of modification can be summarised as follows by considering the **judgements** required by the auditor in two key respects – **nature (cause)** and **pervasiveness (impact)**:

Nature of matter giving rise to the modification	Auditor's judgement about the pervasiveness of the effects or possible effects on the financial statements	
	Material but not pervasive	Material and pervasive
Financial statements are materially misstated (The term 'Disagreement' is used in the UK)	**Qualified opinion** ('except for the effects of the matter described in the basis for qualified opinion section...')	**Adverse opinion** ('because of the significance of the matter discussed...the financial statements do not give a true and fair view...')
Inability to obtain sufficient appropriate audit evidence (The term 'Limitation on scope' is used in the UK)	**Qualified opinion** ('except for the possible effects of the matter described in the basis for qualified opinion section...')	**Disclaimer of opinion** ('we do not express an opinion ...because of the significance of the matter described...')

5.2 Material misstatements

The circumstances leading to a modification due to material misstatement could include:

- The **appropriateness** of selected accounting policies (either inconsistent with the applicable financial reporting framework or those that do not lead to fair presentation)
- The **application** of selected accounting policies (through either inconsistency or error)
- The appropriateness or adequacy of **disclosures** in the financial statements

5.3 Inability to obtain sufficient appropriate audit evidence

The circumstances leading to a modification due to being unable to obtain sufficient appropriate audit evidence are as follows:

- Circumstances **beyond the control of the entity** (such as the loss of records in a fire)
- Circumstances relating to the **nature or timing of the auditor's work** (eg the auditor being appointed after the date of counting physical inventory stocks)
- Limitations on the scope of the audit **imposed by management** (such as management denying access to third parties for external confirmations)

 Essential reading

See Chapter 11 of the Essential reading for illustrations of the wording used when the auditor's opinion is modified.

The Essential reading is available as an Appendix of the digital edition of the Workbook.

5.4 Modifications within the report when the audit opinion is modified

When the auditor has to issue a **modified opinion**, the 'Basis for opinion' section should provide a description of the matter giving rise to the modification, the **details** of any **corrections** required (only possible with misstatement due to being able to quantify such issues, or recommend the required disclosure) or the **uncertainty** remaining (by definition, usually unquantifiable). This should be titled 'Basis for qualified/adverse/disclaimer of opinion' and follows the opinion paragraph.

Similarly, for modified opinions, the **opinion paragraph** should be titled 'Qualified/Adverse /Disclaimer of opinion' and should use the relevant modification terminology depending on the opinion chosen.

5.4.1 Actions when an auditor's opinion is modified

When a modified opinion is likely, the auditor should consider the following implications:

TCWG need to be informed of any such issue and the reason for it (allowing TCWG opportunity to respond)	**External consultation** with regulators or others may be required	**Management integrity** may be called into question (including any representations supplied) meaning an EQCR is required	**Possible withdrawal** from the engagement (and seek legal advice?)

Activity 2: Santa

You are an audit partner. Your firm carries out the audit of Santa, a listed company. Because the company is listed, you have been asked to perform a second partner review of the audit file for the year ended 31 December 20X3 before the audit opinion is finalised. Reported profit before tax is $2.35 million and total assets are $9.5 million.

You have read the following note from the audit file.

'Debt: Rudolph

There is a debt outstanding from Rudolph, a limited liability company, from January 20X3 in respect of a vehicle developed by Santa to Rudolph's own specification. Rudolph has disputed the quality of the vehicle and also does not agree that it was made completely to the specification. The company has submitted the dispute with Santa to arbitration, in accordance with its contractual agreement. Rudolph was a major customer up until the time of the dispute, often accounting for 50% of sales ledger total. It has not placed any orders with Santa in 20X3 or 20X4, preferring a French supplier which is Santa's only real competitor in the European market.

The directors of Santa are confident that at arbitration Rudolph will be required to pay the full bill, which is in the region of $1 million. They state that the quality of the machine is irrefutable and that any amendments to the specification were only safety improvements. The arbitral decision, which is not subject to appeal, is expected after the date of the AGM. Given their confidence, the directors of Santa have refused to refer to the dispute in the financial statements.

Given that the outcome of this arbitration is by no means certain, the potential overstatement of the debt is material and the permanent loss of Rudolph's custom could affect the going concern opinion, the following modification to the auditor's report is proposed:

Disagreement on Accounting Policies – Inappropriate Accounting Method – Adverse opinion

No allowance has currently been made for the impairment of an outstanding debt from Rudolph in respect of a dispute over a contract which has currently been submitted to arbitration, which, in our opinion, is not in accordance with International Financial Reporting Standards. An allowance of $1 million should be made in respect of this debt. Accordingly, receivables, profit for the period and retained earnings should be reduced by $1 million. Also, due to its significance, this allowance should have been disclosed separately in accordance with IAS 1 *Presentation of Financial Statements*.

In our opinion, because of the effects of the matters discussed in the preceding paragraph, the financial statements do not give a true and fair view of the financial position of Rudolph as of 31 December 20X3, and of its financial performance and its cash flows for the year then ended in accordance with International Financial Reporting Standards.'

Required

Comment on the appropriateness of the proposed audit opinion, and critically appraise the form and content of the proposed auditor's report, recommending improvements where necessary.

Note. You are **not** required to redraft the extracts from the auditor's report.

Solution

 Essential reading

See Chapter 11 of the Essential reading for further details of how to critically appraise an auditor's report.

Chapter summary

```
                              ┌─────────────┐
                              │  Reporting  │
                              └─────────────┘
```

ISA 700 – an overview

- ISA 700 *Forming an Opinion and Reporting on Financial Statements*
- ISA 701 *Communicating Key Audit Matters in the Auditor's Report Outside of F/S*
- ISA 720 *The auditor's responsibilities relating to other information*

Standard unmodified report with unmodified opinion

Key contents:
- Title – independent auditor's report
- Addressee
- Opinion
- Basis for opinion
- Key audit matters
- Other information
- Responsibilities
- Legal and regulatory
- Signature
- Date

ISA 260 Communication with those Charged with Governance
- ISA 260 addresses points made in the report to management – matters of audit importance (eg adjustments required, disagreements over treatment)
- ISA 260 also defines those charged with governance (TCWG) at engagement stage

---

ISA 265 Communicating Deficiencies in Internal Control to those Charged with Governance

ISA 265 ensures that any specific internal control weaknesses identified during the audit are brought to the attention of those charged with governance and not subject to management bias.

Modified report with unmodified opinion (ISAs 706 and 570)

Emphasis of matter paragraph
- Opinion is **unmodified**
- Draws attention to uncertainty disclosed in F/S (not G/C)

Going concern paragraph
- Opinion is **unmodified**
- Draws attention to **going concern (G/C) issues only**

Other matter paragraph
- Opinion is **unmodified**
- Draws attention to **issues outside of F/S**

Modified audit opinions (ISA 705)

Insufficient or inappropriate audit evidence
- If material to F/S but not pervasive, issue a **Qualified opinion** ('*except for*')
- If unable to form an opinion (both material and pervasive) issue a **Disclaimer of opinion** ('*we do not express an opinion*')

Material misstatement
- If material to F/S but not pervasive, issue a **Qualified opinion** ('*except for*')
- If misstatement is so severe (both material and pervasive) issue an **Adverse opinion** ('*the F/S do not give a true and fair view*')

BPP LEARNING MEDIA

Knowledge diagnostic

1. Reporting

Auditors' reports are the only tangible output produced by the auditor; it is therefore very important that the **opinion** expressed is appropriate in the circumstances and the **report** follows the correct approach.

2. The standard auditor's report

The basic auditor's report uses ISAs 700, 701 and 720 to produce a **standardised report format** depending on the **jurisdiction** applied. ISAs 260 and 265 cover points made in the report to management.

3. Modifications to the auditor's report

It is important that you understand the **different modifications** that can be made to the standard auditor's report, including forms of **additional communication**.

4. Communication of additional information

To ensure that the users of financial statements are not misled, additional information is required such as **Emphasis of matter** (drawing attention to matters adequately disclosed within the financial statements) and **Other matter** (anything outside the scope of the financial statements) paragraphs and disclosure of **going concern** uncertainties.

5. Modifications to the audit opinion

The auditor has to decide on the **nature** and **pervasiveness** of any matters that lead to opinions such as **qualified**, **adverse** or a **disclaimer** of opinion. Such matters can relate to material misstatements ('disagreement' in the UK) or insufficient/inappropriate audit evidence ('limitations on scope' in the UK)

Further study guidance

Question practice

Now try the following from the Further question practice bank (available in the digital edition of the Workbook):

- Question 12 'Illuminations' tests theory and application related to appointments and opening balances, so should be viewed as good revision of what you have covered so far.
- Question 15 Recognition' requires you to think about what's really happening and consider the implications for the auditor's report.
- Question 23 'Maple' is a more traditional question testing fraud as well as your knowledge of reporting.
- Question 24 'Petrie' blends together a number of syllabus areas but requires you to know the impact on the auditor's report and opinion.

Further reading

There are some technical articles on the ACCA website written by members of the AAA examining team which are relevant to some of the topics covered in this chapter that you should read:

- *Exam technique for Advanced Audit and Assurance – part 5 auditor reporting*
- *Auditor's reports to those charged with governance*

Own research

- Obtain a copy of a recent set of financial statements for an organisation and find as many real-life examples of auditor's reports as you can.

Activity answers

Activity 1: Spot the ball

> **Approach**
>
> Find the relevant content for each element of the auditor's report in the Workbook and the work out where it should go on the proforma for each of the four situations outlined.

Suggested solution

INDEPENDENT AUDITOR'S REPORT

Opinion

Basis for opinion

Material uncertainty related to going concern – after the 'Basis for opinion' section.

Emphasis of matter paragraph – before or after 'Key audit matters' (if used) depending on severity and likely to be below any going concern issue.

Misstatement in the other information – below 'Basis for opinion' but above 'Key audit matters' and likely to be below any Emphasis of Matter paragraph.

Key audit matters

Emphasis of matter paragraph – before or after 'Key audit matters' (if used) depending on severity and likely to be below any going concern issue.

Other matter paragraph – after the 'Basis for opinion' and 'Key audit matters' (if used) and then after any Emphasis of Matter paragraph.

~~Other information~~

(**Misstatement in the other information** – this will **not** appear here any longer.)

Responsibilities of management and those charged with governance for the financial statements

Auditor's responsibilities for the audit of the financial statements

Report on other legal and regulatory requirements

Signed

Note. 'Key audit matters' is presented here as best practice, although it is only required for listed entities.

Activity 2: Santa

> **Approach**
>
> You should work your way through the scenario and challenge every statement made – is it consistent with the rest of the information presented here? Does it conform with the approach that we know an auditor's report should follow? Is the opinion appropriate under the circumstances? Are there any other issues here that we need to pick up outside the auditor's report that might be relevant?

Suggested solution

Allowance for receivables

The receivables balance for the year is potentially overstated by $1 million, depending on the outcome of arbitral proceedings. The amount is material, being 43% of profit and 11% of total assets, and any settlement by which the price is reduced by more than 10% would be **material** to the statement of profit or loss:

Profit before tax = $2.35 million. Materiality = (say) 5% of PBT.

5% × $2.35m = $117,500 which is nearly 12% of contract price ($1,000,000)

The outcome of the arbitration does not appear certain, despite the directors' feelings on the subject. It is clear that they did make amendments to the specification, albeit for what they saw as the right reasons, and therefore, as auditor we must be aware of the possibility that this price will be materially reduced, rendering the reported debt overstated.

In these circumstances, an allowance for the impairment of the debt should be made to some extent. We should take advice from the company's legal advisers as to whether they estimate the price will be reduced at arbitration, and if so, by how much (suitable comments about IAS 37 *Provisions, Contingent Liabilities and Contingent Assets* could be made here).

If Santa's directors refuse to make any necessary allowance in the financial statements, the auditor's opinion should be modified on the grounds of **material misstatement** due to this lack of allowance as has been suggested on the audit file. However, this opinion should probably only be a **qualified ('except for')** rather than an adverse opinion as suggested on the audit file as, although it would be material, it does not appear to be pervasive to the financial statements, but rather confined to one item.

Inappropriate paragraph headings, contents and placement

The proposed auditor's report shows almost all the right content but is presented in the wrong order – the opinion section needs the heading '**Qualified opinion**' and should be positioned at the start of the auditor's report. However, the company referred to within the opinion section should be 'Santa', not 'Rudolph'.

The details of the various disagreements represent the basis of that opinion and should therefore be presented in the next section, headed '**Basis for qualified opinion**'. However, reference to IAS 37 *Provisions, Contingent Liabilities and Contingent Assets* should be made here to explain the reasons for the allowance that should be made against receivables.

IAS 1 disclosure

If a material allowance against this debt is required, as discussed above, separate disclosure will be required in respect of it in the notes in accordance with IAS 1 *Presentation of Financial Statements*. Again, if the directors fail to amend the financial statements to reflect this **disclosure**, the auditor's report should be modified on the grounds of **material misstatement** due to this lack of disclosure. Again, this is not pervasive to the financial statements, so a **qualified ('except for')** opinion, rather than the suggested adverse opinion, would be appropriate.

Going concern

While the outcome of the arbitration might not in itself affect the going concern basis of the company, irretrievable loss of a major customer (representing half of the company's revenue) could have seriously detrimental effects and does at least need to be considered by the auditor.

Hopefully the audit team has reviewed the going concern position of the company and this is all documented on file and has, if necessary, been disclosed in the financial statements. If these events present a material uncertainty for Santa, the auditor's report might also have to be modified.

There could be sufficient uncertainty about the company's future to warrant an additional paragraph from the auditor called '**Material uncertainty related to going concern**' placed after the 'Basis of opinion' section where the auditor would set out the fact that such a material uncertainty existed. If **sufficient disclosure** had been made about this uncertainty by directors, the auditor would use this to draw attention to this disclosure note within the financial statements and state that the opinion was not modified in that respect. However, if **insufficient disclosure**

were given, the auditor would address this within the 'Basis of opinion' section of the auditor's report and **qualify the auditor's opinion ('except for')** on the grounds of lack of disclosure.

Events after the reporting period

The arbitral decision is not expected until after the AGM, when the financial statements will have been issued to members. However, although the IAS 10 *Events After the Reporting Period* time frame for adjustments finishes when the financial statements are authorised for issue, the **auditor's duty** in respect of subsequent events continues under ISA 560 *Subsequent Events*. An early decision before the financial statements are authorised for issue would directly impact the financial statements and might require **further amendment** and a **change in the audit opinion**. A decision after that date may require the financial statements to be **reissued** and the auditor may need to seek legal advice as to possible actions if the directors refuse to do so.

Skills checkpoint 4

Completion and reporting

Overview

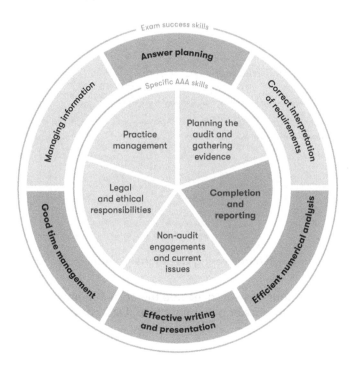

Introduction

The ACCA has confirmed that one of the 25-mark questions will always come from syllabus Section E, and consequently candidates should be prepared to answer a question relating to completion, review and reporting. As a result, this skills checkpoint will cover some of the topics most likely to be seen in these types of questions and the skills required to produce great answers.

Questions on completion and reporting tend to go well together – when you consider issues such as going concern, subsequent events and the evaluation of the auditor's findings, inevitably they will need to considered in the context of the auditor's report and any other communication that might be necessary.

If you struggled with any of the terminology or approaches adopted for this part of the syllabus, you are advised to return to Chapters 10 and 11 now to refresh your memory as this checkpoint assumes you are familiar with the learning materials.

AAA Skill: Completion and reporting

A step by step technique for approaching questions testing this part of the syllabus now follows (you may find that some of these techniques are suitable for other parts of the syllabus as well – why not start practising them now?)

> **STEP 1:**
> Determine which parts of the syllabus the requirement is testing.

> **STEP 2:**
> Actively read the scenario to identify the key issues.

> **STEP 3:**
> Consider the implications of the isues identified in Step 2 for the auditor's opinion (both cause and extent).

> **STEP 4:**
> Consider whether there are any additonal impacts on the auditor's report from the issues identified in Step 2.

> **STEP 5:**
> Write your answer.

Exam success skills

There are some key exam skills that will help you when answering questions from this topic which are summarised below:

- **Answer planning**. In order to help you **tailor your answer** to include the **correct number of points**, a form of '**scaffolding**' to construct your answer plan might help. Let's consider a recent exam question.

Required

For each of the three matters described above:

(i) Explain the matters which should be discussed with management in relation to each of the uncorrected misstatements, and

(ii) Assuming that management does not adjust the misstatements identified, evaluate the effect of each on the audit opinion.

Note. The total marks will be split equally between each matter.

(15 marks)

With 195 minutes to find 100 marks, that works out as **1.95 minutes per mark**, meaning this 15-mark requirement should take **no more than 29 minutes in total**. 25% of that time would mean **7 minutes for reading, thinking and planning**, leaving you 22 minutes to write your answer. What will you need to produce for each of the three matters mentioned in the requirement?

	(i) Matters to be discussed	(ii) Effect on the opinion	Marks for each matter
Matter 1	1) 2) 3)	1) 2) 3)	5 marks

	(i) Matters to be discussed	(ii) Effect on the opinion	Marks for each matter
Matter 2	1) 2) 3)	1) 2) 3)	5 marks
Matter 3	1) 2) 3)	1) 2) 3)	5 marks

During your 7 minutes of reading, thinking and planning time, you should devise something like this and use it as a form of **scaffolding** to support your answer. We are told in the requirement that the 15 marks are split equally between the three matters, so each should score 5 marks, and for each matter, there are two tasks: (i) the matters to be considered and (ii) the impact on the audit opinion. In general, well-explained points score 1 mark, so to score 5 marks for each matter, you will need two or three points for each task. By filling in as many of the shaded gaps in the scaffolding above as you can, you are giving yourself the best chance of tailoring your answer to the requirements.

This approach may seem like a lot to do in only 7 minutes, but it should help you make the most of your valuable reading, thinking and planning time.

- **Efficient numerical analysis.** Questions that test this part of the syllabus are usually going to require two main areas where you will need to consider calculations: the first is to determine the level of **materiality** so you can judge whether or not something is material; the second is to confirm the **amount of any misstatement(s)**. Let's look at both of these using the following example:

  "A company's draft financial statements include an inventory balance of $325,000 for goods which have recently been banned by legislation. A resale market for similar goods has appeared but is not expected to generate more than 50% of cost price at best. The draft profit before tax of the company is $4.25 million. What is the potential impact on the auditor's opinion if the inventory balance is not amended?"

  First, the potential misstatement if no changes are made is going to start at $162,500 (50% of $325,000) but could **rise** as the resale value is 50% of cost price **at best**, so if this value falls, the misstatement would increase. **Secondly**, materiality would start at 5% of $4.25 million = $212,500 meaning that if the resale value fell to $112,500 (calculated as $325,000 - $212,500, around 35% of cost price) the misstatement (the amount that the inventory is overvalued by) would become material, most likely leading to a qualified opinion. Further work would be required to determine the likely resale value before this could be confirmed.

- **Effective writing and presentation.** This should be a fairly quick win – a common criticism of candidates' answers to questions testing completion and reporting is that they are too vague and often cover a variety of points in the hope that the right one is buried somewhere within the text (the so-called 'scatter-gun' approach).

  You can address this by either committing to a course of action and simply stating your conclusion or (if there is further uncertainty that cannot be confirmed without further work being done) presenting a range of options depending on the outcome of that further work. Make your answers as clear as possible to give yourself the best chance of success.

- **Good time management.** In this exam, the ability to manage your time across **all three questions** is **vital**. When reading through the exam you should calculate how long you need to spend on **each question**. However, this should then be broken down into **individual requirements,** and should also show **when each of these will expire**. Therefore you should **annotate the question** with the time for each part and when you should finish it. Remember to use **1.95 minutes per mark** here. Once this is matched up with your 'scaffolding' skills above, you should have a really tight plan.

Continuing the example from above, your plan would have looked like this:

	(i) Matters to be discussed	(ii) Effect on the opinion	Marks for each matter	29 minutes overall Start: 11.25 & End: 11.54
Matter 1	1) 2) 3)	1) 2) 3)	5 marks	5 marks = 10 minutes To 11.35
Matter 2	1) 2) 3)	1) 2) 3)	5 marks	5 marks = 10 minutes To 11.45
Matter 3	1) 2) 3)	1) 2) 3)	5 marks	5 marks = 10 minutes To 11.55

You can permit yourself a **slight time overrun** to try and finish each question, but **no more than a couple of minutes**: you must remember that the more time spent on one question automatically **takes time from the others**. You should only aim to overrun on your **best questions**, when the extra time is likely to score more marks – don't waste time finishing off a question that you are unlikely to score well on at the expense of another **higher scoring requirement**.

Skill activity

STEP 1 Determine which part(s) of the syllabus the requirement is testing.

You are an audit partner. Your firm carries out the audit of Branch Co, a public company. Because the company is a public interest entity, you have been asked to perform a second partner review of the audit file for the year ended 30 June 20X8 before the audit opinion is finalised. Reported profit before tax is $1.65 million and the statement of financial position total is $7.6 million.

You have read the following notes from the audit file.

Earnings per share

As required by IAS 33 *Earnings per share*, the company has disclosed both basic and diluted earnings per share. The diluted earnings per share has been incorrectly calculated because the share options held by a director were not included in the calculations. Disclosed diluted earnings per share are 22.9c. Had the share options held by the director been included, this figure would have been 22.4c. This difference is immaterial.

Financial performance statement

The directors have currently not amended certain financial performance ratios in this statement to reflect the changes made to the financial statements as a result of the auditors' work. The difference between the reported ratios and the correct ratios is minimal.

Opinion

We recommend that an unmodified auditor's report be issued.

A corporate governance statement referring to the UK Corporate Governance Code is to be issued as part of the annual report, but there is no evidence on file that this has been reviewed by the audit team. You are aware that the company does not have an audit committee.

You are also aware that the director exercised their share options last week.

Required

Comment[26] on the suitability of the proposed audit opinion and other matters arising in the light of your review. Your comments should include an indication of what form the auditor's report should take.

[26] Topics covered: 1. Critical appraisal of draft opinion 2. Review of audit evidence collected 3. Other information re: ISA720 4. Subsequent events? 5. Forming an audit opinion 6. Other reporting?

STEP 2 Actively read the scenario to identify the key issues, matching them to the syllabus areas identified in Step 1.

You are an audit partner. Your firm carries out the audit of Branch Co, a public company. Because the company is a public interest entity, you have been asked to perform a second partner review of the audit file for the year ended 30 June 20X8 before the audit opinion is finalised. Reported profit before tax is $1.65 million and the statement of financial position total is $7.6 million.

You have read the following notes from the audit file.

Earnings per share

As required by IAS 33 *Earnings per share*, the company has disclosed both basic and diluted earnings per share. The diluted earnings per share has been incorrectly calculated because the share options held by a director were not included in the calculations. Disclosed diluted earnings per share are 22.9c. Had the share options held by the director been included, this figure would have been 22.4c.

The difference is immaterial[27].

27 2. Review of audit evidence collected – material by nature as relates to a director, plus misstated amount is relevant to investors

Financial performance statement

The directors have currently not amended certain financial performance ratios in this statement to reflect the changes made to the financial statements as a result of the auditors' work. The difference[28] between the reported ratios and the correct ratios is minimal.

28 3. Other information re: ISA 720 – inconsistency – if material, need to amend report

Opinion

We recommend[29] that an unmodified auditor's report be issued.

29 1. Critical appraisal of draft opinion. 5. Forming an audit opinion: Material misstatement re: EPS and possible misstatement re: share options (below)

A corporate governance statement referring to the UK Corporate Governance Code[30] is to be issued as part of the annual report, but there is no evidence on file that this has been reviewed by the audit team. You are aware that the company does not have an audit committee.

30 6. Other reporting – CG does not affect the opinion, but may need to be addressed as part of reporting under ISA 720 or other responsibilities

You are also aware that the director exercised their share options last week[31].

STEP 3 Consider the implications of the issues identified in Step 2 for the auditor's opinion (both cause and extent).

31 4. Subsequent events – why would a director exercise their share options? Usually if a new issue has been made, this would be an adjusting event so if not disclosed, is a material misstatement

When determining the impact of an issue on the audit opinion, there are always going to be two elements to consider if the opinion requires modification: (1) the cause of the modification and (2) the extent. Let's remind ourselves of the various forms of modification that exist.

Applying this to Branch Co, both the share issue and the EPS calculations represent misstatements – as they are (i) fairly self-contained, (ii) do not represent a substantial part of the financial statements and (iii) are unlikely to be fundamental to users' understanding of the financial statements, they are not pervasive, but are material, so a **qualified opinion** would be most appropriate here.

STEP 4 Consider whether there are any additional impacts on the auditor's report from the issues identified in Step 2.

We have already seen the impact on the auditor's opinion from Step 3 – this will require a modification to the standard auditor's report not only for the **opinion section**, but also to the **basis section** as well.

However, while some matters may not affect the audit opinion, they may still require a modification to the standard auditor's report. The completion standards in particular (such as those related to going concern, subsequent events and other information) can fall into this category and we have one such issue to consider from Branch Co:

The directors have currently not amended certain financial performance ratios in this statement to reflect the changes made to the financial statements as a result of the auditors' work.

The difference between the reported ratios and the correct ratios is minimal[32].

STEP 5 Write your answer.

Earnings per share

The problem in the earnings per share (EPS) calculation relates to share options held by a director. As they are held by a director, it is unlikely that they are immaterial, as matters relating to directors are generally considered to be material by

[32] If the inconsistency is not amended by Branch Co's management, we would need to determine whether or not the inconsistency was material – if material, this should be disclosed using the 'Other Information' section of the auditor's report

their nature. The fact that EPS is a key shareholder ratio, which is therefore likely to be material in nature to the shareholders, should also be considered.

As the incorrect EPS calculation is therefore material to the financial statements, the auditor's report should be modified in this respect, unless the directors agree to amend the EPS figure. This would be an 'except for' modification on the grounds of material misstatement.

Share options

The share options have not been included in the EPS calculations. The auditors must ensure that the share options have been correctly disclosed in information relating to the director, both in the financial statements and the other information, and that these disclosures are consistent with each other. If proper disclosures have not been made, the auditor will have to express a modified opinion due to lack of disclosure in this area.

Exercise of share options

The fact that the director has exercised their share options after the year end does not require disclosure in the financial statements. However, it is likely that they have exercised them as part of a new share issue by the company and if so, the share issue would be a non-adjusting event after the reporting period that would require disclosure in the financial statements. We should check if this is the case and, if so, whether it has been disclosed. Non-disclosure would be further grounds for modification.

Financial performance statement

In line with ISA 720, the financial performance statement is 'other information' in the annual report. The auditor is required to read this other information to identify material inconsistencies with the financial statements. The whole of the other information must therefore be read.

An inconsistency has been discovered between the ratio figures, and it is the figures in the other information that are misstated. The figures in the financial statements are not misstated. Therefore the auditor should request that management revises the other information.

The ISA refers to '**material inconsistencies**'. The ratios will be of interest to shareholders, being investor information and this fact may make them material by their nature. However, as the difference is negligible in terms of value, on balance, the difference is probably not material. If the ratios are considered to constitute material inconsistencies, then the 'Other Information' section in the auditor's report will need to be amended and moved further up to come after the 'Basis' section.

Corporate governance statement

As having an audit committee is a requirement of the UK Corporate Governance Code and the company does not have one, the corporate governance statement should explain why the company does not comply with the Code in this respect.

We would not modify our auditor's opinion over the corporate governance statement, as we have no other reporting responsibilities in relation to it. The statement that the company has complied with the UK Corporate Governance Code would be a material misstatement under ISA 720. We should first discuss the matter with management and ask them to include the necessary explanations. If the corporate governance statement is not amended, then we should ask company management to consult with the company's legal counsel. We should then consider the advice given before taking any further action.

Overall conclusion

None of the matters discussed above, either singly or seen together, are pervasive to the financial statements. The auditor's opinion should be modified on the material matter of the incorrect EPS calculation. We should ensure that all the other disclosures are in order and also review the corporate governance statement. If the corporate governance statement does not adequately address the issue of the company not having an audit committee, then we may need to take legal advice.

Exam success skills diagnostic

Every time you complete a question, use the diagnostic below to assess how effectively you demonstrated the exam success skills in answering the question. The table has been completed below for Branch Co to give you an idea of how to complete the diagnostic.

Exam success skills	Your reflections/observations
Good time management	This was not explicitly tested here but remember to consider the total time to answer the question (up to 1.95 minutes per mark) and the split between reading/thinking/planning time and writing time (something like ¼ to ¾ respectively of the total time)?
Managing information	Did you pick up on all the information you needed to satisfactorily answer the question – for example, did you identify the various completion and reporting issues?
Correct interpretation of requirements	Although you were only asked to 'comment', the requirement did go on to ask you to 'indicate' what form of auditor's report would be most appropriate – did you spot this?
Answer planning	Did you differentiate between the issues related to the audit opinion and those that would only affect the auditor's report?
Effective writing and presentation	Did you manage to carry all the points from your plan through into your final answer?
Efficient numerical analysis	Calculations were not required for this question, but materiality was assessed qualitatively instead of quantitatively. Did you mention this?
Most important action points to apply to your next question	

Summary

Completion and reporting will always be tested in the AAA exam, so you cannot afford to ignore it! Use the Practice & Revision Kit to attempt as many different questions as you can, including those from different parts of the syllabus. Make sure you consider the exam skills related to 'scaffolding' and time management when attempting practice questions so the skills become second-nature.

Audit-related services and other assurance services

Learning objectives

On completion of this chapter, you should be able to:

	Syllabus reference no.
Describe the nature of audit-related services, the circumstances in which they might be required and the comparative levels of assurance provided by professional accountants and distinguish between: • Audit-related services and an audit of historical financial statements • An attestation engagement and a direct engagement.	F1(a)
Describe the main categories of assurance services that audit firms can provide and assess the benefits of providing these services to management and external users.	F1(b)
Describe the level of assurance (reasonable, high, moderate, limited, negative) for an engagement depending on the subject matter evaluated, the criteria used, the procedures applied and the quality and quantity of evidence obtained.	F1(c)
Specific assignments • Due diligence • Review of interim financial information For each of the other assignments listed above:	F2(a)
Define and describe the purpose of each type of assignment and analyse the appropriate level of assurance which may be offered by a professional firm in relation to these assignments.	
Evaluate the matters to be considered before accepting the engagement, including any ethical and professional considerations.	F2(b)
Plan the assignment, applying professional scepticism, to gather suitable evidence and provide an appropriate level of assurance in line with the objectives of the assignment.	F2(c)
Discuss the level of assurance that the auditor may provide and explain the other factors to be considered in determining the nature, timing and extent of examination procedures.	F2(d)
Describe and recommend appropriate substantive, examination or investigative procedures which can be used to gather sufficient and	F2(e)

	Syllabus reference no.
appropriate evidence in the circumstances.	
Analyse the form and content of the professional accountant's report for an assurance engagement as compared with an auditor's report.	F5(a)
Discuss the effectiveness of the 'negative assurance' form of reporting and evaluate situations in which it may be appropriate to modify a conclusion.	F5(c)

Business and exam context

In this chapter we look at audit-related services and other assurance services.

Audit-related services include review engagements, such as interim financial information reviews and due diligence reviews. We consider the differences between the external audit and audit-related services.

Assurance services are also considered in this chapter and we examine the different levels of assurance that can be provided on such engagements. In particular we look at risk assessments, performance measurement and value for money audits. Finally in this chapter we look at the ways in which companies are using IT in their organisations and how this affects business risks.

Assurance and audit-related services are very important areas for auditors in practice. Questions in this area may come up in Section B of the exam.

Chapter overview

1 Introduction to assurance and audit-related services

> **Assurance engagement:** Where a professional accountant (or 'practitioner') evaluates or measures a subject matter that is the responsibility of another party against suitable criteria, and expresses an opinion which provides the intended user with a level of assurance about the subject matter. It is implied that such an opinion requires evidence to be reached and a report to communicate it.

Professional firms may not just be asked for assurance reports – they can also be engaged to deliver a number of **audit-related services**, providing varying amounts of assurance (if any at all) depending on the engagement. Audit-related services allow firms to use their skills to support their clients in any way possible and include **reviews**, **agreed-upon procedures** and **compilations**.

2 ISAE 3000 *Assurance Engagements*

ISAE 3000 provides standards for assurance engagements **other than audits or reviews of historical financial information**. In substance, many of the requirements are similar to those required for an audit or a review, including the need for **professional scepticism**.

Acceptance, planning and completion

Before accepting such an engagement, the practitioner needs to meet the requirements of both the **IESBA** *Code of Ethics* and **ISQC 1**, which includes agreeing on the **terms** of the engagement with the client and confirming these in an engagement letter. Effective **planning** is required as with an audit. The **appropriateness** of the **subject matter** and the **suitability** of the **criteria to be used in the engagement** should be assessed: such criteria must be relevant, complete, reliable, neutral and understandable. Sufficient appropriate **evidence** is required on which to base the conclusion. **Documentation** of matters significant in providing evidence to support the assurance **conclusion** and **report** is also required to show that the engagement was performed in accordance with ISAE 3000.

Elements of an assurance engagement

In order to qualify as an assurance engagement, the practitioner will confirm during acceptance and the agreement of terms that it exhibits **all** the following **elements**:

(a) A **three-party relationship** involving:

    (i) A **practitioner**;

    (ii) A **responsible party**; and

    (iii) **Intended users** (ie the person(s) for whom the report is prepared).

(b) An appropriate **subject matter**;

(c) Suitable **criteria**: ie the benchmarks used to evaluate or measure the subject matter;

(d) Sufficient appropriate **evidence**; and

(e) A written assurance **report** (providing either **reasonable** or **limited** assurance).

The **subject matter** under review can vary enormously:

(a) **Physical characteristics**, such as the capacity of a facility

(b) **Performance** of an entity: this could include **performance indicators** both **internally** and **externally** required, such as those produced within an **integrated report** or as part of **public sector governance** (covered separately in these materials) as well as **formal** or **informal**, **financial** and **non-financial** performance, such as the requirement to secure **value for money** (VfM) often against budgets or targets

(c) The operation and reliability of **systems** and **processes**: for example, an entity's **internal controls** (as seen in AA) or controls over specific **IT systems**.

Activity 1: KPIs

Suggest **FOUR** non-financial key performance measures (KPIs) that a manufacturing business could use internally that a practitioner could be asked to report on in an assurance engagement.

Solution

Activity 2: IT risks

What risks are a business exposed to as a result of unreliable IT systems?

Solution

There are a number of engagements where assurance may still be given but where a different ISAE applies:

(a) **Prospective financial information** where the practitioner reviews planned financial performance of an entity (**ISAE 3400** *The Examination of Prospective Financial Information* is covered separately in these materials).

(b) **Due diligence** of any potential business change (covered later in this topic).

(c) **Assurance reports on service organisations** – ISAE 3402 *Assurance Reports on Controls at a Service Organisation* provides guidance for practitioners who have been asked to report on the quality of controls in place at a service organisation which provides financial reporting information on an outsourced basis for an audited client (these reports can be produced on either a 'Type 1' or 'Type 2' basis and are covered in Chapter 7 when **ISA 402** *Audit Considerations Relating to An Entity Using a Service Organisation* is discussed).

2.1 Assurance provided

2.1.1 Reasonable assurance

Reasonable assurance engagement: The objective of a reasonable assurance engagement is to reduce assurance engagement risk to an acceptably low level as the basis for a **positive** form of expression of the practitioner's conclusion:

Eg in the case of assurance on effectiveness of internal controls, the report would be worded: 'In our opinion internal control is effective, in all material respects, based on XYZ criteria.'

2.1.2 Limited assurance

Limited assurance engagement: The objective of a limited assurance engagement is to reduce assurance engagement risk to a level that is acceptable as the basis for a **negative** form of expression of the practitioner's conclusion:

Eg 'Based on the work described in this report, **nothing** has come to our attention that causes us to believe that internal control is **not effective**, in all material respects, based on XYZ criteria.'

2.2 Engagement type

2.2.1 Attestation engagement

Attestation engagement: In an attestation engagement, the **client** measures or evaluates the underlying subject matter against the necessary criteria and prepares the outcome subject matter information, about which the **practitioner** provides assurance of whether or not it is free from material misstatement. The auditor's report on the financial statements is an illustration of this (except that auditors' reports obviously fall outside the scope of ISAE 3000):

Eg 'In our opinion, the financial statements present fairly, in all material respects...'

2.2.2 Direct reporting engagement

Direct reporting engagement: In a direct reporting engagement, the **practitioner** measures or evaluates the underlying subject matter against the criteria, the outcome of which is the subject matter information, and the **practitioner** then **also** issues an assurance conclusion on that subject matter information. This may involve performing **additional tasks** during or after the assurance process which, alongside the **independence** brought by the practitioner, enhances the assurance given – this is what distinguishes a direct reporting engagement from a compilation engagement where typically no assurance is given (compilations are covered later in this topic). Using a Type 2 report on a service organisation as an illustration:

Eg 'In our opinion, internal control is effective, in all material respects, based on XYZ criteria.'

2.3 Form and content of reports

ISAE 3000 does not stipulate a standardised format for the report. Different wording will have to be used depending on the engagement. The report should include the following basic elements as a **minimum**:

(a) A title that clearly indicates that the report is an independent assurance report;

(b) An addressee;

(c) An identification and description of the subject matter information and, when appropriate, the subject matter;

(d) Identification of the criteria;

(e) Where appropriate, a description of any significant inherent limitation associated with the evaluation or measurement of the subject matter against the criteria;

(f) When the criteria are available only to specific intended users/relevant only to a specific purpose, a statement restricting the use of the assurance report to those users/that purpose;

(g) A statement to identify the responsible party and to describe the responsible party's and the practitioner's responsibilities;

(h) A statement that the engagement was performed in accordance with ISAEs, ISQC 1 and the IESBA Code of Ethics;

(i) A summary of work performed;

(j) The practitioner's conclusion;

(k) The assurance report date; and

(l) The signature, name of the firm or practitioner, and a specific location.

(ISAE 3000 (revised): para. 69)

3 Reviewing historical financial information

ISAE 3000 does not cover audits or reviews of historical financial information – this is because there are different types of historical financial information produced and different types of client who require some form of assurance on this information. You already know that **reasonable assurance** is expressed in a **positive manner** for **audits** which are governed by ISAs covered elsewhere on this course, but what about situations when an audit is **not required** but a **limited form of assurance** is still desired by a client?

Limited assurance engagements are increasingly **popular** for entities **exempt from audit** which still value the **benefit** that such an engagement can bring – these so-called 'mini-audits' are carried out either on an ad hoc basis or using the standards explained below. **Audited entities** can also have such engagements completed for them by their auditor to supply additional information to various stakeholders **in advance of the audit**: for example, listed entities may require reviewed financial statements to be submitted to the stock market for an initial assessment of the company's most recent full year performance.

3.1 ISRE 2400 *Engagements to Review Historical Financial Statements*

As with any assurance engagement, the practitioner should ensure that they are able to **accept** the engagement in line with the **IESBA Code of Ethics**, that the **terms** of the engagement are agreed in a **signed engagement letter** and that the engagement will be **planned** and **performed** in line with **ISQC 1**, with an attitude of **professional scepticism** recognising that circumstances may exist which cause the financial statements to be **materially misstated** or not in line with the **applicable financial reporting framework**.

The practitioner should obtain **sufficient appropriate evidence** to support their conclusion primarily through **enquiry** and **analytical procedures** (ISRE 2400: para.7).

The **review report** is usually addressed to the **directors** of the company (not to the shareholders) to indicate who has requested this engagement to be performed. The conclusion delivered within this review will enable the practitioner to state that **nothing** has come to their attention that causes them to believe that the historical financial statements contain **material misstatement** and are not prepared in accordance with an applicable financial reporting framework (ie **limited assurance**).

As with an audit, such a conclusion can be **modified** depending on the nature and extent of the issue(s) identified, with such modifications requiring an explanatory **basis** paragraph immediately preceding the conclusion. In the same way, **Emphasis of matter** and **Other matter paragraphs** can be added if appropriate (ISRE 2400: paras. 87 and 90, Appendix).

3.2 ISRE (UK and Ireland) 2410 *Review of Interim Financial Information Performed by the Independent Auditor of the Entity*

As entities become more accountable to their various stakeholders, the need for **timely** and **reliable** financial information increases, especially at certain times of their reporting period (such as **retailers** who need to report **peak trading** figures). ISRE 2410 provides guidance for assurance engagements where the subject matter does not contain historical financial information for a full reporting period. Broadly speaking, it follows the same approach as ISRE 2400, primarily using **enquiry** and **analytical procedures** to deliver a conclusion.

Essential reading

See Chapter 12 of the Essential reading for illustrations of the reports produced under ISRE 2400 and ISRE 2410.

The Essential reading is available as an Appendix of the digital edition of the Workbook.

4 Audit-related services

Reviews of historical financial information using both ISRE 2400 and ISRE 2410 provide a degree of assurance and are sometimes referred to as audit-related services to differentiate them from the more general types of assurance that we saw earlier in this topic. However, not all audit-related services offer assurance.

4.1 ISRS 4410 *Compilation Engagements*

Practitioners may be asked to **produce subject matter information** and **report** on how this matches the criteria used to assess such subject matter. In other instances (most notably the **preparation of financial statements for small entities**) the practitioner produces the subject matter but **does not provide any assurance** as once complete, no procedures to verify the information are carried out – it is simply a demonstration of the practitioner's accounting skills.

4.2 ISRS 4400 (Revised) *Engagements to Perform Agreed-Upon Procedures*

Practitioners may also be asked to perform **specific procedures** that have been **agreed upon** by both the practitioner and the engaging party. The practitioner will **complete** these agreed-upon procedures (AUP) and **communicate** their **findings** in a **report**. As the report only confirms the procedures that were agreed upon and subsequently performed, **no assurance is given** and the engaging party and the intended users are left to draw their **own conclusions**.

Examples of AUP engagements could include **fraud investigations** or situations where **increased accountability** is necessary for entities claiming **grants** or **other funding**. Both **forensic accounting** and **forensic auditing** engagements could also be considered to be AUP engagements, but they are covered separately in this Workbook.

4.3 Due diligence reviews

Due diligence reviews are a specific type of review engagement. A typical due diligence engagement is where a practitioner is engaged by one company planning to **take over** another to identify the material **risks** associated with the transaction (including a review of all the **assumptions** underlying the purchase) in order to ensure that the acquirer has all the necessary facts. This is important when determining purchase price. Similarly, due diligence can also be requested by sellers.

It may include some or all of the following aspects.

Financial due diligence (a review of the financial position and obligations of a target to identify such matters as covenants and contingent obligations)	**Environmental** due diligence (environmental, health and safety and social issues)	**Regulatory** due diligence (review of the target's level of compliance)

Operational and **IT** due diligence (extent of operational and IT risks, including quality of systems, associated with a target business)	**People** due diligence (key staff positions under the new structure, contract termination costs and costs of integration)

Due diligence work is primarily limited to **enquiry** and **analytical procedures**.

A typical due diligence review could include enquiries into:

- **Assets/liabilities**, in order to **value** the company
- **Management's representations** about the company, which may need to be substantiated by evidence
- **Structure**, including how the target is owned and constituted and what changes will be necessary
- **Acquisition planning**, looking at potential benefits/drawbacks of the acquisition (eg synergies with the acquirer's business, or potential economies of scale)
- **Financial health**, based on a detailed examination of past financial statements and an analysis of the existing asset base
- **Credibility of the owners**, directors and senior managers, including validation of the career histories of all the main players in the business
- **Future potential**, reflected in the strengths of its products or services and the probability of earnings growth over the medium to long term
- **Assessment of the risk** to the acquiring business, in terms of its markets, strategy and likely future events
- **The business plan,** in terms of how realistic it is, how solid the assumptions used are and how well it conveys the potential

Due diligence can sit in a number of **engagement categories** because it can be performed as any of the following.

- As a review of historical financial information (limited assurance)
- As an assurance engagement (limited assurance)
- As agreed-upon procedures (no assurance)

There is no international standard on due diligence engagements, so in practice the engagement would be conducted in accordance with whichever standard best fits the particular engagement being conducted – perhaps ISRE 2400, ISAE 3000 or ISRS 4400.

Note that although due diligence uses the techniques of a review engagement, it is **unlikely** that **any assurance** will be provided. It is normally a report of factual findings such as agreed-upon procedures.

Essential reading

See Chapter 12 of the Essential reading for more detail on each of these engagements.

The Essential reading is available as an Appendix of the digital edition of the Workbook.

Chapter summary

Audit-related services and other assurance services

ISAE 3000 *Assurance Engagements*

Acceptance, planning and completion

- Agree terms of engagement
- Planning – as an audit
- Assess appropriateness of subject matter and criteria
- Obtain sufficient appropriate evidence
- Documentation
- Conclusion and reporting

Assurance and engagement types

- Elements of an assurance engagement:
  - 3 party relationship
  - Subject matter
  - Criteria
  - Evidence
  - Written report
- **Reasonable 'positive'** assurance: ('...*in our opinion, the F/S show a true and fair view...*')
- **Limited 'negative' assurance:** ('...*nothing has come to our attention to suggest the F/S do not show a true and fair view...*')
- **Attestation based** – client measures the subject matter and the practitioner provides a conclusion
- **Direct reporting** – the practitioner both measures the subject matter and provides a conclusion

Reviews of historical financial information

ISRE 2400 *Engagements to Review Financial Statements* & ISRE 2410 *Engagements to Review Interim Financial Statements*

- Report to directors
  - Primarily enquiry and analytical review
- Limited assurance expressed negatively:
  - 'nothing has come to the auditor's attention that the statements do not show a true and fair view'

Other examples of limited assurance

- ISAE 3400 *The Examination of Prospective Financial Information* (see Chapter 13)
- ISAE 3402 *Assurance Reports on Controls at a Service Organisation* (see Chapter 7)

Audit-related services

ISRS 4400 Agreed-upon Procedures

- Factual findings
- Examples are fraud investigations, verifications of claims for funding and forensic audits (see Chapter 14)
- No assurance given as the practitioner just reports what they have done (ie performing the agreed-upon procedures)

ISRS 4410 Compilations

- Producing subject matter information
- Examples are often accounts preparation for smaller clients
- No assurance given as the practitioner just reports what they have done (effectively a test of their skills)

Due diligence reviews

- Provision of advice to purchasing company in a transaction
  - Financial
  - Operational and IT
  - People
  - Regulatory
  - Environmental
- Ensures acquirer has all necessary facts
- Usually enquiry and analytical review only
- Normally no assurance given

Knowledge diagnostic

1. Non-audit engagements

Non-audit engagements can still offer some **assurance**, depending on the nature of work undertaken, or they may be classed as **audit-related** with either **limited** or **no assurance** granted at all.

2. Assurance engagements

Any engagement can be an assurance engagement provided it satisfies the elements of an assurance engagement as laid down in **ISAE 3000**. The subject matter reviewed can vary enormously (including **prospective financial information** and **reviews of service organisations**).

3. Performing assurance engagements

Engagements are planned and conducted in a similar manner to the external audit: assurance reported can be either **reasonable** or **limited** and engagements can be either **attestation** or **direct reporting**.

4. Reviews

Only a **limited (negative) level of assurance** is provided due to a review consisting mainly of **enquiries** and **analytical review** – this could be a full year (ISRE 2400) or interim review (ISRE (UK and Ireland) 2410).

5. Non-assurance services

There are many **additional services** an audit firm can offer their clients. Some of these engagements provide **no assurance at all** and involve the auditor using their skills to perform **agreed-upon procedures (ISRS 4400)** or a **compilation (ISRS 4410)** of financial statements.

6. Due diligence

Due diligence engagements are used for a variety of purposes, so their nature and the level of assurance granted (if at all) can vary too.

Further study guidance

Question practice

Now try the following from the Further question practice bank (available in the digital edition of the Workbook):

- Question 25 'Aquinas' only presents a limited amount of information, so you are going to need to work hard for the marks, but it is a good opportunity to test the theory in this chapter.
- Question 26 'Audit' is also light on detail, but is still a good opportunity to practise something unusual which you may not expect to see in the AAA exam.

Further reading

At the time of writing there are currently no technical articles relevant to this chapter on the ACCA website, but you should continue to look out for any by accessing the website regularly: www.accaglobal.com/an/en/student/exam-support-resources/professional-exams-study-resources/p7/technical-articles.html

Own research

Enter the term 'due diligence' into an online search engine – you should be presented with a range of technical and commercial examples of this kind of engagement – read as many as you can to get a better flavour for this topic.

Activity answers

Activity 1: KPIs

> **Approach**
>
> The secret to success here is to remember that this is a manufacturing business, so you need to recommend key performance indicators (KPIs) relevant to a factory or workshop with its own cost structure, where labour and/or technology is used to turn raw materials into finished goods.

Suggested solution

Non-financial performance measures (any four of these)

- Customer rejects or returns vs sales
- Customer satisfaction
- Wastage of materials
- Staff morale
- Machine down time or idle time per employee
- Items produced per employee
- Staff turnover
- Sickness/absenteeism rates per head

Activity 2: IT risks

> **Approach**
>
> Again, this is a very practical activity that requires a logical solution – even if you do not work for a business like Amazon, eBay or Facebook, you can probably imagine could go wrong with their IT systems (however unlikely) and the impact that each issue could have.

Suggested solution

Businesses are exposed to the following risks if their systems are unreliable:

- Assets are misappropriated or tampered with.
- They are at risk of being unable to trade with their customers (eg service interruption) leading to customer dissatisfaction and loss of customers to a competitor.
- Systems are damaged and shut down.
- Data is tampered with and unauthorised amendments made.
- Confidential data is stolen.
- Data protection legislation is not complied with (eg GDPR in the UK and beyond) leading to fines, loss of reputation and possibly going concern problems.

13

Prospective financial information (PFI)

Learning objectives

On completion of this chapter, you should be able to:

	Syllabus reference no.
Specific assignment • Prospective financial information For the assignment listed above:	F2(a)
Define and describe the purpose of this assignment and analyse the appropriate level of assurance which may be offered by a professional firm in relation to this assignment.	
Evaluate the matters to be considered before accepting the engagement, including any ethical and professional considerations.	F2(b)
Plan the assignment, applying professional scepticism, to gather suitable evidence and provide an appropriate level of assurance in line with the objectives of the assignment.	F2(c)
Discuss the level of assurance that the auditor may provide and explain the other factors to be considered in determining the nature, timing and extent of examination procedures.	F2(d)
Describe and recommend appropriate substantive, examination or investigative procedures which can be used to gather sufficient and appropriate evidence in the circumstances.	F2(e)
Discuss the content of a report for an examination of prospective financial information.	F5(b)

Business and exam context

Reporting on prospective financial information (PFI) is covered by ISAE 3400 *The Examination of Prospective Financial Information*.

Forecasts are of significant interest to users. Some would say that PFI is of more interest to users of accounts than historical financial information (HFI) which, of course, auditors report on in the external audit.

This is an area in which the auditors can therefore provide an alternative service to audit, in the form of a review or assurance engagement. This chapter looks at the factors that the auditor should think about when taking on such an engagement. The basis for this chapter has been laid in Chapter 12 but, in this chapter, we consider issues specific to PFI.

PFI can only be examined in Section B of the exam. The difficulties of reporting on PFI could be examined in an exam question. Section A questions can easily be set in the context of a PFI assignment.

Chapter overview

1 ISAE 3400 *The Examination of Prospective Financial Information*

1.1 Terminology

Prospective financial information means financial information based on assumptions about events that may occur in the future and possible actions by the entity (ISAE 3400: para. 3).

Auditors are regularly engaged to provide assurance on prospective financial information.

Prospective financial information can be of two types (or a combination of both).

> **Forecast:** Prospective financial information based on assumptions as to future events which management expects to take place and the actions management expects to take (best-estimate assumptions).
>
> **Projection:** Prospective financial information based on hypothetical assumptions about future events and management actions, or a mixture of best-estimate and hypothetical assumptions. (ISAE 3400)

There are two other terms commonly associated with prospective financial information:

> **Hypothetical illustration:** Prospective financial information based on assumptions about uncertain future events and management actions which have not yet been decided on.
>
> **Target:** Prospective financial information based on assumptions about the future performance of the entity. (ISAE 3400: paras. 4–5)

Listed companies should have procedures that allow them to generate reliable prospective financial information (PFI), compare it to market expectations, publish it when necessary and subsequently report actual performance against it.

Activity 1: PFI examples

PFI has a key role for businesses in terms of providing information to third parties as well as an internal management tool. Can you think of some examples of different types of PFI?

Solution

2 Matters to consider before accepting an engagement to report on PFI

Before deciding to accept such an engagement, the audit firm should also consider the following.

(a) The **intended use** of the information. For example, is it intended for internal or external use?

(b) Whether the information will be for **general** or **limited distribution**.

(c) The nature of the **assumptions** on which the information is based.

(d) The **information** to be included.

(e) The **period covered** by the information (ISAE 3400: para. 10)

The auditor should not accept, or should withdraw from, an engagement when the assumptions are clearly unrealistic or when the auditor believes that the prospective financial information will be inappropriate for its intended use (ISAE 3400: para. 11).

3 Level of assurance provided

Due to the nature of PFI, the audit firm will be unable to conclude on whether the results forecast will be achieved. Also there may be insufficient evidence available to conclude that the assumptions are free from material misstatement. Therefore, the audit firm can generally only provide a **limited level of assurance**.

The audit firm will normally provide negative assurance. This means they will state that **'nothing has come to their attention'** which causes them to believe that the assumptions are **not** a reasonable basis for the forecast.

Example of an unqualified report on a forecast

REPORT TO....

We have examined the forecast in accordance with the International Standard on Assurance Engagements applicable to the examination of prospective financial information. Management is responsible for the forecast including the assumptions set out in Note X on which it is based.

Based on our examination of the evidence supporting the assumptions nothing has come to our attention which causes us to believe that these assumptions do not provide a reasonable basis for the forecast. Further, in our opinion the forecast is properly prepared on the basis of the assumptions and is presented in accordance with International Financial Reporting Standards.

Actual results are likely to be different from the forecast since anticipated events frequently do not occur as expected and the variation may be material.

AUDITOR

Date

Address

(ISAE 3400 (revised): para.28)

The auditor can express a qualified (material misstatement or insufficient/inappropriate audit evidence) opinion if he believes:

(a) The presentation and disclosure of the PFI is not adequate

(b) One or more of the assumptions do not provide a reasonable basis for the PFI

4 Examination procedures

The auditor should obtain sufficient appropriate evidence as to whether:

- Management's **assumptions** on which the PFI is based are **not unreasonable**
- The information is **properly prepared** on the basis of the assumptions
- The information is **properly presented** and all material assumptions are **adequately disclosed**
- The PFI is prepared on a **consistent basis** with historical financial statements, using appropriate accounting policies

The auditor should obtain **sufficient knowledge** of the business to be able to evaluate whether the assumptions are justified. The historical information will be used as a yardstick to assess the assumptions underlying the information.

In carrying out their review of the accounting bases and calculations for forecasts, and the procedures followed by the company for preparing them, the **main points** which the reporting accountant will wish to consider include:

Whether the forecast under review is based on forecasts regularly prepared for the purpose of management, or whether it has been separately and specially prepared for the specific purpose	Where forecasts are regularly prepared for management purposes, the degree of accuracy and reliability previously achieved, and the frequency and thoroughness with which estimates are revised	Whether the forecast under review represents the management's best estimate of results which they reasonably believe can and will be achieved rather than targets which the management have set as desirable
The extent to which forecast results for expired periods are supported by reliable interim accounts	The details of the procedures followed to generate the forecast and the extent to which it is built up from detailed forecasts of activity and cash flow	The extent to which profits are derived from activities having a proven and consistent trend and those of a more irregular, volatile or unproven nature
How the forecast takes account of any material extraordinary items and prior year adjustments, their nature, and how they are presented	Whether adequate provision is made for foreseeable losses and contingencies and how the forecast takes account of factors which may cause it to be subject to a high degree of risk, or which may invalidate the assumptions	Whether working capital appears adequate for requirements (normally this would require the availability of properly prepared cash flow forecasts) and, where short-term or long-term finance is to be relied on, whether the necessary arrangements have been made and confirmed

The auditor should confirm the **arithmetical accuracy** of the forecast and the supporting information and whether forecast statements of financial position and statements of cash flows have also been prepared (as these help to highlight arithmetical inaccuracies and inconsistent assumptions).

The auditor should also obtain **written representations** from management regarding the intended use of the information, the completeness of significant assumptions and management's acceptance of its responsibility for the PFI.

Activity 2: Prism

Prism, a public company, is one of the world's leading suppliers of fast-moving consumer goods. The company is looking to increase its operations in Eastern Europe and requires some additional finance.

You are the manager of a firm of Chartered Certified Accountants and have been approached by Paul Robinson, the Chief Executive of Prism. He is trying to obtain some additional finance from the bank and they have asked that he obtain an independent review of the figures that have been produced to support the loan application.

Statement of profit or loss

	Forecast 20X4	Actual 20X3
	$m	$m
Revenue	47.6	40.9
Cost of sales	(33.3)	(30.7)
Gross profit	14.3	10.2

	Forecast 20X4	Actual 20X3
	$m	$m
Profit on disposal of investment	1.0	0.6
Other expenses	(5.3)	(4.6)
Profit before tax	10.0	6.2

Statement of financial position

	Forecast 20X4	Actual 20X3
	$m	$m
Non-current assets		
Property, plant and equipment	14.9	10.9
Intangible assets	22.1	25.0
Investments	–	2.3
	37.0	38.2
Current assets		
Inventories	5.6	4.1
Receivables	9.1	7.3
Cash	2.5	2.4
	17.2	13.8
	54.2	52.0
Equity		
Share capital	5.3	5.3
Revaluation surplus	3.2	3.2
Retained earnings	9.8	8.3
	18.3	16.8
Non-current liabilities	18.1	18.3
Current liabilities	17.8	16.9
	54.2	52.0

Required

Describe the audit work that a professional certified accountant would perform on the forecast statement of profit or loss and statement of financial position.

BPP
LEARNING
MEDIA

Solution

Chapter summary

Prospective financial information (PFI)

ISAE 3400
The Examination of Prospective Financial Information

Distinction between:
- A forecast (based on events and assumptions expected to occur)
- A projection (based on expectations and hypothetical assumptions)
- A hypothetical illustration (based on decisions not yet made eg 'flying kites')
- A target (based on possible future performance of an entity)

Matters to consider before accepting an engagement to report on prospective financial information

- Intended use
- General vs limited distribution
- Nature of assumptions
- Information to be included
- Period covered by PFI

Level of assurance provided

- Due to nature of engagement likely to be limited (negative) assurance
  '...nothing has come to our attention...'
- An opinion (effectively reasonable positive assurance) that the forecast has been prepared in line with the assumptions and relevant reporting framework

Examination procedures

- Limited assurance comes from approach – usually enquiry and analytical review
- Auditor should obtain sufficient appropriate evidence that:
  - Management assumptions are not unreasonable
  - Information is properly prepared on the basis of the assumptions
  - Information is properly presented and assumptions disclosed
  - PFI is prepared on basis consistent with historical financial statements (eg accounting policies; activity rates etc)

Knowledge diagnostic

1. Prospective financial information (PFI)

PFI relates to any financial data prepared based on assumptions relating to **future** events or actions. Such PFI can relate to **forecasts, projections, hypothetical illustrations** and **targets.**

2. Accepting a PFI engagement

Auditors must consider some additional factors before accepting an engagement to report on PFI, such as who the information is for and what it is to be used for.

3. Assumptions

In practice the **level of assurance** given in a PFI engagement will always be **limited**, expressed in a **negative form,** for the **reasonableness of the assumptions.**

4. Application

However, the **level of assurance** given in a PFI engagement for the **application of those assumptions** will always be reasonable, expressed in a **positive form (ie an opinion).**

5. Procedures

The type of audit work performed will, in the main, be restricted to **enquiry** and **analytical review** – enough to ensure sufficient appropriate evidence exists for whatever report is required.

Further study guidance

Question practice

Now try the following from the Further question practice bank (available in the digital edition of the Workbook):

- Question 27 'Verity' which is essential exam standard question practice for the contents of this chapter.

Further reading

At the time of writing there are currently no technical articles relevant to this chapter on the ACCA website but you should continue to look out for any by accessing the website regularly: www.accaglobal.com/an/en/student/exam-support-resources/professional-exams-study-resources/p7/technical-articles.html.

Own research

When you are next at work, ask someone in a position of authority whether your employer has ever created forecasts or business plans – why were they required, were they ever reviewed by anyone and were they successful?

Activity answers

Activity 1: PFI examples

> **Approach**
>
> This is a practical exercise in thinking about why PFI would be required and who would benefit from it. Try and consider both internal and external stakeholders for this kind of information.

Suggested solution

Prospective financial information can include financial statements or one or more elements of financial statements and may be prepared:

(1) As an internal management tool, for example, to assist in evaluating a possible capital investment; or

(2) For distribution to third parties in, for example:

    (i) An annual report to provide information to shareholders, regulatory bodies and other interested parties

    (ii) A document for the information of lenders which may include, for example, cash flow forecasts

Activity 2: Prism

> **Approach**
>
> This is definitely exam-standard and demonstrates a key piece of advice – if financial information is presented in a question, you need to do something appropriate with it. However, what will you do here? The solution is laid out in three categories: (i) general procedures over the creation of the PFI; (ii) profit or loss items, which should be considered in terms of the story of how the company's fortunes are going to change; and (iii) the financial position and what it will be in a year's time.
>
> Consider what you have been told and how likely it is that the company will either continue as it is or will change from the figures presented.
>
> Finally, remember that performing analytical procedures is important, but you must do more than just say 'Revenue has increased' – you need to work out whether such an increase is reasonable, whether other factors would support this, whether you need further information to understand this increase etc.

Suggested solution

General procedures

(1) Meet with Paul to determine the process for preparing the forecast information.

(2) Identify and document internal controls over the process. Consider the role played by the Internal Audit department.

(3) Obtain backing schedules for the information, cast and ensure they are numerically accurate.

(4) Review the accounting policies used and ensure they are consistent with previous periods.

(5) Discuss the need to produce a full statement of profit or loss, taking account of the proposed tax, interest and dividend payment.

(6) Produce a letter of engagement.

(7) Obtain management representation with regard to the completeness and accuracy of information and assumptions used. This should also contain a statement that it is management's responsibility to produce the information.

Statement of profit or loss

(1) I would compare the forecast revenues for the year with those in the previous audited financial statements. Challenge Paul's assumption that revenue will increase by 17%.

(2) Agree the increase to contracts, review the management accounts for the start of the year: do they show an increase in revenue?

(3) Consider the likelihood of such an increase in revenue by reviewing the performance of similar companies in the same sector and reviewing the wider economic climate.

(4) Obtain a detailed analysis of revenue and cost, perform a detailed analytical review and discuss the unusual movements with Paul or other relevant directors of Prism.

(5) Compare the gross profit margin with that achieved in the past. The forecast shows an increase of 5% – how has this been achieved? Is it a realistic expectation?

(6) I would compare the level of expenses with those in prior year. Certain expenses should be fixed and remain static. Others will vary according to revenue levels. Any significant fluctuations would be investigated further.

(7) Review the expected profit on disposal of investment to supporting documentation and recalculate it.

Statement of financial position

(1) I would confirm the value of non-current assets to the most recent audited accounts. Possible impairment of assets will be discussed with the directors.

(2) I would recalculate depreciation for each period and compare the accounting policies against those used in previous financial statements.

(3) I would calculate the age of inventories, receivables and payables and compare them with past financial statements. Any significant variations would be investigated further.

(4) Discuss with management the possibility of obtaining equity finance.

(5) Calculate key ratios and compare them year on year such as ROCE, asset turnover, current asset and quick asset ratios. Review any current bank agreements and confirm that bank covenants are not breached.

(6) Discuss the need to include any provisions for contingencies, such as warranties.

(7) I would agree the cash figure and the level of overdraft and loans to agreements with the banks and financial institutions.

14

Forensic audits

Learning objectives

On completion of this chapter, you should be able to:

	Syllabus reference no.
Specific assignment • Forensic audits For the assignment listed above:	F2(a)
Define and describe the purpose of this assignment and analyse the appropriate level of assurance which may be offered by a professional firm in relation to this assignment.	
Evaluate the matters to be considered before accepting the engagement, including any ethical and professional considerations.	F2(b)
Plan the assignment, applying professional scepticism, to gather suitable evidence and provide an appropriate level of assurance in line with the objectives of the assignment.	F2(c)
Discuss the level of assurance that the auditor may provide and explain the other factors to be considered in determining the nature, timing and extent of examination procedures.	F2(d)
Describe and recommend appropriate substantive, examination or investigative procedures which can be used to gather sufficient appropriate evidence in the circumstances.	F2(e)

Business and exam context

In the current globalised business world there is an increasing demand for forensic services. Audit and assurance professionals are well-placed to provide these. This chapter introduces forensic accounting and auditing and discusses its applications in practice and continues with a look at investigative procedures and evidence.

This topic is often examined in a very practical way. It is important to have an understanding of the framework but case study questions will involve the application of procedures similar to those used in traditional audits of financial statements. Some specific knowledge is required of basic definitions, but otherwise the application of audit-style procedures is used. Questions on forensics may only come up in Section B of the exam.

Chapter overview

Forensic audits

Terminology

Applications of forensic auditing

The forensic accountant as expert witness

1 Terminology

KEY TERM

Forensic auditing: The process. Relates to the **procedures** followed by the firm and can be defined as gathering, analysing and reporting on data, in a pre-defined context, for the purpose of finding facts and/or evidence in the context of financial/legal disputes and/or irregularities and giving preventative advice in this area.

Forensic investigation: An example of a forensic auditing engagement. Applies similar procedures to a forensic audit but is carried out for specific civil or criminal cases. Such cases could involve fraud or asset tracing in money laundering cases.

Forensic accounting: The skills involved. Involves undertaking a financial investigation in response to a particular event, where the findings of the investigation may be used as evidence in court or to otherwise help resolve disputes.

2 Applications of forensic auditing

The range of assignments in this area is vast so to give specific definitions for each is not always practicable. In a publication of the Chartered Professional Accountants of Canada, *Standard practices for investigative and forensic accounting engagements* (November 2006), the following definition is established.

Investigative and forensic accounting engagements are those that:

(a) Require the application of professional accounting skills, investigative skills, and an investigative mindset

(b) Involve disputes or anticipated disputes, or where there are risks, concerns or allegations of fraud or other illegal or unethical conduct (CPA Canada (2006): p2)

Forensic audit and accounting is a rapidly growing area. The major accountancy firms all offer forensic services, as do a number of specialist companies. The demand for these services arises partly from the increased expectation of corporate governance codes for:

Company directors to take seriously their responsibilities for the prevention and detection of fraud (for example, to quantify the extent of the losses	Governments concerned about risks arising from criminal funding of terrorist groups

Otherwise, in a case where an auditor or accountant is being sued for **negligence**, both parties may wish to employ forensic accountants, either to investigate the standard of work performed or to establish the losses suffered by the plaintiff.

Insurance companies often engage forensic accountants to verify and report on the amounts of losses suffered by a claimant where there is a dispute between the claimant and the company.

2.1 The forensic accountant as an expert witness

Due to the nature of this work, forensic accountants will very often be called as **expert witnesses** in civil or criminal cases. This is a very important function and some jurisdictions have specific rules governing their duties.

For example, in England and Wales, experts have a duty to exercise reasonable skill and care to those instructing them, and to comply with any relevant professional code of ethics. **However**, when they are instructed to give or prepare evidence for the purpose of civil proceedings they have an overriding **duty to help the court** on matters within their expertise. This duty **overrides** any obligation to the person instructing or paying them. Experts must not serve the exclusive interest of those who retain them.

The **Forensic Science Regulator** has produced guidance for experts in England and Wales to follow when producing reports for criminal prosecutions. The main contents are outlined below.

Expert reports should contain the following:

(a) Statements regarding the objectivity of the expert and that no conflicts of interest exist

(b) Confirmation that any fees are not paid on a contingent basis

(c) Acknowledgement that the expert's duty is to the court and not the party who engaged them to give evidence

(d) An overview of the sources of information used in creating the report

(e) Confirmation that the expert has complied with the relevant Code of Conduct in producing the evidence used in the case

(f) A declaration of the following:

    (i) That they are an expert in their field

    (ii) Their qualifications and experience

    (iii) That the contents of their report are true to the best of their knowledge

    (iv) Acknowledgment that any false statements may lead to their prosecution

    (v) Name, signature, date and occupation

(Forensic Science Regulator, 2019)

Essential reading

See Chapter 14 of the Essential reading for further information on planning and conducting a forensic audit engagement.

The Essential reading is available as an Appendix of the digital edition of the Workbook.

Activity 1: Sam Seel

You are a manager in an audit firm with a small team dedicated to forensic investigations. You have been approached by the Finance Director of SL Co to perform an investigation into a fraud perpetrated by a purchase ledger clerk.

You have ascertained the following.

The fraud came to light after another employee drew attention to the activities of the purchase ledger clerk, Sam Seel. Initial investigations have identified that Sam had been paying money into his own bank account by raising false invoices and paying them through SL Co's purchase ledger. The fraud had gone undetected for an unknown amount of time because SL Co's controls only require invoices in excess of $1,000 to be authorised by a senior member of staff. Invoices below this amount are processed and authorised for payment by the relevant purchase ledger clerk.

SL Co is a very large company with revenue in excess of $100m and operates in the construction industry. Sam Seel joined the finance department nine months ago and has since been suspended from duties pending this investigation.

The Finance Director has requested that your firm perform such procedures as necessary to quantify the extent of the loss suffered by the business.

Required

1   In the context of the ACCA's fundamental ethical principles, what factors should you take into account before accepting this engagement?

2   Assuming you accept the engagement, what specific procedures would you perform to allow you to quantify the loss suffered by SL Co?

Solution

Chapter summary

```
                    ┌─────────────────────┐
                    │   Forensic audits   │
                    └─────────────────────┘
            ┌──────────────────┴──────────────────────────┐
  ┌──────────────────┐              ┌──────────────────────────────────┐
  │   Terminology    │              │  Applications of forensic auditing │
  └──────────────────┘              └──────────────────────────────────┘
```

Terminology

- **Forensic auditing** is the process of gathering, analysing and reporting on data, in a pre defined context, for the purpose of finding facts and/or evidence in the context of financial/legal disputes and/or irregularities and giving preventative advice in this area.
- **Forensic investigation** applies similar procedures to a forensic audit but is carried out for specific civil or criminal cases. Such cases could involve fraud or asset tracing in money laundering cases.
- **Forensic accounting** involves undertaking a financial investigation in response to a particular event, where the findings of the investigation may be used as evidence in court or to otherwise help resolve disputes.

Applications of forensic auditing

- **Fraud investigations:**
  Used to quantify the possible amount lost, for example.
- **Negligence cases:**
  To establish the standards of work actually done.
- **Verification of insurance claims:**
  In the event of dispute between claimant and company.

The forensic accountant as expert witness

The accountant's duty to help the court overrides any duty owed to clients who may have paid for their services.

Knowledge diagnostic

1. Forensic engagements

Auditors are increasingly being called upon to use their skills in forensic work. Engagements in this area can include **forensic auditing, forensic investigations** and **forensic accounting.**

2. Applications

The work can involve **fraud investigations, evidence gathering** where an auditor is being sued for negligence or performing work for insurance companies to **verify customer claims.**

3. Expert witnesses

Due to the nature of the work, it is likely the forensic accountant will be called to a court of law as an **expert witness** and care must be taken to ensure that this function is fulfilled in the appropriate way.

Further study guidance

Question practice

Now try the following from the Further question practice bank (available in the digital edition of the Workbook):

- Question 28 'Painswick Co' is further practise of the content introduced here and the skills required if a question on forensics comes up in the exam.

Further reading

There is one technical article on the ACCA website written by members of the AAA examining team which is relevant to some of the topics covered in this chapter that you should read:

- *Forensic auditing*

Own research

- There are plenty of accounting firms that offer forensic audit services – compare what they do and see if there are any significant differences in their approach.

- There are many other resources online that can help this subject come to life: try this as an example of what forensic audit can include:

  corporatefinanceinstitute.com/resources/knowledge/accounting/what-is-a-forensic-audit/

Activity answers

Activity 1: Sam Seel

> **Approach**
>
> This requirement has two parts: for the first part, you need to list the five fundamental ethical principles (hopefully not a struggle, but refer back to Chapter 2 in this Workbook if you can't remember them all!) before you consider how each one could be compromised by accepting this engagement.
>
> For part two you should try and visualise the fraud and explore everything that Sam could have been connected with to see how far it has spread throughout SL. Remember to make your procedures active, explaining what you will be doing, why and how – this will make for a thorough answer.

1 **Suggested solution**

   Integrity

   SL Co has been a victim of fraud perpetrated by at least one of its own staff. It appears that this is isolated to one, junior, member of staff. Despite this, prior to accepting the engagement, we should consider the risk that the fraud was assisted by more senior members of staff or that there is a weak control environment which could call into question the integrity of some or all of the senior staff at SL Co. If we feel there is a significant risk of our own integrity being compromised, we should not accept the engagement.

   Objectivity

   Should this case come to court in the future there is a very real chance staff from our firm could be called as an expert witness. We would need to consider our relationship with the client and whether that would restrict our ability to provide testimony to the court in an objective manner. An expert witness should seek to provide evidence independently, regardless of the interests of their client.

   Professional competence and due care

   As with any engagement, we should consider our ability to perform the engagement with the required level of expertise and competence. Our firm has a forensic department (albeit a small one) so it is likely that we have performed similar engagements in the past. We should note, however, that SL Co is a construction company and we would need to carefully consider whether we have sufficient knowledge of the business and the industry to perform a meaningful investigation.

   Confidentiality

   As with all other engagements, this will carry a duty of confidentiality to SL Co. However, this will be overridden should we be called to court as an expert witness and we should inform SL Co of this in the engagement letter. Additionally, this is likely to be a sensitive investigation and we should discuss the levels of secrecy required whilst we are at the client's premises.

   Professional behaviour

   There is a chance that this case could enter the public domain in a court case that could be relatively high profile. We should be careful to conduct ourselves in a professional manner and do nothing which brings our firm or the profession into disrepute, particularly if we are called as an expert witness.

2 **Suggested solution**

   - Enquire of the Purchasing Manager as to the contracts/jobs for which Sam Seel dealt with the invoices.

- Perform an analytical review on purchases for contracts/jobs that Sam wasn't involved in to identify any unusual trends that may imply the fraud is more widespread.

- Inspect **all** (materiality is not relevant) invoices that Sam dealt with below $1,000. Be alert for invoices to suppliers not on the company's approved list or purchase ledger for the previous year (Sam was only employed for nine months). Unusual suppliers should be contacted to confirm their existence; where the supplier cannot be verified, the invoice should be listed as being fraudulent.

- Perform an analytical review of all invoices dealt with by Sam in excess of $1,000. Consider any unusual trends in purchasing costs, margins and so on compared to the prior year. Unexplained fluctuations could indicate more extensive fraud and collusion with senior staff.

- Depending on the results of this analytical review, select a sample of invoices greater than $1,000 and ensure the existence of the suppliers as above.

15

Social, environmental and public sector auditing

Learning objectives

On completion of this chapter, you should be able to:

	Syllabus reference no.
Plan an engagement to provide assurance on integrated reporting (performance measures and sustainability indicators).	F3(a)
Describe the difficulties in measuring and reporting on economic, environmental and social performance and give examples of performance measures and sustainability indicators.	F3(b)
Describe substantive procedures to detect potential misstatements in respect of socio-environmental matters.	F3(c)
Discuss the form and content of an independent verification statement of an integrated report.	F3(d)
Explain the auditor's main considerations in respect of social and environmental matters and how they impact on entities and their financial statements (eg impairment of assets, provisions and contingent liabilities).	D3(c)
Describe the audit of performance information (pre-determined objectives) and differentiate from performance auditing.	F4(a)
Plan the audit of performance information (pre-determined objectives) and describe examination procedures to be used in the audit of this type of information.	F4(b)
Discuss the audit criteria of reported performance information, namely compliance with reporting requirements, usefulness, measurability and reliability.	F4(c)
Discuss the form and content of a report on the audit of performance information.	F4(d)
Discuss the content of an audit conclusion on an integrated report of performance against pre-determined objectives.	F4(e)

Business and exam context

In this chapter we investigate the impact of social and environmental issues on assurance services.

Increasing importance is being placed on social and environmental issues in business. Recent years have seen a substantial weight of environmental legislation passed, which puts a significant burden of compliance on companies. The danger of non-compliance (fines, bad publicity, impact on going concern) is an aspect of the environmental risk which companies face.

We also examine the work of the auditor in the context of public sector organisations. Auditors may take on varied roles here, and we focus on the audit of performance information.

Finally, integrated reporting is a recent innovation and current issue in the profession.

The topics in this chapter may be examined as part of a Section B question, and are unlikely to be more than a sub-section of a question as opposed to being the subject of a full question.

Chapter overview

1 Practical context

Activity 1: Social and environmental factors

The importance of social and environmental factors is increasingly recognised by the business community. Many businesses now have specific policies governing their relationship with their employees, society and the environment.

Required

What factors have led to the rapid growth in business awareness of these issues?

Solution

2 Impact on practitioners

Social and environmental issues cannot be ignored by external auditors. Potential impacts on their work may arise from:

The application of environmental **laws** and **regulations** during the audit	The operation of processes that may cause **pollution** or the use of **hazardous substances**	The holding of an interest in **land and buildings** that have been **contaminated** by previous occupants

Dependence on a **major customer segment** whose business is threatened by **environmental pressures**	The voluntary reporting of any initiatives undertaken by an organisation to address social or environmental **concerns** of stakeholders (such as **integrated reporting**)

2.1 General financial statement impacts

Auditors do not necessarily have a specific knowledge of environmental or social matters. However, in planning the audit, they should obtain sufficient knowledge of the business (under **ISA 315** *Understanding the Entity*) to understand the social and environmental events, transactions and practices (**ISA 250** *Laws and Regulations*) that may have a significant effect on the financial statements or the audit and respond appropriately to them (**ISA 330** *Risk Response*).

2.1.1 Substantive procedures

The auditor may perform substantive testing to obtain evidence in relation to social and environmental matters. Below are some **suggested procedures**: it is not intended that all of the procedures will be appropriate in every case (in many cases, the auditor may judge it unnecessary to perform any of these procedures and may apply others instead) so overall, **common sense** and **commercial awareness of the scenario** should play a part here.

Documentary review

(a) Review **minutes** from meetings of directors, audit committees, or any other subcommittees of the board specifically responsible for environmental matters.

(b) Read **publicly available information** regarding any existing or possible future environmental matters.

Where relevant, consider:

- **Reports** by **environmental experts** about the entity, such as site assessments, due diligence investigations or environmental impact studies
- **Internal audit reports** and other internal reports dealing with environmental matters
- Reports issued by, and correspondence with, **regulatory** and **enforcement agencies**
- **Publicly available registers** or **plans** for the restoration of soil contamination
- **Environmental performance reports** issued by the entity
- Correspondence with the entity's **lawyers**

(c) Obtain **written representations** from management that it has considered the effects of environmental matters on the financial statements, and that it:

- Is not aware of any **material liabilities** or **contingencies** arising from environmental matters, including those resulting from illegal or possibly illegal acts;
- Is not aware of environmental matters that may result in a material **impairment** of assets; or
- If aware of such matters, has **disclosed** to the auditor all related facts

Asset impairments (IAS 36)

(a) Enquire about any planned changes in capital assets, for example, in response to **changes** in **environmental legislation** or **business strategy** and their impact on the valuation of those assets or the company as a whole.

(b) For any asset impairments related to environmental matters that existed in **previous periods**, consider whether the **assumptions** underlying a write down or related carrying values **continue to be appropriate.**

Liabilities, provisions and contingencies (IAS 37)

(a) Enquire about policies and procedures operated to **identify** liabilities, provisions or contingencies arising from environmental matters.

(b) Enquire about **events** or **conditions** that may give rise to liabilities, provisions or contingencies arising from environmental matters, for example:

- **Penalties** or **possible penalties** arising from breaches of social or environmental laws and regulations; **or**
- **Claims** or **possible claims** for environmental damage.

(c) For property abandoned, purchased, or closed during the period, enquire about requirements or intentions for site **clean-up** and **restoration.**

(d) For property sold during the period (and in prior periods) enquire about any **liabilities** relating to environmental matters retained by contract or by law.

(e) For liabilities, provisions, or contingencies related to environmental matters, consider whether the **assumptions** underlying any **estimates** continue to be appropriate.

(f) Review the adequacy of any **disclosure** of the effects of environmental matters on the financial statements, especially in relation to **going concern (ISA 570)**.

3 Assurance on integrated reports

Increasingly, practitioners are being asked to provide **assurance** on (and even **produce**) **reports** for clients that explain more fully their **responsibilities** to their various **stakeholders**. This includes a blend of **financial** and **non-financial information**, covering areas such as **governance**, **sustainability** and **remuneration**. The term used to describe such a report is **integrated reporting**.

3.1 Planning and performing an engagement to review an integrated report

The process of planning and performing any engagement follows a number of key steps, so when reviewing an integrated report, the practitioner will consider the following:

1   **Acceptance issues** – Does the engagement present any ethical issues (such as fee dependency, self-review, competence to act and required experience) or risks (such as liability or reputation factors)?

2   **Quality control** – Policies and procedures within the firm to manage the engagement

3   **Agreeing the terms of the engagement** via an engagement letter (this may need to be very specific, given the non-statutory nature of such integrated reports)

4   **Planning** – This will depend on the engagement but risk assessment and collecting evidence will need to be considered (see next section)

5   **Conclusions and reporting** – There is no required format as long as the terms of reporting and concluding are agreed in the engagement letter

3.1.1 Measuring social and environmental performance

While such engagements are a good source of revenue for many assurance firms, they do present **challenges**, as very often the **outputs** that need to be reported on are either **difficult to measure** (eg emissions of a pollutant) or **intangible** in nature (eg impact on the local community).

It is therefore accepted that measuring social and environmental performance is **difficult**, so when planning this kind of engagement, the practitioner will need to consider either **how** to **validate** the measurements made by the client, or **how** they can **measure** the information themselves. Understandably, this could affect acceptance (but conversely, this may make those firms that choose to specialise in providing this kind of engagement very sought after).

Essential reading

See Chapter 15 of the Essential reading for more detail on measurement difficulties.

The Essential reading is available as an Appendix of the digital edition of the Workbook.

The following types of measures may be used:
- **Direct** – For example, kilograms (kg) of contaminant emitted
- **Relative** – For example, kg of contaminant emitted per kg of product manufactured
- **Indexed** – Measured over a period of time to identify longer-term trends
- **Aggregated** – Information of the same type, but from different sources expressed as a combined value (for example, volume of waste recycled or employees supported by training)
- **Weighted** – Information modified by applying a factor relating to its significance

Examples of **specific indicators** included in environmental and social elements of integrated reports on which the auditor may be asked to provide assurance include:

- Toxic gas emissions
- Energy usage, recycling levels and progress against waste reduction targets (such as reducing packaging)
- Average wage levels vs minimum wage
- Employee satisfaction and/or staff turnover levels
- Customer complaints
- Financial assistance to charitable organisations
- Investment in infrastructure, such as schools and roads

3.1.2 IAASB Discussion Paper on integrated reporting

In August 2016, the IAASB released the **Discussion Paper**, *Supporting Credibility and Trust in Emerging Forms of External Reporting: Ten Key Challenges for Assurance Engagements.*

The paper introduced a new piece of jargon for social and environmental reporting: **EER, E**merging forms of **E**xternal **R**eporting. The issue debated by the IAASB was **credibility and trust**, and how best to achieve this with EER (both in terms of its creation and the assurance that can be provided on it).

One of the key issues is that the external auditor's opinion does **not** include EER as it is part of the 'Other information' reviewed under ISA 720. While there is a strong overlap with existing assurance services (especially the audit, where credibility and trust are enhanced) **flexibility** is required to meet the ongoing needs of stakeholders as this EER is not legally required but clearly still has great significance.

In conclusion, some other form of engagement to provide assurance on this EER is required, but determining exactly how to arrive at the desired level of assurance is not straightforward – hence the core of the paper: the 'Ten Key Assurance Challenges':

Ten key assurance challenges
Determining the scope of an EER assurance engagement, which can be **complex**
Evaluating the **suitability of criteria** in a consistent manner
Addressing **materiality** for diverse information with little guidance in EER frameworks
Building assertions for subject matter information of a diverse nature
Lack of maturity in governance and internal control over EER reporting processes
Obtaining assurance with respect to **narrative information**
Obtaining assurance with respect to **future-oriented information**
Exercising **professional scepticism** and **professional judgement**

Ten key assurance challenges
Obtaining the **competence** necessary to perform the engagement
Communicating effectively in the assurance report

(IAASB, 2016: pp 34–39)

Following a period of **consultation** with many different stakeholders, IAASB issued a **Feedback Statement** in January 2018 which delivered the following messages:

- There should be greater awareness of the **limitations of ISA 720** among stakeholders so they can decide on the best way of providing assurance on EER alongside the audit opinion

- While the use of a **specific standard** to provide assurance consistently on EER is favoured (probably ISAE 3000 as mentioned in Chapter 12) it should still reflect the fluid nature of such reporting and should therefore **not be too specific or rigid**

- Respondents felt that the **top three assurance challenges** from the original list of ten were suitable criteria, materiality and the form of reporting that should be used

- While this is still an evolving area of reporting, EER will **inevitably grow in significance** as more stakeholders get on board and this growth will drive the way that EER should be both created and reviewed (IAASB, 2018: pp 5–14)

3.1.3 Auditing integrated reports

Auditors may be engaged to produce an independent verification statement on an integrated report. This is an assurance report and would therefore need to be performed in line with the guidance contained in ISAE 3000 *Assurance engagements other than audits or reviews of historical financial information* (covered in detail in Chapter 12 of this Workbook).

This could be either a direct or an attestation engagement, with the practitioner presenting the integrated report themselves (direct), or providing a report on information presented by the entity.

Practitioners in this area face many of the difficulties outlined above in relation to the audit of public sector performance information. The measurement of financial or even physical capital is relatively unproblematic because these areas may be readily subject to quantification. But intellectual, human and social capital are much more difficult to present objectively; their measurement involves a good deal of judgement. It is therefore difficult to see how an assurance engagement on an integrated report could offer much more than **limited assurance**, sticking as much as possible to the factual assertions made by the report and wording its conclusion negatively.

Essential reading

See Chapter 15 of the Essential reading for a reminder of how the various capitals are used within the International Integrated Reporting Framework.

The Essential reading is available as an Appendix of the digital edition of the Workbook.

Activity 2: Integrated reporting

1   What are the perceived benefits from an entity's point of view of paying for assurance on its integrated report?

2   What would you expect to be the key contents of the practitioner's conclusion on an integrated report?

Solution

4 The audit of performance information in the public sector

Countries face **conflicting demands** from their inhabitants – they crave **prosperity** and the ability to **enjoy** their own hard work, yet at the same time there is a desire to meet **social need** (**health, education, welfare** and **democracy** are some examples) but there is no consensus on **how** this is to be **achieved** or **funded**. The public sector caters for these needs but often from public money, either directly from government or from other sponsors. In each case, **accountability** of how social need is addressed using public funds represents a significant governance challenge, which assurance providers will try to meet.

The **financial statements** of public sector entities have been subject to audit for many years, often using their own interpretations of accounting standards due to the specific nature of their objectives and funding structures. However, it is not always about financial performance, so the role of **non-financial information** to support the assessment of public sector entities is important to understand.

There are two **definitions** that may be useful to compare and contrast here:

Performance audit (which is **not** examinable in AAA) is part of the process of reviewing financial statements for public sector entities by assessing **value for money** (VfM) which only uses **quantitative** data (financial and non-financial) to assess the relative level of service for a set financial amount (eg the **cost per procedure in a hospital**, compared across similar sites).	The **audit of performance information** (which **is** examinable under AAA) can include these VfM indicators but is more about assessing **operational performance** by looking at **qualitative** as well as both financial and non-financial quantitative measures against stated objectives (eg **standards of educational attainment** within and across school boundaries).

4.1 Problems with performance information

The example quoted above on educational attainment may **seem** straightforward as performance information, but let's consider it in more detail:

Does this information exist?	Standards are designed to assess performance against

BPP LEARNING MEDIA

	objectives: **exam pass rates** may say something about whether the objective of educational attainment has been met but are they enough? Are there any other methods of assessing performance?
Can you measure this information?	Alternative information may be available (eg inspections) but are they measurable and do they **support** the findings of pass rates?
How relevant is this information?	The measure requires **comparison** with other entities to become meaningful, so these other entities must be **representative** in terms of size or demographics.

The **challenge** for practitioners engaged to audit measures such as these becomes more apparent as each gets **defined** in enough detail to fully understand the task – this makes **acceptance procedures** extremely important before agreeing to perform such work.

4.2 Planning and performing the audit of performance information

Assuming all **ethical, quality control** and **acceptance** issues are addressed satisfactorily, the practitioner can commence **planning** the engagement to ensure **procedures** are documented and **evidence** is collected that meets the required standards against set objectives in order to allow a **valid conclusion** to be drawn – this will take into account the earlier problems identified with auditing such performance information.

Procedures may include:

- Tests of controls on the systems used to generate performance information
- Performing analytical review to evaluate trends and gauge the consistency of quantitative data
- Analysis of service-user activity data
- Review of service-user experience surveys
- Surveys of key management and staff
- Interviews with key management and staff
- Review of minutes of meetings where performance information has been discussed
- Confirmation of performance information to source documentation; this may be performed on a sample basis
- Conducting case studies
- Review of existing literature
- Review of results of internal and external challenges

The auditor must keep **documentation** of the planning process and of the audit evidence obtained.

Activity 3: New Evenham

The country of New Evenham provides public sector hospitals which operate accident and emergency (A&E) departments treating patients requiring emergency admissions (admissions that are not planned and happen at short notice because of perceived clinical need). The New Evenham Government is considering the introduction of a system for reporting A&E departments' performance that goes beyond the current aim of value for money (VfM) and incorporates many additional forms of quantitative and qualitative information.

Required

1   You work as an audit manager in the New Evenham Public Sector Audit (NEPSA) inspection unit. You have been asked to draft a briefing note that explains how the audit of A&E performance information will work in practice. Your briefing note should address the following:

(a) Identify **FOUR** examples of performance information that would help both hospital managers and members of the public assess each A&E department's performance.

(b) For each example, recommend audit procedures that NEPSA's inspection unit would carry out to reach a conclusion about each A&E department's performance (your answers should consider the likely sources of evidence available).

2 What problems might NEPSA experience while carrying out its work?

Solution

4.3 Concluding and reporting on the audit of performance information

The practitioner expresses a **conclusion** on the entity's **achievement of its objectives** however it sees fit (**there is no standard report format**) so it will depend on the nature of the **engagement** as agreed with the entity. The entity's report may take the form of an **integrated report** of performance against its objectives, compared with the performance information itself, so the **practitioner's conclusion** would be included within this document (this may require an assessment of the consistency of the entity's performance compared with other information in the integrated report on which a conclusion has already been given, such as the audited financial statements).

Chapter summary

Social, environmental and public sector auditing

Practical context

- Increased importance – why?
  - Social and environmental issues now politically and economically important
  - Growth of ethical investors, consumers and employees
  - Increase in social and environmental legislation affecting businesses

Impact on practitioners

- Affects auditors through:
  - Application of environmental laws and regulations
  - Potential pollution by client
  - Contamination of land and buildings on statement of financial position
  - Dependence on major market affected by environmental issues
  - Greater use of voluntary reporting to satisfy stakeholders

General financial statement impacts
- No specific knowledge of environmental matters required
- Should obtain sufficient knowledge of the business to understand impact on audit

Substantive procedures
- **General:** Board minutes, reports, media etc
- **Assets:** Impairments and changes in asset usage policy.
- **Liabilities, provisions and contingencies:** Restructuring, fines and penalties, estimates
- **Disclosure:** Sufficient for stakeholders?

Assurance on integrated reports

- Additional assurance engagements – no formal structure for reports
- Integrated reports use the six capitals: Financial; Manufactured; Human; Intellectual; Natural; Social

Planning and performing an engagement to review an integrated report
- Types of measurement:
  - Direct (eg kg emitted)
  - Relative (eg kg per capita)
  - Indexed (eg over a period)
  - Aggregated
  - Weighted
- Items for measurement include gas/liquid emissions, waste amounts, staff turnover, customer complaints and even donations to charity

The audit of public sector performance information

- Performance audit
  - Assessing value-for-money using quantitative measures
- Auditing performance information
  - Using quantitative (non-financial) and qualitative information as well to assess operational performance
- What are the problems?
  - Does the information exist? How easily can it be measured and relied upon?

Knowledge diagnostic

1. Social and environmental matters

Social and environmental issues are now of **critical importance** to the vast majority of businesses, customers and employees and therefore cannot be ignored.

2. Impact on financial statements

The auditor must have an understanding of the **impact** of these issues on their work, as social and environmental issues can generate significant **risks** for audits. (Although auditors do not have to be experts, they should respond to any significant risks with **appropriate substantive procedures**.)

3. Integrated reports

Stakeholders are demanding **accountability** from businesses and increasingly, they are responding by producing **social** and **environmental information** as part of an **integrated report**. In many cases, the auditor will provide **assurance** on this information although the precise nature of this information can vary enormously.

4. Performance information

There is a distinction between **performance auditing** and the **audit of performance information** but for practitioners, the main challenge lies in **planning** and **performing** an engagement that addresses the **inherent risk** of auditing this information but still allows valid **conclusions** to be drawn and **reported**.

Further study guidance

Question practice

Now try the following from the Further question practice bank (available in the digital edition of the Workbook):

- Question 29 'Rank' is further practice of acceptance and procedures for a non-audit engagement – in this case, a social and environmental report for an ethical company.

Further reading

There is one technical article on the ACCA website written by members of the AAA examining team which is relevant to some of the topics covered in this chapter that you should read:

- *Performance information in the public sector*

Own research

- Try and find some real-life examples of social and environmental reports – have they been reviewed and if so, what did the review report contain?
- For an example of what an integrated report could look like, why not have a look at what ACCA has done?

  annualreport.accaglobal.com/assets/downloads/ACCA-Integrated-Report-2018.pdf

Activity answers

Activity 1: Social and environmental factors

> **Approach**
>
> You will definitely have covered content related to social and environmental issues in your studies so far (both ACCA and others) so this activity should be a way of summarising what you know. Remember to consider your answer by thinking: 'Social and environmental issues have become more important to business in recent years because...' and proceed from there.

Suggested solution

Social issues – family-friendly issues such as **paternity leave** and **flexible working conditions** for parents and carers – have become more important now due to changes in society.

There has been a growth in the importance of **the environment** as a political and economic issue – climate change (which has major social aspects to it) plus the importance of sustainability and the impact of the environment on business (fuel costs and climate change issues etc).

This has led to the growth of so-called **ethical consumers, investors** and **employees.** These key groups are now very selective about who they will purchase goods from, which companies they invest in and who they would work for. Food miles are more important now than ever before, as is the role of plastic carrier bags (now to be charged for in many jurisdictions to reduce their adverse environmental impact).

As a result of this, **businesses** are keen to be seen to be engaging with **key stakeholder groups** and demonstrating a commitment to ethical, social and environmental behaviour. This, in turn, helps to attract and retain customers and employees.

From an alternative perspective there has been, in many countries, a growth in the volume of domestic and supra-national **legislation** regulating the behaviour of businesses in these areas. This leads to penalties and fines in certain jurisdictions for breaches of social issues (working time directive, discrimination policies etc) and environmental legislation (Environment Agency in the UK).

Social and environmental issues have evolved over time and made us look at things in a different way. Consider the coal industry: a coal mining company's financial statements will include the costs of employee wages, plant and machinery used, licences and future dismantling costs. The coal industry is usually seen as bringing economic benefits to society, through providing energy to consumers and employment for workers.

But the costs of the coal industry to the social and natural environment may be much more widespread than this. The environmental impact of the coal industry as a whole includes the following factors, which are not part of financial statements.

- **Land use.** Mining radically changes the landscape, eg by eliminating vegetation, changing soil profiles and stopping current land uses.
- **Waste management.** Burning coal (eg to make electricity) creates ash, much of which must be stored in the ground, which both uses up land and creates a potential hazard to communities.
- **Wildlife.** Mining damages wildlife principally by changing or destroying habitats, which can result in the depletion or total extinction of species from affected areas.
- **Air pollution.** Coal is the largest contributor to the man-made increase of carbon dioxide (CO_2) in the atmosphere, which is associated with climate change.

Activity 2: Integrated reporting

> **Approach**
>
> As integrated reporting is such an evolving issue, you should be prepared for it to form part of a discussion-style question (such as that seen on the specimen exam for AAA). Consequently,

this is excellent practice for you to consider the benefits of having an assurance report reviewed (remember to do this from the perspective of the entity creating the integrated report).

When answering the second part of this question, think about the contents of an auditor's report and any other reports that you have seen so far in AAA and then consider what might be most appropriate to use in the context of an integrated report.

1   **Suggested solution**

Perceived benefits of assurance work on integrated reports include:

- The assurance report adds credibility to the data reported.
- It reassures investors by promoting transparency (and may improve stock market price).
- There is added prestige of having the information audited.
- It gives a competitive advantage over those whose reports are not audited.
- It identifies areas of weakness which can be addressed.
- It may be a requirement for trading with some companies/countries or governments.
- Social and environmental performance is taken more seriously, which in turn will improve performance and (hopefully) reduce costs.

2   **Suggested solution**

Contents of the practitioner's reported conclusions

- Note of the objectives of the review
- Opinion (if the engagement was agreed-upon procedures rather than assurance, there will be no opinion given)
- Basis on which the opinion (if any) has been reached
- Work performed
- Limitations (if any) to the work performed
- Limitations (if any) to the opinion given

Note. There is **no specific guidance** on the contents of a practitioner's conclusion on an integrated report on social and environmental issues; the above points represent the **minimum** you should expect to see included. The International Integrated Reporting Framework (denoted by the term <IR>) supported by ACCA is a voluntary scheme that suggests the areas where companies might wish to report on their social and environmental credentials in a combined format with other financial and non-financial performance. It is likely that you will have already met integrated reporting (for example, as part of your studies for Strategic Business Leader).

Activity 3: New Evenham

Approach

There is an underlying assumption here that each hospital would produce the performance information first and the NEPSA inspection unit would then audit that information.

There are more than four examples of performance information presented here – answers could vary considerably depending on the provision of healthcare in your own country and your own point of view. Our answers take a UK perspective where the National Health Service (NHS) operates most hospitals in the public sector and where patient care is sometimes played off against private competition, usually (inevitably) in a political context. The following report was referred to when constructing this example: www.nao.org.uk/wp-content/uploads/2013/10/10288-001-Emergency-admissions.pdf.

Value for money (VfM) is not covered here as this example is supposed to show performance information going beyond the purely financial (as well as to differentiate it from performance auditing per syllabus area F4(a), but obviously VfM is important information for any service funded by public sector money.

You may wish to try and answer parts (a) and (b) together and consider what you know about a casualty department before moving on to part (c) when a healthy dose of scepticism may be required to consider how such an audit may not always be possible.

1 The correct answers are as follows.

    (a) Any four of the following:

        (1) Availability of treatment

        (2) Waiting times for treatment

        (3) Quality of diagnosis (A&E is often a gateway to other services but is also used inappropriately)

        (4) Quality of patient care

        (5) Patient safety

        (6) Mortality rates

    (b)

Examples of performance information used to assess A&E	Audit procedures to reach conclusions about performance (including evidence)
(1) Availability of treatment	Consider demand for A&E services and compare with departmental capacity (this would require evidence about patient volumes, staffing levels and floor space/throughput rates). Recalculate the percentage of patients sent elsewhere or who left without treatment and consider reasons why – inadequate space, resource or facilities? (Ambulance transport data may exist to support this as well as patient records that show no treatment was received).
(2) Waiting times for treatment	For a sample of patients, recalculate length of stay using times between first admission and treatment time (requires accurate records of reception, triage and treatment time).
(3) Quality of diagnosis (A&E is often a gateway to other services but is also used inappropriately)	Recalculate the percentage of inappropriate admissions (ie those not acute) and the percentage of incorrect diagnoses by reviewing quality of triage assessment (Requires data recording whether A&E was required and readmission data for patients given inappropriate treatment).
(4) Quality of patient care	Consider from evidence presented whether treatment is in line with agreed care standards (Requires analysis of treatment and comparison with standards, as well as patient satisfaction surveys and interviews). Recalculate the percentage of shifts operated without a consultant to supervise staff (Requires staffing records).
(5) Patient safety	Recalculate the percentage of serious incidents recorded per shift (Requires inspection of incident logs and interviews with staff, as well as definition of 'serious').
(6) Mortality rates	Recalculate the percentage of patients treated who die in

Examples of performance information used to assess A&E	Audit procedures to reach conclusions about performance (including evidence)
	A&E and the percentage who die within a set time of discharge (eg five days) – mortality rates should be collected so would be straightforward to analyse (but drawing conclusions less so).

2 **Suggested solution**

Data may not exist or may just not be recorded; even if recorded, though, it may not be accurate, consistent, trustworthy or comparable enough for use in producing and auditing the performance information (often due to workload and because recording data is seen as too bureaucratic).

Some measures may be intangible (quality of healthcare, for example) requiring care in their use and interpretation as meaningful performance information.

Auditors will need to ensure a balanced view is presented (eg ensuring both positive and negative patient comments are reflected fairly within the information).

Auditors may not possess the clinical skills to fully understand the data before them (eg an A&E department may record higher than average mortality rates due to the demographics of their location) leading to clinical staff displaying either reluctance to engage with audit or plain hostility.

Political pressure to manipulate data in order to report inappropriate levels of performance (the lack of controllability of underlying causes of both illness and necessary treatment may also devalue any conclusions reached about performance).

BPP
LEARNING
MEDIA

16

Current issues

Learning objectives

On completion of this chapter, you should be able to:

	Syllabus reference no.
Discuss current developments in auditing standards including the need for new and revised standards and evaluate their impact on the conduct of audits.	G2(a)
Discuss current developments in business practices, practice management, audit methodology and evaluate the potential impact on the conduct of an audit and audit quality.	G2(b)
Discuss the proposed changes to the audit profession and critically evaluate the implications of these changes for companies and audit firms and their impact on audit process and quality.	G2(c)
Discuss current developments in emerging technologies, including big data and the use of automated tools and techniques such as data analytics and the potential impact on the conduct of an audit and audit quality.	G2(d)
Discuss the impact of significant global events on audit practice.	G2(e)

Business and exam context

At this level in your studies you are expected to be familiar with current developments affecting the audit and assurance profession. Currently, many of these relate to international regulation.

You must read *Student Accountant* and the wider professional press to keep up to date with these.

You may be asked to discuss current developments and must be prepared to argue for or against any new proposals from the point of view of either a preparer or user of assurance reports.

Chapter overview

Current issues

- Current developments in auditing standards and their impact on the audit
- Current developments in business practices and their impact on the audit
- Current developments in emerging technologies and their impact on the audit
- The examining team's technical articles and other publications
- Impact of professional changes and significant global events on auditors and their clients

BPP
LEARNING
MEDIA

1 Current issues

Syllabus section G on current issues may be examined in Section A or B as appropriate. The topic of current issues is unlikely to form the basis of any question **on its own** but instead, will be **incorporated** into the Case Study or either of the Section B questions, dependent on question content and the topical issues affecting the profession at the time of writing.

For example, Question 3 part (a) of the specimen exam contained the following requirement following a comment made by the IESBA on the subject of auditors performing non-audit work:

Discuss the changes made to the Code in relation to non-assurance services and evaluate the arguments for and against auditors providing non-assurance services to audit clients. (8 marks)

Clearly, producing a sound answer to this would require the following:

Awareness of the current changes made to the IESBA Code – you can get this from reading Chapter 16 of the Essential reading (found in the digital edition of this Workbook) and from keeping an eye on the ACCA's website for any recent technical articles written by the examining team for AAA.	Good technique for writing solutions using all the elements of the requirement: • A discussion of the changes • Arguments in favour • Arguments against • An overall conclusion Use the 'Further Question Practice' at the back of the Workbook to work on your technique (available in the digital edition of this Workbook).

Essential reading

See Chapter 16 of the Essential reading for further details of all the relevant current issues that ACCA and BPP think you need to be aware of to be prepared for the AAA exam.

The Essential reading is available as an Appendix of the digital edition of the Workbook.

Chapter summary

BPP
LEARNING
MEDIA

Knowledge diagnostic

1. Essential reading

It is vital that you access the material from the Essential reading section available in an Appendix of the digital edition of the Workbook for all the information relevant to this part of the syllabus.

2. ACCA technical articles

You must keep accessing the ACCA website for any last-minute technical articles published that might be examined.

Further study guidance

Question practice

Now try the following from the Further question practice bank (available in the digital edition of the Workbook):

- Question 30 'Merger of audit firms' – there is no way of knowing what (if any) current issues the exam will contain, but you should get used to being able to discuss things in this manner.

Further reading

There is one technical article on the ACCA website written by members of the AAA examining team which is relevant to some of the topics covered in this chapter that you should read:

- *Auditing disclosures in financial statements*

Own research

- You **must** keep reading the business press and a quality news source for regular updates on what is relevant to the auditing and accountancy profession.
- You also **must** keep up to date with any last-minute technical articles published by the ACCA AAA examining team in case they are tested in your exam.

Skills checkpoint 5

Non-audit engagements and current issues

Overview

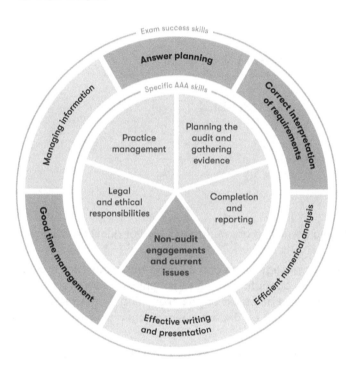

Introduction

Remember that although this is an audit exam, the words '...and Assurance' are also in the title. The syllabus contains a number of non-audit elements that you could be tested on, so this checkpoint will consider how you can prepare for these if required. Part F of the syllabus covers these subjects.

The AAA examining team also periodically publishes technical articles on subjects deemed to be of interest to candidates. In some cases, they may recommend exam techniques for syllabus topics that have been poorly answered in previous exam sittings; in others, they may relate to current issues which the examining team want candidates to be aware of.

Traditionally, whenever a technical article is published, the content is often examined within the next couple of sittings, so keeping up to date with these technical articles is essential. You will find references to relevant technical articles with the 'Further reading' sections of this Workbook.

AAA Skill: Non-audit engagements and current issues

A step by step technique for approaching questions testing this part of the syllabus now follows (you may find that some of these techniques are suitable for other parts of the syllabus as well – why not start practising them now?)

> **STEP 1:**
> Think about the question and list all the things that you will need to do.

> **STEP 2:**
> Read the scenario and identify all the areas that are relevant to producing an answer.

> **STEP 3:**
> Is there any other technical knowledge that will help you to produce an answer?

> **STEP 4:**
> Draw up an answer plan based on your outputs from Steps 1, 2 and 3.

> **STEP 5:**
> Write your answer.

Exam success skills

There are some key exam skills that will help you when answering this kind of question which are summarised below:

- **Answer planning.** Questions on non-audit engagements can be quite **technical** – for example, the specific matters to be considered before accepting an engagement to review prospective financial information (PFI) – but they may also be based on the examining team's **technical articles.** You can access technical articles written by the examining team online (available from the ACCA website) which will help you to build a plan.

  Questions on topics like this can also be more applied and require sound **commercial awareness** and **common sense** to score well. A previous exam question was set in the context of a company which would receive substantial government funding only if it achieves targets in three specific areas, one of which is 'accidents in the workplace'. The following requirement relates to this:

  (i) **Describe the procedures to verify the number of serious accidents in the year ended 30 November 20X7. (4 marks)**

The examining team reported that for this question:

'*Many candidates seemed to think that the auditor has access to absolutely any kind of evidence that they could wish for. Common sources of evidence referred to included:*

- *The private medical records of employees*
- *Police reports on 'dangerous' incidents*
- *Hospital admissions data*
- *Interviews with ambulance drivers/paramedics/doctors*
- *Death certificates*

Candidates need to appreciate that although the auditor will have access to books and records held by their client, they will not be able to access external and possibly highly confidential information as a means to gather evidence. The above examples show of a lack of commercial, or even, common sense.'

- **Correct interpretation of requirements**. It is vital that you read the data in the scenario and then consider the requirements of the question **in that context**. All too often, candidates read the requirements and then produce an answer to **the question they think has been asked or the question they think they can answer, not the actual question itself.**

  Consider the following question from a recent exam sitting:

  Your audit client, Mulligan Co, designs and manufactures wooden tables and chairs. The directors want to secure a loan of $3 million in order to expand operations and have approached LCT Bank for the loan. The bank's lending criteria stipulate the following:

  'Loan applications must be accompanied by a detailed business plan, including an analysis of how the finance will be used. LCT Bank need to see that the finance requested is adequate for the proposed business purpose. The business plan must be supported by an assurance opinion on the adequacy of the requested finance.'

  Your firm has agreed to review the business plan and to provide an assurance opinion on the completeness of the finance request. A meeting will be held tomorrow to discuss this assignment.

  Required

  (a) Identify and explain the matters relating to the assurance assignment that should be discussed at the meeting with Mulligan Co. **(8 marks)**

  What matters should be discussed at this meeting? Issues of an acceptance nature perhaps: 'Do we want the work?'; 'Are we competent to act?'; or even, 'Have we got the necessary resources?' Maybe issues of a client acceptance nature might also be appropriate here, such as, 'Is this client legitimate?'

  Reading the scenario is vital – the following comes from the AAA examining team's report:

  '*The vast majority of answers to requirement (a) stated that at the meeting they would discuss 'whether we are competent to take on the work'. Surely this is not something you would raise at a meeting with your client __having just agreed to do the work__... Many candidates (also) wanted to discuss at the meeting matters such as, 'Do we have the experience to perform the work?' Again, I would think that the client would be surprised to learn that you may not be knowledgeable enough to conduct the assignment, especially considering that you are the auditor of their business. I would urge candidates to stop and think, and consider if the matters they are suggesting discussing at the meeting... fit in with the scenario provided.*'

- **Good time management**. Finally, it may seem obvious, but the rule of 1.95 minutes per mark applies all the way through the exam. If you have over run on any earlier questions, eventually it will catch up on you. The logic we discussed in an earlier skills checkpoint still applies – always attempt those questions that you feel most confident about first, and leave the ones you feel less confident about until the end of the exam.

  If tested, the question relating to current issues and non-audit engagements may be the 'rogue variable' in your AAA exam, which means you leave it to the end to attempt. However, you will always score more marks for the first half of an answer than the second, so if time is getting tight, make sure you have at least started every question, even if it is unpopular!

Skill Activity

STEP 1 Consider the following question and write a short list of the things you are going to need to consider in order to satisfactorily answer the requirement.

You are a manager in the forensic investigation department of an audit firm. You have been approached by the Finance Director of Arnold Co to investigate a possible fraud. The Finance Director has identified a number of unresolved discrepancies between inventory records and the quarterly physical inventory counts which are performed. Her suspicions have been increased by the fact that the discrepancy always relates to the same product line and approximately the same number of items appear to be missing each time.

Required

(a) Explain the procedures you would perform to determine whether a fraud has taken place and to quantify the loss suffered by the company. **(6 marks)**

List of things to consider

- 6 marks = 12 minutes (3 minutes reading, thinking and planning time; 9 minutes writing)
- Usually 1 mark per well-explained point, so will need 6 things to score well
- Procedures to determine whether a fraud has taken place (maybe 3 or 4 things)
- Procedures to quantify the loss suffered (maybe 2 or 3 things)

This should start to become second nature to you when starting to answer a question – the requirement, the time, the points required.

STEP 2   Read the scenario, identifying those areas most relevant to producing an answer.

In this case, the approach to answering the question is likely to include the elimination of legitimate reasons as to why the discrepancies may have arisen, leaving fraud as the only plausible reason for the missing inventory. However, you have not been asked to explain how the fraud arose though. Let's look at the scenario again:

You are a manager in the forensic investigation department of an audit firm. You have been approached by the Finance Director of Arnold Co to investigate a fraud. The Finance Director has identified a number of unresolved discrepancies[33] between inventory records and the quarterly physical inventory counts which are performed[34]. Her suspicions have been increased by the fact that the discrepancy always relates to the same product line[35] and approximately the same number of items[36] appear to be missing each time.

[33] Who completes the count and how are discrepancies normally resolved?

[34] How is the count performed? Are there any issues that could explain the discrepancy?

[35] Need to confirm what these are to see if there is a reason for their disappearance

[36] Confirm amounts to see if this helps with the investigation

STEP 3   Identify any areas of technical knowledge that may help you to answer the question.

Discrepancies between accounting records and real evidence usually tend to occur for one of two reasons – either fraud or error. In this case, we are trying to eliminate as many of the legitimate reasons why this may have occurred, leaving fraud as the only plausible reason (from that point on, the collection of evidence would need to be more cautious in case any 'tipping off' occurs).

Remember what you have already learned about inventory counts and how they work – you are trying to find any shortcomings in any of the three stages:

- Beforehand – Usually related to the count instructions, the timing of the count and the staff involved
- During – Were the instructions followed, has anything unusual happened, were goods being issued at the same time etc?
- After – How were results reported and scrutinised, what follow-up work was done etc?

You should also consider what you have learned about the controls usually present in warehouses regarding inventory and establish whether there are any deficiencies here.

STEP 4   Draw up an answer plan using the outputs from Steps 1, 2 and 3.

Note how practical this requirement actually is – there's very little (if any) knowledge of forensic auditing to add to this, other than the general context of the scenario and the ability to understand it as an engagement in its own right.

Here's an example of a plan which may help:

Has a fraud taken place?	1 – Who completes the count?
	2 – How are discrepancies followed up?
	3 – What controls are in place?
	4 – Understanding the business and inventory items
How much has gone missing?	1 – Confirm book values and count values
	2 – Cost up differences
	6 points in total = 6 marks which should take around 12 minutes
	Start: 10.06
	End: 10.18

STEP 5 Write your answer.

Procedures would involve the following.

To establish whether a fraud has taken place:

- Obtain an understanding of the business and in particular, the roles and responsibilities of those involved in processing inventory transactions and those in the warehouse.

- Discuss with management the method adopted for conducting the quarterly inventory count and review the detail of the count instructions. Any weaknesses in the controls should be identified and considered as a possible explanation for the discrepancies, eg double counting of this particular line of inventory.

- Obtain confirmation of whether inventory is held at more than one location. If so, confirm that this has been included in the physical inventory counts.

- Review procedures for the identification of obsolete and damaged items and in particular, the disposal of such items. Determine who is responsible for making the decision and the procedures for updating records for these adjustments. If items have been disposed of but records not maintained, this could explain the discrepancy.

- Obtain an understanding of the system for the processing and recording of despatches and in particular, consider the effectiveness of controls regarding completeness of despatches. Trace transactions from order to despatch in respect of the inventory line in question to confirm that all goods out have been recorded.

- Obtain an understanding of the system for the processing and recording of goods received for this inventory line. Controls over the initial booking in of inventory should be reviewed. If inventory is double counted at this stage, this could account for the discrepancy.

- Review the system for subsequent processing of goods received, in particular the controls and procedures regarding the accuracy of input. If goods in are processed more than once, this would give rise to a discrepancy between the book records and actual inventory.

- Assess the existence of general controls affecting access to the warehouse and inventory.

To quantify the loss

The evidence obtained above should enable the auditor to determine the accuracy of the book records and the accuracy of the physical inventory records. A reconciliation of the two figures should provide the number of units missing. The cost of each unit should then be agreed to recent purchase invoices.

Exam success skills diagnostic

Every time you complete a question, use the diagnostic below to assess how effectively you demonstrated the exam success skills in answering the question. The table has been completed below for Arnold Co to give you an idea of how to complete the diagnostic.

Exam success skills	Your reflections/observations
Good time management	6 marks, taking up to 1.95 minutes per mark, should take up 12 minutes in total.

Exam success skills	Your reflections/observations
	The split between reading/thinking/planning time and writing time (something like ¼ to ¾ respectively of the total time) should be 3 to 9 respectively – did you follow this?
Managing information	Did you pick up on all the information you needed to satisfactorily answer the question?
Correct interpretation of requirements	Do you think you were able to 'explain' sufficiently well, distinguishing between the two issues of establishing whether there was a fraud and quantifying it?
Answer planning	Did you complete a plan for such a short requirement? If so, did it help? If not, how did you get on and will you do the same in future?
Effective writing and presentation	Did you manage to carry all the points from your plan through into your final answer?
Efficient numerical analysis	Not applicable for this question
Most important action points to apply to your next question	

Summary

In some respects, questions on this part of the syllabus are the hardest to answer as they relate to infrequently tested topics and the subject of current issues. However, as this question shows, the technical knowledge required to produce an answer is often outweighed by the need to display sound commercial awareness and common sense, both of which you should possess as a nearly-qualified accountant.

In addition, the fact that such questions are tested infrequently means that as long as you have practised examples from each of the key syllabus areas (including assurance, due diligence, prospective financial information, forensic, social and environmental audits) and kept up to date with the examining team's technical articles, you should be ready for anything!

Index

Bibliography

ACCA (2008) *Technical Factsheet 84* [Online]. Available at: www.accaglobal.com/content/dam/ACCA_Global/Technical/fact/technical-factsheet-84.pdf [Accessed 03/2021]

ACCA (2012) *Obtaining professional work* [Online]. Available at: www.accaglobal.com/content/dam/acca/global/PDF-members/2012/2012p/professional_work.pdf [Accessed 03/2021]

ACCA (2020) *Rulebook* [Online]. Available at: www.accaglobal.com/content/dam/ACCA_Global/Members/Doc/rule/commentary/Rulebook-update-01-02-20-commentary.pdf [Accessed 10/2020]

ACCA (2019) *Student accountant* [Online]. Available at: www.accaglobal.com/ie/en/student/sa.html [Accessed 03/2021]

BBC (2018) *UK accountancy firms face major overhaul under new plans* [Online]. Available at: www.bbc.co.uk/news/business-46591575 [Accessed 03/2021]

Competition and Markets Authority (CMA) (2018) *CMA launches immediate review of audit sector* [Online]. Available at: www.gov.uk/government/news/cma-launches-immediate-review-of-audit-sector [Accessed 03/2021]

CPA Canada (2006) *Standard practices for investigative and forensic accounting engagements* [Online]. Available at: www.cpacanada.ca/en/business-and-accounting-resources/other-general-business-topics/forensic-and-investigative-accounting/publications/standard-practices-investigative-forensic-accounting-engagements [Accessed 03/2021]

Economia (2019) *Brydon lays out scope of audit review* [Online]. Available at: economia.icaew.com/news/april-2019/brydon-lays-out-scope-of-audit-review [Accessed 03/2021]

FATF (2013) *Politically exposed persons (recommendations 12 and 22)* [Online]. Available at: www.fatf-gafi.org/media/fatf/documents/recommendations/Guidance-PEP-Rec12-22.pdf [Accessed 03/2021]

Forensic Science Regulator (2019) *Expert Report Guidance: FSR-G-200, Issue 3* [Online]. Available at: assets.publishing.service.gov.uk/government/uploads/system/uploads/attachment_data/file/796387/Statement_and_Report_Guidance_Appendix_Issue_3.pdf [Accessed 03/2021]

FRC (2014) *Guidance on risk management, internal control and related financial and business reporting* [Online]. Available at www.frc.org.uk/getattachment/d672c107-b1fb-4051-84b0-f5b83a1b93f6/Guidance-on-Risk-Management-Internal-Control-and-Related-Reporting.pdf [Accessed 03/2021]

FRC (2015) *Audit Quality – Practice Aid for Audit Committees* [Online]. Available at: frc.org.uk/Our-Work/Publications/Audit-and-Assurance-Team/Audit-Quality-Practice-Aid-for-Audit-Committee-(1).pdf [Accessed 03/2021]

FRC (2015b) *Audit Quality Inspections, Annual Report 2014-15* [Online]. Available at: www.frc.org.uk/getattachment/d83b5d16-de6f-4fb0-b230-f5de62989daf/AQR-2014-15-Annual-Report-final.pdf [Accessed 03/2021]

FRC (2016d) *Conduct Committee* [Online]. Available at: www.frc.org.uk/About-the-FRC/FRC-structure/Conduct-Committee.aspx [Accessed 03/2021]

FRC (2016e) *Guidance on Audit Committees* [Online]. Available at: www.frc.org.uk/getattachment/6b0ace1d-1d70-4678-9c41-0b44a62f0a0d/Guidance-on-Audit-Committees-April-2016.pdf [Accessed 03/2021]

FRC (2019) *FRC Structure* [Online]. Available at: www.frc.org.uk/about-the-frc/structure-of-the-frc [Accessed 03/2021]

IAASB (2009) *Emerging Practice Issues Regarding the Use of External Confirmations in an Audit of Financial Statements* [Online]. Available at: www.ifac.org/publications-resources/staff-audit-practice-alert-emerging-practice-issues-regarding-use-external-co [Accessed 03/2021]

IAASB (2015) *Auditor Reporting—Illustrative Key Audit Matters* [Online]. Available at: www.ifac.org/publications-resources/auditor-reporting-illustrative-key-audit-matters [Accessed 03/2021]

IAASB (2016) *Discussion Paper, Supporting Credibility and Trust in Emerging Forms of External Reporting* [Online]. Available at: www.ifac.org/publications-resources/discussion-paper-supporting-credibility-and-trust-emerging-forms-external [Accessed 03/2021]

IAASB (2016b) *Determining and Communicating Key Audit Matters* [Online]. Available at: www.ifac.org/publications-resources/determining-and-communicating-key-audit-matters [Accessed 03/2021]

IAASB (2016c) *More Informative Auditor's Reports – What Audit Committees and Finance Executives Need to Know* [Online]. Available at: www.ifac.org/publications-resources/more-informative-auditors-reports-what-audit-committees-and-finance [Accessed 03/2021]

IAASB (2018) *Feedback Statement, Supporting Credibility and Trust in Emerging Forms of External Reporting: Ten Key Challenges for Assurance Engagements* [Online]. Available at: www.ifac.org/system/files/publications/files/IAASB-EER-Feedback-Statement_0.pdf [Accessed 03/2021]

IAASB (2018) *Feedback Statement Prepared by the Staff of the IAASB: Exploring the Growing Use of Technology in the Audit, with a Focus on Data Analytics* [Online]. Available at: www.ifac.org/system/files/publications/files/Data-Analytics-Feedback-Statement.pdf [Accessed 03/2021]

IAASB (2019) *Exposure Draft - Proposed ISA 220 (Revised) Quality Management for an Audit of Financial Statements* [Online]. Available at: www.ifac.org/system/files/publications/files/IAASB-Proposed-ISA-220-Revised-Explanatory-Memorandum.pdf [Accessed 03/2021]

IAASB (2019) *Exposure Draft - Proposed International Standard on Quality Management (ISQM) 1 Quality Management for Firms that Perform Audits or Reviews of Financial Statements, or Other Assurance or Related Service Engagements* [Online]. Available at: www.ifac.org/system/files/publications/files/IAASB-Proposed-ISQM-1-Explanatory-Memorandum.pdf [Accessed 03/2021]

IAASB (2019) *Exposure Draft - Proposed International Standard on Quality Management (ISQM) 2 Engagement Quality Reviews* [Online]. Available at: www.ifac.org/system/files/publications/files/IAASB-Proposed-ISQM-2-Explanatory-Memorandum.pdf [Accessed 03/2021]

IAASB (2019) *The IAASB's Exposure Drafts for Quality Management at the Firm and Engagement Level, including Engagement Quality Reviews* [Online]. Available at: www.ifac.org/system/files/publications/files/IAASB-Covering-Explanatory-Memorandum.pdf [Accessed 03/2021]

IAASB (2019) Introduction to ISA 315 (Revised 2019) *Identifying and Assessing the Risks of Material Misstatement* [Online]. Available at: www.ifac.org/system/files/publications/files/IAASB-Introduction-to-ISA-315.pdf [Accessed 10/2020]

IAASB (2020) Exposure Draft – *Proposed International Standard on Auditing 600 (Revised) Special Considerations – Audits of Group Financial Statements (Including the Work of Component Auditors)* [Online]. Available at: www.iaasb.org/publications/proposed-international-standard-auditing-600-revised-special-considerations-audits-group-financial [Accessed 10/2020]

IAASB (2020) Fact Sheet – Introduction to ISRS 4400 (Revised) *Agreed-Upon-Procedures Engagements* [Online]. Available at: www.ifac.org/system/files/publications/files/ISRS-4400-Revised-Fact-Sheet-final.pdf [Accessed 10/2020]

IAASB (2020) ISRS 4400 (Revised) *Agreed-Upon-Procedures Engagements* [Online]. Available at: www.ifac.org/system/files/publications/files/ISRS-4400-Revised-Agreed-Upon-Procedures-final.pdf [Accessed 10/2020]

IAASB (2020) *Non-authoritative support material related to technology: Audit documentation when using automated tools and techniques* [Online]. Available at: www.ifac.org/system/files/publications/files/FINAL-Non-Authoritative-Support-Material_Audit-Documentation-When-Using-Automated-Tools-And-Techniques.pdf [Accessed 10/2020]

IAESB (2014) *International Accounting Education Standards Board Fact Sheet* [Online]. Available at: www.ifac.org/system/files/uploads/IAESB/IAESB-Fact-Sheet-2.pdf [Accessed 03/2021]

IBM (2018) *The Four V's of Big Data* [Online]. Available at https://www.researchgate.net/figure/IBM-Four-Vs-of-Big-Data_fig1_320799079 [Accessed: 03/2021]

ICAEW (2016) *Data Analytics for External Auditors* [Online]. Available at: www.icaew.com/-/media/corporate/files/technical/iaa/tecpln14726-iaae-data-analytics—-web-version.ashx [Accessed 03/2021].

ICAEW (2016b) *Framework for Resolving Ethical Problems* [Online]. Available at: www.icaew.com/en/technical/ethics/framework-for-resolving-ethical-problems [Accessed: 03/2021]

IESBA (2012) *Responding to a Suspected Illegal Act* [Online]. Available at: www.iaasb.org/system/files/publications/files/IESBA-Code-of-Ethics-Illegal-Acts-Exposure-Draft.pdf [Accessed 03/2021]

IESBA (2016) *Responding to Non-Compliance with Laws and Regulations* [Online]. Available at: www.ifac.org/publications-resources/responding-non-compliance-laws-and-regulations [Accessed 03/2021]

IESBA (2019) *Exposure Draft - Proposed Revisions to the Code to Promote the Role and Mindset Expected of Professional Accountants* [Online]. Available at: www.ifac.org/system/files/publications/files/IESBA-Exposure-Draft-Role-and-Mindset.pdf [Accessed 03/2021]

IESBA (2020) Exposure Draft – *Proposed revisions to the fee-related provisions of the code* [Online]. Available at: www.ifac.org/system/files/publications/files/FINAL-IESBA-ED_Proposed-Revisions-to-the-Fee-related-Provisions-of-the-Code_0.pdf [Accessed 10/2020]

IESBA (2020) Exposure Draft – *Proposed revisions to the non-assurance services provisions of the code* [Online]. Available at: www.ifac.org/system/files/publications/files/FINAL-IESBA-ED-Proposed-Revisions-to-the-NAS-Provisions-of-the-Code.pdf [Accessed 10/2020]

IFAC (2017) *Toward enhanced professional skepticism: Observations of the IAASB-IAESB-IESBA Professional Skepticism Working Group* [Online]. Available at: www.iaasb.org/publications-resources/toward-enhanced-professional-skepticism [Accessed 03/2021]

IIRC (2013) *The international IR framework* [Online]. Available at: integratedreporting.org/wp-content/uploads/2015/03/13-12-08-THE-INTERNATIONAL-IR-FRAMEWORK-2-1.pdf [Accessed 03/2021]

Norton (2019) *Norton Cyber Safety Insights Report* [Online]. Available at: us.norton.com/nortonlifelock-cyber-safety-report [Accessed 10/2020]

PCAOB (2016) *Mission and vision* [Online]. Available at: pcaobus.org/About/History/Pages/default.aspx [Accessed 03/2021]

Rolls Royce (2014) *Annual report – other information* [Online]. Available at: www.rolls-royce.com/~/media/Files/R/Rolls-Royce/documents/investors/annual-reports/rr-full-annual-report-2014.pdf [Accessed 03/2021]

TAC (2010) *Who we are* [Online]. Available at: www.ifac.org/who-we-are/committees/transnational-auditors-committee-forum-firms [Accessed 03/2021]

Corporate governance code

FRC (2018) *FRC UK Corporate Governance Code* [Online]. Available at: www.frc.org.uk/getattachment/88bd8c45-50ea-4841-95b0-d2f4f48069a2/2018-UK-Corporate-Governance-Code-FINAL.pdf [Accessed 03/2021].

FRC Audit and Assurance Standards and Guidance

FRC (2018) *Standards and guidance* [Online]. Available at: www.frc.org.uk/auditors/audit-assurance/standards-and-guidance [Accessed 03/2021].

International Audit and Assurance Standards Board guidance

IAASB (2018) *Publications* [Online]. Available at: www.ifac.org/system/files/publications/files/IAASB-2018-HB-Vol-1.pdf [Accessed 03/2021].

IAASB (2019) *ISA 315 (Revised 2019) and Conforming and Consequential Amendments to Other International Standards Arising from ISA 315* (Revised 2019) [Online]. Available at: www.ifac.org/system/files/publications/files/ISA-315-Full-Standard-and-Conforming-Amendments-2019-.pdf [Accessed 10/2020].

International Ethics Standards Board for Accountants guidance

IESBA (2018) *Publications* [Online]. Available at: www.ethicsboard.org/system/files/publications/files/IESBA-Handbook-Code-of-Ethics-2018.pdf [Accessed 03/2021].

International Financial Reporting Standards

IFRS Foundation (2019) *IFRS* [Online]. Available at: eifrs.ifrs.org [Accessed 03/2021].

UK Law

Companies Act 2006 [Online]. Available at: www.legislation.gov.uk/ukpga/2006/46/contents [Accessed 03/2021]

Open Parliament Licence v3.0: www.nationalarchives.gov.uk/doc/open-government-licence/version/3/ [Accessed 03/2021]

US Law

Sarbanes-Oxley Act 2002 [Online]. Available at: www.sec.gov/answers/about-lawsshtml.html#sox2002 [Accessed 03/2021]

Tell us what you think

Got comments or feedback on this book? Let us know.
Use your QR code reader:

Or, visit:
https://bppgroup.fra1.qualtrics.com/jfe/form/SV_9TrxTtw8jSvO7Pv